CRITICAL DIRECTIONS

A series of criticism selected and edited by
J.R. (Tim) Struthers
Department of English, University of Guelph

The volumes chosen for this series explore directions through which criticism can uphold its most urgent responsibilities: to the honouring of literature and language, to the cultivation of a more profound, more valuable experience of art and life, and to the building of a more enlightened society.

1. *Volleys,* Sam Solecki, John Metcalf and W.J. Keith

2. *An Independent Stance: Essays on English-Canadian Criticism and Fiction,* W.J. Keith

An Independent Stance

CRITICAL DIRECTIONS

Essays on English-Canadian Criticism and Fiction

W.J. KEITH

The Porcupine's Quill

CANADIAN CATALOGUING IN PUBLICATION DATA

Keith, W.J. (William John), 1934-
An independent stance : essays on English-Canadian criticism and fiction

(Critical directions)
Includes bibliographical references and index.
ISBN 0-88984-121-7

1. Canadian fiction (English) – 20th century – History and criticism.* 2. Criticism. I. Title. II. Series.

PS8187.K45 1991 C813'.5409 C91-094679-5
PR9192.5.K45 1991

Published by The Porcupine's Quill, Inc., 68 Main Street, Erin, Ontario NOB 1TO with financial assistance from The Canada Council and the Ontario Arts Council.

Distributed by The University of Toronto Press, 5201 Dufferin Street, Downsview, Ontario M3H 5T8.

Edited for the press by J.R. (Tim) Struthers. Assisted by Doris Cowan.

Cover is after a painting, 'Via Dolorosa', oil on canvas, 1983, by Hiroko Keith.

Printed and bound by The Porcupine's Quill. The stock is Zephyr Antique laid, and the type, Ehrhardt.

Contents

PART TWO: FICTION

On the Need for an Independent Stance

SOME MONTHS AGO I stumbled on some critical formulations by W.H. Auden that deserve wider currency:

> What is the function of a critic? So far as I am concerned, he can do me one or more of the following services:
>
> 1. Introduce me to authors or works of which I was hitherto unaware.
> 2. Convince me that I have undervalued an author or a work because I had not read them carefully enough.
> 3. Show me relations between works of different ages and cultures which I could never have seen for myself because I do not know enough and never shall.
> 4. Give a 'reading' of a work which increases my understanding of it.
> 5. Throw light upon the process of artistic 'Making'.
> 6. Throw light upon the relation of art to life, to science, economics, ethics, religion, etc. (8-9)

I was impressed by the lucidity and good sense of all this. It seems to me that, as a statement of literary-critical principles, it can hardly be bettered. At the same time, I could not help feeling that it had a rather old-fashioned air about it – though I hasten to add that I employ the term 'old-fashioned' without any pejorative connotation whatsoever. How many contemporary literary critics would see their function in this way? How many perform the service that Auden asks for and approves of?

By coincidence (or synchronicity), on the same day as I uncovered Auden's remarks I was leafing through the most recent issue of *Canadian Literature* (No. 119), and the following sentences caught my attention:

> Within the context of its special topological system described above, ethnic discourse clearly tries, and is conscious of trying, to recompose the binary isotopies deriving from its spatial organization. (173)

> Through its mnemotechnical strategies and its use of genealogy as an alternative ordering principle, ethnic semiosis offers a double perspective of postmodern identity. (176)

Would Auden, I wondered, have considered this helpful? Does anyone? Above all, I found myself asking why the editor had allowed such sentences to pass, why he hadn't at the very least returned them for translation into English. But again, if they were so translated, would they lead to genuine insight?

The contrast between Auden and this writer is, of course, extreme, but it conveniently points up the dilemma of modern criticism. It seems to me that the writer in *Canadian Literature* is no longer interested in providing any of the services that Auden respects. He is unconcerned about the general reader – who is now virtually identical with the intellectually curious student – and has not paused to ask whether a discussion of communication should itself be capable of communicating in a clear and civilized fashion. If such commentary is now acceptable, doesn't it follow that our literary-critical priorities have gone seriously astray? It so happens that I began teaching and writing about the time that Auden made the remarks that I have quoted. As I finish reading through some fifteen years of my later literary-critical writings in order to prepare this book, I am saddened by the realization that passages like these from *Canadian Literature* have become, if not the norm, at least no more than somewhat extreme examples of established practice. A return to more traditional critical methods seems to be urgently needed. If this gathering of articles, addresses, and reviews of mine has any justification, it will be because I have consistently endeavoured, without being aware of Auden's statement, to perform in modest fashion some of the functions that he lists.

INTRODUCTION

WHEN J.R. (TIM) STRUTHERS and John Metcalf first broached the possibility of my collecting together the contents of this book, my first reaction was one of scepticism. Too much literary criticism is published nowadays; most of these pieces have already enjoyed their brief moments in print; why revive them? But I was eventually persuaded to delve into this material, to sift it, and to decide whether a judicious selection would in fact create a book – whether such a gathering resulted in a whole that might be considered more significant than the sum of its constituent parts. I have persuaded myself that this may indeed be so.

One of the reasons for this may well be found in the curious background that I bring to my interest in Canadian literature. Not only do I approach the material as an immigrant who first came to this country at the age of twenty-four, but I turned my attention to Canadian criticism and fiction after I had established myself as a specialist in Victorian and modern British literature. This means that my critical attitudes were formed in another area of study and even (originally) in another country. As a result, although I may fail to appreciate some of the finer points that only the Canadian-born can fully savour, by the same token I may be in a better position to recognize the particular Canadian achievement within the broader context of literature in English. But more is involved, I think, than the mere accidents of biography. Reading through these articles and reviews *en masse,* I detect (or, at least, hope I detect) a continuing literary-critical purpose that suggests a reasonable consistency of approach without, I trust, solidifying into inflexibility. This is due in part to the fact that I have always made a point of trying to read all writers on their own terms. It would be absurd to analyse the work of Margaret Laurence with the identical critical tools that were appropriate for, say, Hugh Hood, and an approach to Jack Hodgins needs to be different again.

While I avoid adherence to any particular critical theory, I do, of course, embrace certain literary principles. Indeed, it is now clear to me that three basic principles lie at the root of all my work. These are: a) literary criticism is an art, not a science;

b) literary criticism and evaluation are ultimately inseparable; c) although literary criticism is an art, it is not one of the creative arts and should not put on airs. I would like to comment briefly on all of these.

That literary criticism is an art and not a science ought to be so self-evident that it does not need to be spelled out, let alone argued. Yet the plain fact is that, because we live in an age when scientific method reigns supreme, a discipline that does not try at least to disguise itself behind a pretence to scientific method is not likely to be accepted as important. As a result, recent decades have seen an upsurge of literary classification in the tradition of Linnaean botany, by which literary works are described, measured, broken down into generic divisions and subdivisions, duly labelled and docketed. (Yes, I know that, from an up-to-date scientific viewpoint, fixed categories are themselves suspect, but that is the categorizers' problem, not mine.) Similarly, literary-critical articles are often adorned with complex, scientific-textbook diagrams which, though superficially impressive, prove – ninety-nine times out of a hundred in my experience – more confusing than helpful. Above all, literary theories are propounded and propagated like scientific hypotheses, individual works examined not for their own sakes but as counters to be fitted (too often, forced) into a pretentious all-embracing *schema.* Literature is therefore constantly being *used*: for its historical significance, its sociological relevance, its psychological insights, its political implications – for everything, indeed, except its literary *quality*.

The results are generally lamentable. *Gorboduc* and *Romeo and Juliet* may both be classified as five-act Elizabethan tragedies in blank verse written for the unlocalized stage, but these common characteristics tell us nothing about the basic qualities that make them, in performance, as different as chalk and cheese. As for diagrams, a containing literary circle may be constructed that moves from comedy through romance to tragedy to irony and satire and back to comedy again, but this can provide no more than a convenient parking lot in which a specific work of art can be located: it does not help us to understand the individual work or to identify its unique features. A literary theory may banish intentionality, insist that there are no ideas but in things, communicate in seemingly clear language an insistence on the incommunicability of language, or attempt (systematically!) to deconstruct everything that lies in its way. Yet novelists obstinately continue to write novels after the novel as a form has (theoretically) been pronounced dead; poetry is still produced after Auschwitz; literary butterflies broken on theoretical wheels persist in flying. Because it is in the nature of any genuine work of art to be different from any other, rules are powerless to incorporate it into a generalized system. Art remains art, and can only be appreciated in what F.R. Leavis was fond of calling the 'third realm' where the artistic imaginations of maker and reader merge.

The argument for the inevitability of evaluation is made so consistently and conspicuously throughout the articles to follow that it would be absurdly repetitious to add anything further here. Struthers and Metcalf have invited me rather than someone else to compile this particular book; I have made a selection out of the materials available, admitting some while discarding others. In both cases, evaluative decisions were involved. The evaluation may or may not have been justified, but the fact of evaluation remains, as it does in virtually all aspects of life.

That literary criticism is not, however, one of the creative arts needs, I think, to be asserted forcefully. The concept of criticism or critical theory as an autonomous field of study, a conceptual universe with its own rules and justifications, needs to be resisted. Ultimately, individual literary critics, though they have an honourable part to play in cultural matters, are of little importance in themselves. Their function is to assist in the understanding and appreciation of artistic creations. If this book is of any interest, it will be because Canadian literature is an important subject. Literary commentators like myself are middle-men, and should be prepared to admit the fact. If this book succeeds in helping readers to appreciate the works of Canadian writers that I discuss, and to derive increased pleasure and insight from them, it will have served its purpose. I can see no other justification for it – or for any other work of criticism.

* * *

A FEW PRELIMINARY DETAILS. Part One gathers together various statements on literary-critical matters as they relate to Canadian literature in general and Canadian fiction in particular. They are arranged chronologically in order of composition since it may be useful to present one man's attempt over the years to respond to the ever-changing intellectual challenges. Part Two contains discussions of specific authors and specific texts, and is arranged in terms of the publication dates of the works discussed rather than the order in which I wrote the articles. They are offered as specimens of 'criticism in practice' – attempts, with varying degrees of success, to discuss individual works in ways best suited to them.

The individual texts reproduced here have been adapted so that stylistic 'house-rules' are rendered consistent. Typographical errors have been corrected. I have sometimes introduced stylistic changes to render the meaning clearer, but have made no alterations to the arguments themselves. Some additional notes have been inserted when it seemed necessary or desirable to comment on more recent developments. In all cases, these are identified by the date: [1989].

Finally, I would like to thank John Metcalf for his flattering encouragement, Sam Solecki for sage (and frank) counsel, and especially J.R. (Tim) Struthers for his meticulous editorial assistance over and above the call of duty.

PART ONE

Criticism

Canadian Literature, Criticism, and Evaluation: The *Literary History of Canada*

This review, originally untitled, appeared in the Summer 1977 issue of the *University of Toronto Quarterly*. It may well seem strange to begin a collection of this kind with a review of a book that had first appeared over a decade earlier, and is, as I write, about to be enlarged by a further volume. I do so not only because this review is chronologically the earliest expression of my continuing plea for an increased evaluative component in Canadian criticism, but also because the literary-critical principles briefly discussed here are developed and refined in various subsequent articles reproduced in this book.

The *Literary History of Canada*, under the general editorship of Carl Klinck, first appeared in 1965 and is now revised in three volumes, the first two involving a reprint (with additions and revisions) of the original text, the third comprising new chapters written to bring the record up to 1973. On its initial appearance, A.J.M. Smith contributed a brilliant review to the *University of Toronto Quarterly* – a discussion that deserves to become a *locus classicus* of Canadian criticism – and I can do no better than take up some of his leads in examining the new material.

Any useful criticism of the principles involved in the whole enterprise must start from a much-quoted statement by Northrop Frye in his 'Conclusion' to what is now the second volume:

> Its authors have completely outgrown the view that evaluation is the end of criticism, instead of its incidental by-product. Had evaluation been their guiding principle, this book would, if written at all, have been only a huge debunking project, leaving Canadian literature a poor naked *alouette* plucked of every feather of decency and dignity. (2: 333)

Smith registered a fervent protest against both sentences quoted here, but I am more concerned at the moment with the matter of evaluation. 'I have always believed', Smith wrote, 'that evaluation *is* the end, purpose, and *raison d'être* of criticism, and that criticism without evaluation would be, if it could be called criticism, the least rewarding of the pastimes available to the dwellers in an ivory tower'(115). I had better state here that all my own principles, instincts, and prejudices align me with Smith, but, even after making allowance for this, I am convinced that, in the eleven years that have passed between the two editions, Smith's position has worn much better than Frye's.

Evaluation, while primarily concerned with quality, arises inevitably as a response to quantity. George Woodcock opens his discussion of poetry in the new third volume with the following statistics:

> In 1959, 24 books of English verse were published in Canada; ... in 1970 more than 120 books of verse were published.... When I finally closed the list at the end of 1973 I found that I had traced some 1,125 books of verse – not counting anthologies – that had been published by Canadian writers in the English language during the fourteen years in question. (3: 284)

With thirty-four pages at his disposal, Woodcock has no alternative but to undertake a radical evaluative act before even putting pen to paper. He makes no claims to omniscience, admitting openly and properly that his choice has been 'guided largely by personal taste' (3: 316).

Even in the original edition, whatever Frye may claim, evaluations were everywhere implicit. Gordon Roper reported that 'during the years 1880 to 1920, more than 400 Canadians published over 1,400 volumes of fiction' (1: 275); he and his assistants could obviously do no more than survey the mass. In the more successful chapters, value-judgements explicitly determined the arrangement of the material. Thus Roy Daniells devoted a seventeen-page chapter to Lampman and Roberts, and another one of sixteen pages to Crawford, Carman, and D.C. Scott; their less important contemporaries were surveyed in a nine-page chapter entitled 'Minor Poets: 1880-1920'. This is surely as it should be. The general editor makes the point clearly in his introduction to the third volume: 'The problems are still those of weighing, sorting out, selecting, discarding, and describing, and of passing over nothing of true significance' (3:xii). His order is accurate and revealing: evaluation comes first. I believe, moreover, that weaknesses in the book arise when contributors have not approached their subjects with sufficient evaluative rigour.

If blanket coverage takes precedence over judicious evaluation, numerous dangers can arise. First, of course, the discussion of minor (in some cases, worthless) writers precludes adequate consideration of significant work. There is something seriously wrong in the proportions of a book that can devote three times as much space to the novels of Lily Adams Beck as to those of Ernest Buckler. Besides, if too much attention is paid to scraping the bottoms of barrels ('The Reverend Frank Baird ... wrote two quite good adventure stories for boys' (2: 183)), something may well escape from the top. While the late Desmond Pacey, responsible for the last quotation, can be forgiven for missing Howard O'Hagan's fine novel *Tay John* in the first edition, there is no excuse for the editors to fail to remedy the omission by 1976. Again, I happened to be rereading Wallace Stegner's *Wolf Willow* while preparing this review, and was amazed to discover that no mention is made of either author or book in the *Literary History.* Stegner, admittedly, is an American (in his own words, he 'missed becoming a Canadian by only about one inch of rain' (299)), but I can think of no more brilliant evocation and analysis of a segment of the Canadian consciousness, and if Samuel Hearne, an Englishman, can qualify as a contributor to eighteenth-century Canadian literature, why not Stegner in the twentieth? The answer to that question is unkind, but critical honesty compels me to state it quite bluntly: the scholarly (as distinct from the critical) mind cannot be trusted with literary judgements until they have been safely consecrated by history. For all its usefulness (and I should be the last to minimize its value as a reference work), the *Literary History of Canada* is seriously weakened by a deadening 'academic' bias.

I must now turn my attention to the new third volume. The first point to be noted is the eccentric allocation of space. The editors have clearly followed Matthew Arnold's definition in 'Literature and Science': 'Literature ... may mean everything written with letters or printed in a book. Euclid's *Elements* and Newton's *Principia* are thus literature. All knowledge that reaches us through books is literature' (385). While this broadness of scope was evident in the earlier edition, it becomes positively conspicuous in the third volume which contains chapters not only on 'Canadian History' and 'Philosophical and Religious Writings' but also on 'The Physical Sciences and Engineering', 'The Biological Sciences', and 'Writing in the Social Sciences'. When the writers stick to their topics, these last become little more than lists ('Of books on economic nationalism, the following sample may suffice'; 'On other standard topics there have also been new books' (3: 140, 141)). When they try to intersperse their surveys with supposed literary commentary, the results are disturbing. W.O. Mitchell may be surprised to find himself rubbing shoulders with Grey Owl in the biological sciences (alas, he will probably not be surprised to find his best-known novel mistitled). Far be it from me to slight the contributions of the social, natural, and physical sciences. I am merely questioning the feasibility of including any adequate treatment of them in 1976 in even a three-volume work, especially since consideration of *la littérature canadienne-française,* surely a much more relevant area of study for a literary history, has been deliberately excluded. The editorial intentions were doubtless admirable; the result is lopsided.

But even if we confine ourselves to what Arnold would call *belles-lettres,* the proportions are surprising. We find no fewer than three essays on criticism (taking up sixty-three pages in all) while poetry and fiction are rationed to thirty-four and fifty-one pages respectively. One begins to question the priorities. Lauriat Lane, Jr., given the thankless task of covering Canadian scholarship, names some 350 books (not to mention articles) in thirty pages. I cannot help asking: why bother? Why, for example, should a book I wrote about an English Victorian be immortalized in Canadian literary history just because it was written on Canadian soil? Why indeed, when a novel as fine as Henry Kreisel's *The Betrayal* fails to gain a mention in the fiction section (where, however, I find my favourite example of desperate academic pigeon-holing: 'Two novels about escaping to the Balearic Islands ...' (3: 251-52)). Even George Woodcock feels the constriction in the poetry section; although, as one might expect, he is more concerned with genuine literary values than most of the contributors, he is inevitably forced back upon the listing of trends, presses, and statistics. He can allow himself only one poetic quotation in the whole essay. It seems clear that his talents have not been employed to the best advantage.

In such circumstances the maintaining of high critical standards becomes virtually impossible. If the writer tries to be specific, little can be said. In his survey of essayists, Brandon Conron is reduced to covering the contributions of Robertson Davies, Hugh MacLennan, Pierre Berton, Mordecai Richler, and Hugh Hood in one dizzying paragraph. Small wonder that nothing helpful emerges. Again, if the writer falls back on generalization, the results are often staggering: 'Television in particular brought children into the adult world [*sic*!] more quickly than ever before' (3: 204). Similarly, a bald value-judgement without evidence or illustration achieves nothing. If all that can be said about Judith Copithorne's *Heart's Tide* is that it is 'stylistically unpolished' (3: 270), why mention the book at all? On the other hand, an objectively descriptive statement can be equally unsatisfactory. When, for instance, John Ripley tells us in the drama chapter that Tom Hendry's *How Are Things with the Walking Wounded?* 'depicts the second anniversary party of a Montreal homosexual couple during which the guests turn on each other in an orgy of mutual destructiveness' (3: 229), is he merely indicating the theme or subtly drawing attention to a tedious jumble of contemporary clichés? I hope the latter but suspect the former.

I must now redress the balance of my criticism and acknowledge that there are some very good things to be found in the volume. One of the best is Malcolm Ross's article on critical theory. This is because he is thinking rather than listing, exploring an area rather than producing an inventory. He is not crudely evaluative, but firm standards emerge throughout. Moreover, he writes both wittily and wisely, offering a strange, subtly balanced mixture of irony and aplomb that underlines (and sometimes deliberately undercuts) his argument. I admire even when I occasionally disagree. He has been helped, I suspect, by the fact that the other writers on criticism have relieved him of the burden of issuing a roll-call. I emphasize this chapter because it exemplifies what might have been achieved in other areas.

I am still conscious, however, of appearing excessively negative in my general response. Obviously, when a work of such mammoth proportions is involved, it is easy to find niggling deficiencies. But the instances I have cited, often minor in themselves, are cumulatively symptomatic of a general attitude to the materials. Pervading the whole enterprise (though clearly not intended by the editors) is a sense of rather naïve patriotism ('Look, we've got a literature too!'). Although most contributors pay lip-service to the end of the 'garrison mentality', the eagerness with which they announce their liberation suggests that they may still remain under its shadow. Indeed, they encourage an interpretation of the whole project as an indirect monument to the Puritan work ethic: it proves indisputably that we have all been very busy. But such an attitude is surely no longer necessary. That the literature exists has been amply demonstrated in almost 1,400 pages. Carl Klinck and his fellow editors may be said to have driven the last literary-historical spike home. What now?

In his new 'Conclusion' Northrop Frye has gone some way towards qualifying his original comparison of Canadian literature to 'a poor naked *alouette*'. He acknowledges now that 'Canadian literature is here, perhaps still a minor but certainly no longer a gleam in a paternal critic's eye' (3: 319). I would argue, though Frye probably would not, that the 'paternal critic' must not only shed his paternalism but become stricter, more exacting, and ultimately more evaluative. The cultural explosion which this volume documents renders a rigorous critical function essential. Individual critics will not be performing their duty if they do not assess, if they are not prepared to say 'this (rather than that) is worthy of detailed attention.' True, these will only be individual opinions, and they may well be wrong, but others (if they are doing *their* duty) will present the counter-statement, as Smith did to Frye in 1965. Criticism, as we should know by now, is a collaborative venture – 'the common pursuit [dare I quote Leavis quoting Eliot in this context?] of true judgement' (*Common Pursuit* v). In his original 'Conclusion' Frye raised the possibility of 'another book: *A Literary Criticism of Canada*' (2:358). That, I suppose, is what I am asking for, and it was what Smith was asking for in his original review, which concluded as follows:

> What is needed now is a comprehensive 'critical history' by a single author who can combine scholarly research with imaginative interpretation and who has enough faith in the literary quality of the best work drawn from all kinds of writing ... to make evaluation his first business and let the chips fall where they may. (116)

For all their limitations, the volumes under review can at least be said to have cleared the ground for this necessary undertaking.

The Thematic Approach to Canadian Fiction

This paper was first presented at the Calgary Conference on the Canadian Novel in 1978, and published with the rest of the proceedings in *Taking Stock,* edited by Charles Steele. The conference was controversial, mainly because of the accompanying 'ballot' in which respondents were asked to list what they considered the most important works of Canadian fiction. This, of course, raised the whole issue of evaluative criticism, albeit in a decidedly crude form. I discuss the conference and some of its implications in 'The Quest for the (Instant) Canadian Classic', reproduced later in this section. A number of specific works alluded to in my paper – notably Hugh MacLennan's *The Watch That Ends the Night,* Margaret Laurence's *The Diviners,* the fiction of Ethel Wilson, and Jack Hodgins's *The Invention of the World* – receive further attention in essays in the second section of this book.

PERHAPS I CAN BEST INDICATE my basic response to this subject by describing the circumstances under which I come to be speaking here. When I first received Ernest Ingles's invitation to deliver a lecture on 'Themes in Canadian Fiction', my first reaction was, I confess, one of amusement – amusement because, 'if small things we may with great compare', reasonable equivalents might be to ask René Lévesque to address you on the benefits of federalism or (more to the point here) Mordecai Richler to discourse on the novelistic virtues of Frederick Philip Grove. Not long before, in my capacity as editor of the *University of Toronto Quarterly,* I had, in self-defence and with something approaching desperation, penned a statement on editorial policy that insisted: 'The journal does not normally print thematically oriented criticism.' And only a week or so before, while setting essay topics in my undergraduate course on Canadian fiction, I had appended (as, nowadays, I invariably do) the following instructions: 'You are expected in each case to concentrate on the novels *as works of art*; it is not sufficient merely to compare and contrast themes.'

So I contacted Ingles, thanked him for asking me, but explained my difficulty. Thematic criticism, I said, was my *bête noire*; if I began to talk about 'Themes in Canadian Fiction', I would inevitably end by arguing that the thematic approach was in fact the least promising way of coming to terms with Canadian fiction (or any other). Imagine my surprise when he replied: 'Most interesting. Why don't you come and do just that?' So here I am.

EXACT DEFINITIONS OF LITERARY TERMS always bother me, so my first action upon acceptance was to look up 'theme' and 'thematic criticism' in any literary reference-books that lay to hand. M.H. Abrams, in his *A Glossary of Literary Terms*, referred me from 'theme' to 'motif' and there I found the following:

> A motif is sometimes called a *theme*, but the word 'theme' is more usefully employed to denote the thesis or doctrine of a didactic work.... In modern criticism, the word 'theme' is often used also to signify the abstract concept which is said to be embodied in the structure and imagery of a nondidactic or purely imaginative work. (53)

'Said to be' implies scepticism, and the definition goes on to question the usefulness of the term outside explicitly didactic works. And when I looked up 'Criticism, Types of' in Thrall, Hibbard, and Holman's *A Handbook to Literature*, I discovered that, although they listed no fewer than eight types (impressionistic, historical, textual, formal, judicial, analytical, moral, mythic), 'thematic criticism' was not included. (They admit that 'there are certainly others', but imply that these are relatively unimportant.) I quote these definitions because the results may well come as a surprise to those familiar with the habitual procedures of Canadian literary criticism, in which, presumably because of the influence of Northrop Frye, the emphasis has (especially in the last two decades or so) been predominantly thematic.

I am tempted to say exclusively so. One has only to assemble titles of the most influential essays or volumes for the thematic bias to become evident. They consist either of dominant images suggestive of grand generalization to which literary experience – so it is said – significantly conforms ('Wolf in the Snow'; *The Bush Garden: Essays on the Canadian Imagination*; *Butterfly on Rock: A Study of Themes and Images in Canadian Literature*; *The Haunted Wilderness: The Gothic and Grotesque in Canadian Fiction*) or directly advertise the themes to be extracted from literature (*Survival: A Thematic Guide to Canadian Literature*; *Patterns of Isolation in English-Canadian Fiction*; *Sex and Violence in the Canadian Novel: The Ancestral Present*). Even individual issues of the journal *Canadian Literature* are, more often than not, arranged along thematic lines. All this being so, it was hardly surprising that, when the organizing committee of this conference came to plan topics for these sessions, 'Themes in Canadian Fiction' should, as a response to an almost Pavlovian preconditioned stimulus, inevitably spring to mind. We are, frankly, obsessed with thematics. Indeed, where (one asks with some unease) can we turn for a literary-critical account, not of the subject matter of Canadian fiction, but of Canadian fiction itself? Sad to say (and publishers, please note), the answer is: nowhere.

This matter has been troubling me for some time. I know many individuals similarly dissatisfied with the current emphasis, but, until recently, challenges to the literary-critical *status quo* rarely appeared in print. I have detected, however, ripples of discontent in the last few years, and at least one four-square confrontation of the problem. I refer to Frank Davey's hard-hitting article, 'Surviving the Paraphrase', which appeared in *Canadian Literature* in the issue for Autumn 1976. My own opinion is that Davey begins excellently and presents a number of searching criticisms that desperately needed to be voiced. I would like now to summarize his analysis of the situation and then to explain why I differ from him in his positive recommendations.

Davey's position is contained in the following series of highly selective extracts:

> In its brief lifetime, Canadian criticism has acquired a history of being reluctant to focus on the literary work – to deal with matters of form, language, style, structure, and consciousness as these arise from the work as a unique construct. It has seldom had enough confidence in the work of Canadian writers to do what the criticism of other national literatures has done: explain and illuminate the work on its own terms, without recourse to any cultural rationalizations or apologies. (5)

Davey complains that the thematic critic's role 'is not to attend to language, form, or even to individual works of literature but to something called by Jones in *Butterfly on Rock* "our imaginative life", by Moss in his *Patterns of Isolation* the "national being", and by Frye in *The Bush Garden* "cultural history".' Davey calls these approaches 'extra-literary' and 'at worst, anti-literary' because the 'focus of such criticism invariably rests outside the writing....' The movement, he continues, is towards paraphrase: 'The critic extracts for his deliberations the paraphrasable content and throws away the form. He attends to the explicit meaning of the work and neglects whatever content is implicit in its structure, language, or imagery' (6).

I have quoted Davey at length because, up to this point, I agree wholeheartedly, and could not hope to improve upon his crisp and clear-headed account. I agree also with two of his related points: first, that recent Canadian writing 'has been engaged for the most part at the level of form and language rather than theme' (5) and so needs a critical approach capable of responding to this challenge (Davey specifies the mature work of Rudy Wiebe here, and, since he wrote, Jack Hodgins has come into prominence and added substance to the argument); second, that thematic criticism tries 'to define a national culture but chooses to work with materials – literary themes – that are ...

international in nature' (8). Davey's diagnosis seems to me impeccable – but I have great reservations about his proposed course of treatment. Moreover, I can locate the parting of our ways at a specific point in the following passage:

> The motivations of thematic criticism strike one as essentially defensive in respect to both the culture and the literature. A declared motive has been to avoid evaluative criticism, which Frye has claimed would reduce Canadian criticism to a 'huge debunking project'. An even more important but undeclared motive appears to have been to avoid treating Canadian writing as serious literature. For there are many kinds of non-evaluative criticism which these critics could have practised other than the thematic. (9)

Why 'non-evaluative' – which Davey never questions? The whole of his argument seems to have been moving towards a plea for a more discriminating and so evaluative reassessment. I expected him to say (as I *do* say) that Canadian literature has now attained a sufficient solidity and stature that we can invoke high standards without any fear that the subject might succumb to the process. The plain fact of the matter is that Davey ventures so far and then draws back. 'It is extremely important', he argues, 'that Canadian critics do not forget that there are indeed alternatives to thematic criticism, and that most of these do not involve a return to that *bête noire* evaluation' (9). And he goes on to list possible critical approaches: historical criticism, analytical criticism, genre criticism, phenomenological criticism, even archetypal criticism. This, I must confess, not only disappoints but depresses me. In my view, Davey here shows himself just as much a victim of the pigeon-holing obsession as the thematic critics whose approach he deplores.

At this point I had better lay my own cards on the table. Admittedly, I first studied English at Cambridge and therefore came under the influence of evaluative criticism at what some might call an impressionable age. I still think that 'the words on the page' are the first concern of a literary critic, though I agree that one must be sure that one knows not only what the words mean but what associations attach to them at different literary periods – and words vary, we should remember, not only in different ages but in different countries. But I am above all a critical relativist. I believe that 'taste' consists in knowing the appropriate criteria to bring to the individual work. The critic must be firm (you will not find me – *pace* Warren Tallman – trying to prove that 'crude' is really 'fine'), but one must also be flexible. Obviously, it is no good bringing to *Sunshine Sketches of a Little Town* the same critical approaches that one applies to *Middlemarch.* But one discovers the appropriate criteria by attending in each case to the language and its associated qualities: tone, imagery, rhythm, point of view, authorial attitude – not to mention those larger, vaguer entities like form and structure. One will go astray if one starts extracting thematic plums, like Little Jack Horner. Indeed, if one *does* confine oneself to themes (provincialism, political corruption, religious cant, financial intrigue), *Sunshine Sketches* and *Middlemarch* may well appear to resemble each other – but in doing so one will only succeed in distorting and belittling the art of both.

However, I do not wish to be misunderstood. I am not advocating a total neglect of subject matter and theme. If one ignores what a work of art is about, one soon enters the realm of 'art for art's sake', and any attempt wholly to separate art from life leads either to triviality or to absurdity. I am merely insisting that identification of theme is no more than a tentative first step towards mature literary-critical discussion. Again, some authors clearly invite a greater thematic concern than others. Hugh MacLennan is an obvious instance, though I had better state my conviction that *The Watch That Ends the Night* is far and away MacLennan's finest novel, not because its theme is any more important or appealing (let alone 'Canadian') than the others, but because of all his novels it is the most satisfactorily realized as art. By the same token, I do *not* consider *The Diviners* Margaret Laurence's best novel – or anywhere close to her best – though I grant that it is thematically the most comprehensive. But artistic and thematic criteria are by no means identical – and ultimately it is the artistic that endure.

Yet here I encounter a difficulty. I have a number of points I wish to make (for example, how can one possibly separate the theme of, say, *As For Me and My House* from the artistry that Ross displays in telling the story?), but when articulated they sound so simple and obvious that I wonder if I am not merely offering platitudinous truisms. Surely, it might be asked, everybody believes all this? Unfortunately, everybody does not. It *ought* to be generally accepted that classifying works of art by subject matter, without any attention paid to comparative quality, is a waste of time. Yet we find David Arnason, in his collection of *Nineteenth Century Canadian Stories,* trying to resurrect a feeble tale by Rosanna Leprohon (no, 'resurrect' is the wrong word: how can one resurrect something that has never lived?) with the comment: 'Like Maupassant's later story "The Necklace", it tells of lost jewellery ...' (viii). Only in a critical tradition dominated by pigeon-holing in terms of theme and subject would such a remark pass muster. And it *ought* to be self-evident that in critical analysis theme can never be divorced from treatment. But, in his little book on Morley Callaghan, Victor Hoar does precisely that. He begins as if he had made a great critical discovery: 'Whenever Morley Callaghan has commented upon his apprenticeship as a writer of fiction, he has expressed as much interest in the matter of technique as he has in the matter of theme' (1). But he misses Callaghan's point and so divides his book, simplistically, into two parts: I, The Technique: II, The Themes. I cite both these instances, trivial in themselves, not merely because they are elementary – though they show with painful obviousness the literary-critical inertia that has to be challenged – but because they come from books specifically designed for the edification of students. As it is, they can only teach students bad critical habits. Surely, as critics, we can do better than that?

MY OWN OBJECTIONS to thematic criticism are twofold: first, emphasis on themes and related structural patterns generally reveals comparisons rather than contrasts, and often confuses a novel's weaknesses with its strengths; second, the neglect of language is often reflected in linguistic inadequacy within the thematic critic's own prose, and this in turn leads to distortion and crudity of effect. I would like now to pursue these two points in greater detail.

Because he is in no way remarkable for stylistic subtlety, Frederick Philip Grove is a novelist peculiarly suited to the thematic approach. His main thematic preoccupations are easily listed: the pioneering theme; the conflict between generations; the clash between a man's duty to the land and his duty to his wife and family; the inexorable pressure of Time; the contrast between 'vision' and reality, etc. But in listing these, and illustrating their recurrence in the novels, one has said little or nothing about the distinctive quality of Grove as a novelist. On the contrary, one emphasizes what the novels have in common but neglects what gives them variety. For Grove hardly ever repeats himself. Niels Lindstedt in *Settlers of the Marsh* and Len Sterner in *The Yoke of Life* are both young and sexually naïve idealists but in strikingly different ways; the general pattern of Abe Spalding's life in *Fruits of the Earth* may resemble that of John Elliot, Sr., in *Our Daily Bread*, but the details – Abe's attempt to dominate the land by machinery against Elliot's reliance on traditional methods, for example – vary considerably. Indeed, although the organic unity of Grove's total *oeuvre* is important, the variety of intention and effect from book to book is even more so. Whatever principles and laws Grove may recognize as operating on earth, he always presents them in particular instances as they affect particular human lives. His emphasis in his novels is invariably on *people*, people who share certain basic attitudes but differ subtly in motive and response, and this concern for individual uniqueness is what sets him off from many so-called 'Prairie novelists' who attempt no more than a straight, documentary presentation of the Prairie itself.

If we merely classify his themes instead of examining the ways in which they are transformed into art, we shall fail to do justice to Grove's originality. Moreover, I believe that, if the thematic approach is pursued, some of his best effects will be neglected and some of his weaknesses mistaken for strengths. About two years ago, I remember hearing a 'Radio College' programme in which *Settlers of the Marsh* was the focus of attention. The commentator concentrated on thematic patterns – Ellen and Clara as opposites, the balancing of scene against scene, the contrasts between rural and urban values, nature and artifice, innocence and experience, etc., etc. All these are, of course, to be found in the book, but the lecturer seemed to assume that they automatically constituted artistic strengths. Yet it seems to me that the very fact that these patterns are so conspicuous in the novel is, rather, an artistic weakness. The structure is *too* insistent; the content is too readily detachable from the context. *Settlers of the March* has, I believe, many artistic strengths, but these exist despite rather than because of the too-baldly stated themes, the excessively schematic construction.

But I have already expressed my views on the artistry of this novel in print.[1] To demonstrate how Grove creates situations that transcend the thematic, I prefer to turn to a scene in *Our Daily Bread.* John Elliot, Sr., is a man who has lived through the pioneering period, and by the time the novel opens has established himself as a farmer in the Saskatchewan short-grass country. We get one memorable glimpse of his pioneering days, and this occurs in a flashback placed strategically in the very centre of the novel. Elliot is on a visit to his daughter Cathleen and his professor son-in-law, Woodrow Ormond, in Winnipeg. They hold a party (as Woodrow explains, 'A few guests.... Mostly men. Colleagues of mine, or men in public life' (178)), and Elliot feels uncomfortably out of place in this urban and sophisticated

1 See 'The Art of Frederick Philip Grove: *Settlers of the Marsh* as an Example', reproduced in Part Two of this volume. [1989]

intellectual setting. Suddenly, however, a young man engaged in writing a book on the early history of the West asks Elliot for information about the pioneering period. He begins to reminisce, launches into stories and anecdotes, and gradually the attention of all the guests is centred upon him.

The scene is an extremely complex one, and I can do no more than offer a pale indication of its effectiveness. The main point is that this effectiveness lies not in the pioneering theme itself but in the context that Grove has created for it – a context, moreover, that becomes an inextricable part of the subject. He doesn't have to remind us that eras of historical development (or, to be more accurate, eras of white historical development) were so foreshortened on the Prairies that a single lifetime could span the period from pioneers' sod huts and Red River wagons to cars, sumptuous houses, and maid service at the press of a button. Grove's 'meaning' is to be found, not in a detachable theme that can be measured or tabulated, but in the multi-faceted experience of the scene as a whole. In this case the artistry lies, not in language, but in imaginative, creative construction. Here Grove is indisputably a 'maker'.

But I must now turn to a consideration of language. Thematic criticism, I have said, underestimates the importance of language and style; moreover, thematic critics often demonstrate an insensitivity to language in the way they write about literary works. I detect a vicious circle here. There has been so much ponderous Canadian criticism in the past, dull in more than one sense of the word, that some of our younger critics have rebelled against its standards by writing a direct, forceful, but essentially slangy prose. It is easy to sympathize with their motives, but the fact remains that this is a style in which, to put the matter bluntly, serious literary criticism cannot adequately be written.

Here is a minor example. But first, since I begin by quoting John Moss in a context of disapproval, I should state that Moss is a critic whom I greatly admire when he writes at his best; indeed, I recommend *Patterns of Isolation* to my students as the most useful single book on Canadian fiction at the present time. All in all

I find Moss (and this is sincerely intended as a compliment) a critic worth disagreeing with. Here, however, I quote a sentence from *Sex and Violence in the Canadian Novel*: 'Morley Callaghan, in the 1930s and 1940s, exhibited a fascination with not only the moral but the spiritual implications of violence, but he muted sex somewhat, even in *Such Is My Beloved* which features two hookers and a priest' (23). Margaret Atwood, in *Survival,* casually refers to 'the whores in Callaghan's *Such Is My Beloved*' (206), and D.G. Jones mentions the priest's campaign 'to help two prostitutes' (62). Now Callaghan himself took great care to make the narrative voice in the novel speak not of 'prostitutes' or 'whores' or 'hookers' but of 'the girls'. In other words, he habitually refers to them, not in terms of their trade, but in terms of their humanity. Ironically, that is part of the central theme of the novel, but it is conveyed through language and thematic critics seem to miss it. In the scene where Father Dowling confronts his bishop we are told that 'the way the Bishop said common prostitutes hurt him' (129). To Father Dowling himself they are 'the girls' until late in the novel, and on the few occasions when he does refer to them as 'streetwalkers' or 'prostitutes', he is specifically concerned with their profession rather than themselves. Otherwise it is left to Mrs Robison, the Bishop, the probation officer – and the critics – to classify them merely according to their commercial and sexual function in society.

I don't want to exaggerate the significance of this example. After all, the girls *are* prostitutes, and Callaghan does not disguise this – quite the contrary, in fact. It is, admittedly, extremely difficult to avoid using such words while discussing the novel, but Callaghan himself was certainly not being puritanically evasive in eschewing the direct terms.[2] To say that the novel 'fea-

---

2 A registrant at the conference suggested to me after my lecture that 'the girls' might well imply 'prostitutes' in Callaghan's period and place. This possibility should be considered, though a rereading of the novel

tures two hookers and a priest' is to give a misleading impression ('features', with its suggestion of Hollywood movie-advertising, is as much to blame as the reductive 'hookers'). A reader unfamiliar with the book receives no clue as to what kind of book it is.

Let me quote a few sentences from the text to bring us closer to the centre of Callaghan's subject and his art:

> When Father Dowling saw the girls moved in this way, he was so thankful his whole face beamed with gratitude. He moved his chair closer to the bed. He put his hand lightly and shyly on the little dark girl's head and stroked her hair softly and in him was a joy he had never known before. As he tried to smile at the two girls who had been moved by his presence, he felt more love for them than for any one he had known in his parish, a curious, new love that gave him a strange contentment. (13)

The first thing to notice, surely, is the extraordinary delicacy of this. Callaghan succeeds in being profoundly moving when it would have been so easy to lapse into tasteless vulgarity. He assumes an awareness of modern psychology, but achieves a precision and subtlety that we rarely find in the application of Freudian theories. The novel is, among other things, a study of the relation between *eros* and *agape,* between sexual and spiritual love; this is one of its major themes, but Callaghan embodies it in language that provokes the questioning response but not the crude snigger. We realize that Father Dowling lacks self-knowledge, that he is vulnerably naïve, but we also respect him for his spontaneous goodness, for his genuineness. I am groping awkwardly for the adequate words here, but Callaghan made the

with the suggestion in mind did not convince me of its likelihood. It cannot surely be intended in the passage quoted in the next paragraph of my text. And even if the possibility is allowed, the fact remains that (unlike some of his commentators) Callaghan chose the neutral word that need not carry secondary implications.

distinctions and created the essential balance through his words, in the text. And only through attention to Callaghan's words – their tone, rhythm, combinations, and associations – can we come to a proper appreciation of his art. At this level, thematic criticism cannot help us.

I HAVE TRIED TO DEMONSTRATE by brief reference to individual details and scenes, how the thematic approach has to be supplemented before anything very useful can be said about a novel as a work of art. With the same overall aim in mind, I would now like to offer a more extended treatment of a single work, and the book I have chosen is Ethel Wilson's *Swamp Angel.* This book seems to me unquestionably a masterpiece; a title that ought to appear on anyone's list of the ten best Canadian novels. I shall start on the level of subject matter and theme, and then proceed to more directly artistic matters.

Swamp Angel opens, you will remember, with Maggie Vardoe fleeing from her disastrous second marriage, and the main plot focuses upon her gradual development of a new life and a new equilibrium as cook and general assistant in a fishing lodge in the country north of Kamloops. But this plot is punctuated by scenes in Vancouver dominated by Maggie's friend Nell Severance, a wise, obese septuagenarian continually recalling her early life as a circus juggler. We soon realize that Maggie and Nell are being presented as opposites who are yet, in a curious way, complementary. Maggie, trying to escape from a dead past, goes into 'the wilderness', the traditional journey for the religious contemplative. Nell Severance, herself a contemplative and in her own words 'an unusually religious woman' (128), remains almost completely indoors ('Everything of any importance happens indoors', she claims (149)), and on the one occasion on which she ventures outside she suffers a fall that has serious consequences; she surrounds herself with a protective screen of cigarette smoke and harks back to a probably tawdry but in retrospect exotic past. Maggie acts; Nell theorizes. Maggie finds peace only in the wilds; Nell doesn't enjoy (as she puts it) 'drooling over scenery' (66). Maggie, then, a swimmer and fisherman who follows the northward-flying birds on migration, is attuned to nature; Nell, still practising her juggling techniques, relies on artifice.

Yet there are some curious similarities. Both have the capacity to help others in distress; both have to find their place in the uncertain country between solitariness and loneliness. Each needs the other: '"Maggie,"' writes Nell, '"I miss you very much to talk to and I need humanizing. I'm a bad influence on myself"' (128); and Maggie, in a moment of crisis, thinks: 'I wish Nell Severance were here with her acid good sense' (142). If Nell is attached to the Swamp Angel, a revolver that once formed part of her juggling act, Maggie takes with her on her journey 'the little yellow [Chinese] bowl which was now her household god' (73). If Nell thinks about religious values, Maggie acts upon them in her day-to-day life – as Desmond Pacey remarked, 'Mrs Severance comes closest to articulating the creed; Maggie Vardoe embodies it' (Introduction 7).

Although they have been close friends for many years, within the book itself Maggie and Nell meet only once, in a crucial scene in which they discuss the 'themes' of the novel. But as soon as we try to list these themes, we find ourselves (or *should* find ourselves, unless we are content with a crude parody) acutely conscious of Ethel Wilson's art as a 'maker'. So far, my commentary may have suggested a plot as conspicuously polarized as that of *Settlers of the Marsh*, but *Swamp Angel* does not give this impression. The thematic relations between the parts are by no means obvious as we read. Ethel Wilson's art depends to a considerable extent upon her capacity to lead us surely but indirectly towards her unifying 'vision'.

What, then, are the themes? Well, the nature of marriage, together with the related concern of the individual's place within a larger social unit (often the family unit), is a major one. We do not see Maggie's own marriage (or only the last moments of it), but we see its effects. Nor do we see Nell's marriage, since she has long been a widow, but we see the effects of that too in the attitudes of her daughter Hilda. When Maggie establishes herself at the lodge, we are told that her 'union with Three Loon Lake was like a happy marriage' (84), but there she comes in contact, and sometimes conflict, with another marriage, that of the Gunnarsens, trembling in the balance under the strain of the wife's neurotic jealousy and the husband's stubborn obstinacy. There are numerous other references: the happiness of Maggie's first marriage, destroyed by war; Hilda Severance's marriage towards the end of the novel; Edward Vardoe's later liaison with the shadowy Ireen; the eccentric family to which Nell's husband belonged; the humdrum domesticity of a talkative woman who sits next to Maggie on the bus to Kamloops. Moreover, a whole chapter early in the novel is devoted to the Quongs, despite the fact that only the two brothers, Joey and Angus, play any part – and that secondary – in the main plot. But the Quongs are important because they are a true family; they possess a familial loyalty and morale that endures and blossoms despite their relative poverty, cramped living conditions, and apparent cultural deprivation.

It is only after we have been introduced to all these marriages and families that Maggie and Nell discuss the subject – and then Nell, while expressing her faith, 'I believe in marriage' (150), reveals that Philip was never in fact her legal husband, that they had never married because he did not believe in the 'bonds' of matrimony, and Nell, the 'unusually religious woman', had sacrificed her own principles to his. From time to time, Ethel Wilson allows herself the privilege of authorial intrusion, but the profundity of her treatment of marriage and the family depends almost wholly on the examples fully integrated into the novelistic texture and the 'serious irony' of Nell's statement in the context of her own situation. Ethel Wilson's 'thought' is of the utmost significance; however, it is the thought not of a philosopher or of a theologian or of a sociologist but of a creative artist.

Because Maggie has to build a new life out of the ruins of the old, and because this is inevitably a slow process, *Swamp Angel* is also about Time and the relationship between past and present.

Here once again Maggie and Nell are similar yet dissimilar; both must come to terms with the past but for different reasons. For Maggie, separation (or, to use the word that Ethel Wilson emphasizes by giving it to Nell as a surname, 'severance') is essential to her own interests; the burden of the immediate past has become intolerable, and Maggie must cut all connections. For Nell, however, the past – or, rather, her memory of it – is an indulgence, a sentimentality, an addiction like her chain-smoking. A continual harking back to it can be, like the Swamp Angel itself, beautiful but dangerous. The price of Nell's compulsion is paid by her daughter Hilda in the present. Nell, the wise woman, has sufficient intelligence and courage to cut her links with the past, and she does so, significantly, by sending the Swamp Angel to Maggie for safe-keeping and ultimate disposal. After Nell's death, and according to her wishes, Maggie, who has now established the basis for her new life, throws the Swamp Angel into the middle of the lake in which, as a swimmer, she has found a timeless freedom.

If at this point some of you are complaining that my own critique has not yet ventured far beyond thematics and subject matter, you are quite right. Part of my intention is to demonstrate both the difficulty and the challenge of writing adequate literary criticism about a novel that is at once straightforward and extremely subtle. I have deliberately kept close to the thematic in order to show that even a primarily thematic approach should (must) broaden out if it is at all responsive to the artistry of the work. But, ultimately, this can only be accomplished if the verbal quality is stressed – and so far I have only quoted briefly and in the interest of content rather than stylistic effect. Obviously, one could spend a whole lecture and more on detailed verbal analysis. I have time for only the briefest of indicative hints. Most evident (as well as economical) are the *bon mots* of Nell Severance – wise, compassionate, but with a palpable hint of the sardonic:

> [Nell to Edward Vardoe] 'You've got a new life ahead' (you poor fool, she thought).... (49)

> [Nell of Edward Vardoe] 'He's an unpleasant object but worth salvation I suppose.' (49)

> [Nell's creed] 'I believe in faith, I believe in God ... and in man, to some extent at least.' (103)

The effect here depends upon the tone of the spoken voice, upon the cadences and pauses that combine to convey a meaning existent only in those same words and that precise order. Any 'paraphrase', to borrow Davey's term, destroys the artistic balance. One can draw attention to the effect, praise it, even analyse it, but one cannot recreate it in any other form. The themes can be extracted readily enough, but Nell Severance herself, in all her human intricacy, lives in the words as Ethel Wilson arranges them.

But more subtle and less conspicuous is the effect of the narrator's own commentary. Take, for instance, the description of Maggie offered through the eyes of Mr Spencer, the official in the sports shop to which she has gone to sell her fishing flies: 'She was not beautiful; she was not plain. Yes, perhaps she was beautiful. She took no pains to be beautiful' (14). Or of Nell Severance trying to save Vardoe:

> She smiled a faint smile but her face was not happy because she saw Edward Vardoe in his helplessness and his meanness and his stupidity and she thought again that life is unfair. 'It's not fair ... not fair', she murmured, and then she went into the kitchen and made a tall pot of cocoa. (49)

There is no 'style' here, no 'fine writing' – and I have chosen these examples for that reason. What we have is an exquisite sense of clarity, of finding the right sequence of words to convey a meaning: first, Maggie's appearance poised between the plain and the beautiful, a balance established between the polarized words as they are repeated with variations, and all this presented through an observer in the very act of discovery, of responsive assessment; and then the extraordinarily subtle sense of a whole situation – Vardoe's inadequacy, Nell's inner reaction, her resigned yet positive practicality, all fused into a single experience. These extracts will not seem important in any thematic reading, yet they are of the essence of *Swamp Angel* as an achieved work of art.

Poise, simplicity, profundity, exquisite control of tone, delicate human insight, and above all that compassion that becomes the redeeming feature of so many of her human and therefore imperfect characters: all these are qualities that distinguish Ethel Wilson's work and are communicated through the verbal texture of her novels. One thinks of the elaborate inlaid beauty alongside the potential force of the Swamp Angel, the satisfying but delicate fragility of Maggie's yellow Chinese bowl.

And reference to revolver and bowl leads me to a related point. Through these recurring images and a number of others, Ethel Wilson conveys additional, often complex meanings. We call them symbols – yet how clumsy, how unsatisfactory is that word also! Merely another way of pigeon-holing that proves limiting. Ethel Wilson warns us within the novel of the inadequacy. Nell Severance wakes after her fall, remembers the crowd and remembers its response to the revolver, and knows that the symbolic Swamp Angel must go: 'All this nowadays of symbol symbol symbol ... destroying reality ...' (79). This is not merely Nell's own interior monologue; Ethel Wilson has spoken in her own voice about the limitations of symbolism, and we know that she shares Nell's sentiments (see Pacey, *Ethel Wilson* 36). Nell renounces the Swamp Angel for the very reason that it has become emblematic and therefore unreal, and after it has been sent away Ethel Wilson remarks: 'Her endeared symbol was gone and she would not touch it any more. I have nothing now but the reality, she thought stoically and fairly cheerfully ...' (83). It is a redeeming act, and it reminds us, as serious readers, that our very terminology, in its attractiveness and convenience, can become reductively simplifying. The Swamp Angel is more than a symbol in being itself.

MY TIME IS ALMOST EXHAUSTED, but I must give a few minutes' attention to one more novel. So far, my examples have been drawn from familiar and established works. But it is a responsibility of criticism to be able to assess the contemporary, and I feel the need to comment briefly on a novel that has not yet found a recognized, undisputed place in enduring Canadian fiction. One published within the last twelve months proves admirably suited to my purpose since its qualities cannot in my opinion be properly revealed by the thematic approach. I refer to Jack Hodgins's *The Invention of the World*.

This novel portrays and explores two human communities: the Revelations Colony of Truth, a peculiar quasi-religious group founded by Donal Keneally, a 'messiah-monster' (120), on Vancouver Island at the turn of the century, and a collection of idiosyncratic misfits and their acquaintances who occupy the site of the defunct colony in the early 1970s. Superficially, this loosely knit organization appears to provide no more than a minimal framework roughly linking a collection of separable short stories. Indeed, one is tempted to suggest *Spit Delaney's Island Revisited* as a suitable title. But further consideration shows that this greatly underestimates the subtlety of Hodgins's art.

On a first reading, while brooding over the subject of this paper, I found myself doubting whether any thematic significance could be read into the novel at all. But that, I now see, would be mistaken. Keneally's bringing the whole population of an Irish village to create a new life and a new community in Canada obviously has nationalistic and historical implications, while the suggestion that they may in fact only exchange 'one madman master for another' (97) forms the basis for a possible political allegory. The problem they face on arrival – 'How was it possible to turn this forest into a piece of land where they could do the only thing they knew how to do, which was farm?' (116) –

becomes an archetypal version of the pioneer theme, and it is by no means accidental that their successors on the property, Maggie Kyle and the 'collection of losers' she gathers around her, are referred to as the 'new pioneers' (264). Moreover, the fact that the site of the colony becomes a modern trailer-park patronized by 'American tourists who spend their time out on the strait catching salmon to take home with them' (xi) clearly strikes a number of sensitive contemporary chords.

This kind of approach could be extended, but ultimately such interpretations prove unsatisfying. When one of the immigrants insists that the hero of the land to which they are sailing is a 'fine big red-nosed Irishman named Sir Sean A. McDermott' (112), we realize that it would be easy to take this kind of meaning too solemnly. And one would have to be unusually insensitive not to respond to the bubbling exuberance that pulses through the whole novel. How can we come to terms with the elusive, pigeon-hole-defying richness of this book?

The real title – not *Spit Delaney's Island Revisited* but *The Invention of the World* – may give us the clue we need. Who does the inventing? There are, I think, four possible answers (all undoubtedly correct): 1. Donal Keneally, who claims to keep God in his pocket and, as founder of the Colony, brings his people to 'all the world that anyone ever needs' (253); 2. Maggie Kyle, mother, bride, and 'loggers' whore' (342), who occupies the central place in the novel and who, indispensable to her collection of losers, proves a positive, humane, beneficent alternative to Keneally; 3. Strabo Becker, who 'wants to be God' (x) and who, armed with notebook and tape-recorder, goes out to interview, to collect and preserve the records out of which the story is built (of him we are told: 'Sometimes this god-man almost believes that he owns this island, that he has perhaps invented it ... a shy man, who knows only this much: that the tale ... exists somewhere at the centre of his gathered hoard, in the confusion of tales and lies and protests and legends and exaggerations' (x-xi)); and 4. – of course – Jack Hodgins himself who, by creating the novel, has invented not only its world but Keneally, Maggie, and Becker as well.[3]

But it is, of course, a world built out of words, and the world is vivid and memorable because Hodgins's words are also. Stylistically, the book is a *tour de force.* As many readers must have noted, the story of the journey from Ireland and the founding of the Colony is told as if it were a Celtic myth in that Irish vernacular lilt that comes to us through William Carleton, Charles Lever, Lady Gregory, 'Kiltartanese', and all the verbal blarney of the Irish Literary Revival. And the central section, 'Scrapbook', is Becker's scrapbook in which he types up the recorded statements of his interviewees (who subject the Colony to a many-angled analysis reminiscent of Browning in *The Ring and the Book*), and thus preserves the individual speech-rhythms of a varied cross-section of Vancouver Island residents. Throughout, Hodgins's own ear for varieties of speech is manifest in the crisp, differentiated dialogue; and above all we enjoy his controlled, limpid, exquisitely modulated, but direct and natural-sounding prose. Like Ethel Wilson, Hodgins controls his novel both formally and stylistically: he unifies his plot by showing how Maggie Kyle and her friends can only come to terms with their own problems after coming to terms with Keneally's colony, which constitutes the past of their world; and for all the stylistic variety, we sense the continuing presence of Hodgins's verbal discipline behind the work.

Hodgins's style cannot be properly illustrated because it shifts and adapts with such astonishing ease to the requirements of his subject. Here, then, is a quotation offered not as a representative illustration, but as a (not *quite* random) sample:

---

3 Here I failed to make the distinction between 'invention' and 'creation' that Hodgins insists on. See the interview with Geoff Hancock (61-62), and my later discussion of *The Invention of the World* reproduced in Part Two of this book. [1989]

> They drove north, mostly north, for more than two hours. They moved slowly at first, out of town; down around the highrise apartment block and across the bridge and out past the string of service stations and take-out restaurants and motels that stood where until recently there had been the high old houses and flower gardens of the town's pioneers.... Faster now, on a widened highway, they passed a long series of sprawled-out new-car lots and the long wall of wrecked cars piled ten high, and passed between the two sky-reflecting lakes. Faster still, the hood flapping and shuddering, the tires whining, they roared up through roadside stands of timber and gouged-out subdivisions and trailer sales, out into country, and farms, then dipped down to follow the edge of the strait, a thumbprint bay, where the broken barnacled posts and piles of rubble from an abandoned sawmill lay in the beach gravel and the lace froth of the water's edge, passed a long line of freight cars thundering south on the tracks, and swelled up again to the top of a hill to snake through a village where a woman in a blue-flowered dress stopped walking on the shoulder to watch them go by. In the mirror Maggie saw her turn, a thick woman with her hair in rollers, to waddle away on her short white legs.
>
> North. She needed no maps for this journey.... (324-25)

That represents Jack Hodgins's 'world', microcosm and macrocosm, regional and universal, and, although it suggests a modern (and a quintessentially Canadian) landscape, it is nonetheless his 'invention' – what he calls 'an imitation world that hid a multitude of unsuspected unfamiliar things' (107). It is made not from themes, but from words. And this brings me (you will be relieved to hear) to my final point. The 'world' of a novel is never identical to the 'real' world that it reflects. Often, given the realistic convention that still (and perhaps inevitably) dominates the novel form, the fictive world may seem remarkably similar to the one we inhabit, but there remains always an essential difference. It is a world of imagination, and it is therefore subject, not to the laws of this world, but to those of art. I am not going to launch into pomposities about 'the verbal universe' because such discussion soon becomes arid. I merely point out that the thematic approach to literature, whatever lip-service it may pay to Imagination, Creativity, etc., etc., ultimately reads the world of art as if it were our own – reduces it, I would say, to our terms. True, we should never separate the two worlds – the existence and the necessity of art depend upon the connection – but we must approach the world of art (here, the subsidiary world of fiction) humbly and flexibly, always taking care to remain faithful to the materials from which it is created. For literature in general – and, for our purposes, the novel in particular – the materials are words (with, once again, their tones, rhythms, associations, and implications). If we neglect them – and the thematic approach does, alas, undervalue them – we are neglecting the vital ingredients of that created world.

Poet as Critic: Louis Dudek

This review of Louis Dudek's *Selected Essays and Criticism* (1978) and *Technology & Culture: Six Lectures* (1979) appeared in *Canadian Forum* in April 1980. Most reviews are by their very nature ephemeral, but this one seemed worth preserving because it traces a Canadian poet and teacher's single-minded attempt to work out his own independent literary-critical stance. Dudek's prose writings have not yet been recognized as a major contribution to Canadian intellectual and cultural debate. The publication of a substantial selection of Dudek's criticism in a special issue of *Open Letter* (Spring/Summer 1981) and of his *In Defence of Art: Critical Essays & Reviews* (1988) has, I believe, reaffirmed the high position that I accord his work here. There is a sensitive wisdom in this material that we ignore at our peril.

ON 8 MAY 1977 Louis Dudek presided as chairman over a panel discussion at the University of Ottawa climaxing an academic conference on Isabella Valancy Crawford. In his initial remarks he delivered what he calls in a title of one of the essays in *Selected Essays and Criticism* a 'rib-roasting' of the assembled scholars and critics:

> I have been suffering here for two days listening to papers and discussions that seem entirely out of focus with the needs of Canadian criticism.
>
> I have spent my life, or at any rate the 35 years of my literary life, disinfecting and fumigating against the kind of poetry ... that the papers and panelists have been analyzing and treating with very high seriousness. (Tierney 123)

Read in the published record of the conference, Dudek's remarks shine out as the one ray of critical sense in an oppressive darkness of barren pedantry. Predictably, the other participants seem to have had no idea what he was getting at – the editor even attempts to pass off his remarks as 'humorous' (3)!

Until recently, Dudek's contribution to the Canadian literary scene has seemed a little blurred. Because his poetry wasn't represented in Milton Wilson's influential *Poems of Mid-Century* anthology, his work is less familiar to paperback-reading students of Canadian poetry than it otherwise might have been. And his critical writing has up to now been scattered in newspapers, journals, and little magazines. But thanks to the appearance of his *Collected Poetry* in 1971 and the recent publication of these critical gatherings, we are now in a better position to see his work as something approaching a totality. And a very impressive achievement it proves to be.

First, *Selected Essays and Criticism.* Perhaps Dudek's most significant contribution to Canadian criticism (and the implications of the statement for our current literary-critical situation are staggering) is his continued insistence on the centrality of the value-judgement. As he remarks in an appreciation of Alden Nowlan in 1969,

> ... the real business of literature – to know what is good, and why, to explore the range of possible human 'meaning', and to see how this is anchored properly in the text – [has] been almost forgotten.... What is needed is some kind of total relevant criticism, which would examine the text, relate it to large ideas, and return again to the text for sound evaluation. Criticism really begins and ends with evaluation, whether we know it or not. (282)

This, I think, is the cornerstone to his whole critical position. His quarrel with Northrop Frye and Marshall McLuhan (both of whom, it should be noted, he lists among 'our first genuine critics' (304) – perhaps because they at least have 'large ideas') stems from their hostility to evaluative criticism. Frye 'tells us that in [*The Bush Garden*] he is not interested in evaluation.... But he has never been clear himself as to the role of evaluation in his own criticism' (306). Elsewhere, Dudek notes, Frye 'denied that value-judgement has any function at all in criticism' (306). Dudek counters this by arguing that 'the whole meaning of mythopoeic criticism lies in the kind of judgement that comes out of it' (307). Similarly, in *Technology & Culture* he objects that McLuhanism 'makes technology more important than art, and ... renounces all attempt[s] to make value-judgements about the content of communications' (44). Dudek's own 'large ideas' have very different emphases.

But, despite what I have written about his not infrequent strategic outbursts, Dudek's own criticism is judicious in various connotations of that word. Throughout his *Selected Essays and Criticism*, Dudek constantly weighs the evidence with care and ends with a discriminating verdict. His early critique of Innis and McLuhan, for example, is in the best traditions of practical criticism in that he approaches their theories through detailed examination of representative passages of their prose. At the same time, he is careful not to present his own work as a salvo in the war of conflicting critical schools. He makes every effort to put each subject in perspective; he is never satisfied with a simple taking of sides. Thus in his review of *The Educated Imagination* – despite the dogmatic title, 'Northrop Frye's Untenable Position' – he begins with what is surely a fair statement of the whole critical controversy:

> I have been asking myself what it is about [Frye's] position that makes it so aggravating to myself and some of the poets I know, as well as so appealing to a few disciples (Reaney, Macpherson, Mandel), when we are all of us interested in good poetry and good criticism. (175)

Dudek always (well, nearly always) strives to be fair. His aim is to bring both reason and imagination to bear, and to restore any imbalance he sees in the contemporary response. In one review he combines consideration of F.R. Scott's *The Eye of the Needle* and Jay Macpherson's *The Boatman* because he believes that the former was unfairly dismissed and the latter accepted uncritically. He attempts to qualify the trend rather than to reverse it. He is also careful to display – and make due allowance for – his own preferences. Here is a convenient example:

> Daryl Hine's poems are almost faultless, but they are also without a tremor of excitement, like a seismograph on the moon.... In technical proficiency, Layton is miles behind Daryl Hine, he is often writing pure doggerel – yet he has more original and genuine poetry than any of the Toronto scholar-poets. (154, 155)

Within the whole context of Dudek's relation to Layton, this is both crucial and characteristic. His fluctuating response to Layton's poetry is, in his own view, not a change of mind but a change in keeping with the circumstances of Layton's own development. At any rate, he is acutely conscious of the dangers of his position; as he remarks in 'Layton on the Carpet', 'the old champion uneasily becomes the new fault-finder' (136).

Selected Essays and Criticism is full of shrewd assessments of (for the most part) contemporary Canadian poets and developments in the contemporary poetic scene. But his interest in 'large ideas' is always present, and in *Technology & Culture* he widens his range to consider the entirety of modern (that is, post-modernist) civilization. It is, I think, profoundly characteristic of Dudek that he should refuse to be confined by the boundaries of purely – or merely – literary criticism and should see the function of criticism at the present time (Arnold's phrase inevitably springs to mind) in much broader terms. The very fact that ours is an age of increasing specialization makes him determined not to be a specialist. So he writes in the preface: 'I have never had the fear of specialized knowledge that some scholars have. I believe that specialists do their meticulous work to serve *us,* who must use their knowledge on a comprehensive scale' (vii).

The six lectures contained in the book were delivered at various universities and learned societies between 1969 and 1975. Together they record Dudek's reaction to the various challenges and cultural revolutions of the 1960s. Although they include certain optimistic hints – 'what I have in mind', he remarks at one point, 'is a kind of theory of technological progress that leaves much room for hope' (13) – the predominant impression conveyed by the book is that of a civilized man brooding stoically over clear signs of cultural degeneration. He laments the 'great avalanche from high art to popular noise' (39), pinpoints the decline of the review-section in modern newspapers in the significant title-change from 'Book Reviews' to 'Entertainment', asks rhetorically whether even the best film can compare with Michelangelo's 'David', Beethoven's Fifth, or Milton's *Paradise Lost,* and decides that 'the CBC is no longer a medium for promoting the civilized life' (39).

Some, of course, will dismiss Dudek's position here as blatant reaction (typically, in line with his concern for judiciousness already mentioned, he wonders himself whether these laments for a sick culture represent 'just the gripes of an aging man' (39)). But the years that have passed since Dudek delivered his jeremiad have surely borne out his prognostications. 'The CBC is no longer a medium for promoting the civilized life' – these words were spoken in 1971. Five years earlier, Dudek had presented a series of six talks on the CBC later published as *The First Person in Literature.* I read these for the first time a month or two ago, and my immediate reaction was: what a golden age, when such talks were still possible on radio! At the beginning of the 1980s such a prospect is, simply, inconceivable. The process Dudek identifies has even developed to the point where 'the civilized life' seems a quaintly old-fashioned term in sore need of defence and far removed from 'reality' (the title of the lecture that contains the phrase is, significantly, 'Reality in the Arts and Education').

But: 'There is such a thing as being over-civilized.' This, too, is Dudek – from his poem *Europe* (48). One finds there the articulation of a scrupulous artistic and social conscience along with the same kind of brooding over cultural decline:

As in Genoa, never good for art,

that defeated Pisa,
    says Baedeker,
(judge the decay of the tourist intellect,
        the old guides against the new blue books –
    where do the French girls strip
        for *exhibition*, where are the night clubs:
    'What to See What to Do in Paris') (88-89)

We begin to see a continuing preoccupation in all Dudek's work, both poetry and prose. The long 'travel' poems – *Europe, En México, Atlantis* – continually set past against present, old world against new, the cultivated (dead) against the vulgar (living). Dudek is always a literary tourist, and acutely conscious of the vulnerability of his position. 'Do the arts matter?' (*En México* 7) is a perpetual question, and the affirmative answer is never offered thoughtlessly or glibly. All the more valuable, then, is this firm defence of a discriminated tradition from the past (the dross, including Isabella Valancy Crawford, is ruthlessly excluded) as a model for possible regeneration in the beleaguered present.

I have entitled this review 'Poet as Critic' because Dudek's critical writings buttress the unabashedly intellectual vision of the poetry. With the publication of these two books, the essential unity of his contribution to Canadian letters becomes clear. As he remarks himself in *Technology & Culture*: 'Art is incomplete without interpretation. The "whole event" is a happy cooperation of reason and imagination' (63). There, I submit, is his creative attitude in a nutshell. But Dudek the clear-sighted, agonized poet (in *Europe*) should have the last, humanely balanced word:

The past is something one learns and contemplates
        only to make the present a diamond
as hard as the Duomo of Siena,
brilliant in all facets.
To be torn from these roots is to be dying.

But I would rather have my friend's new poem
            than all the Coliseum,
which is a blood-stained stable, fallen in ruin,
and your kind letters, than all the sculptured words
            in all the crumbling friezes. (97)

Atwood as (Infuriating) Critic

This review of Margaret Atwood's *Second Words: Selected Critical Prose* (1982) appeared in *Canadian Forum* in February 1983. I have taken the opportunity to restore a few sentences at the close that for some reason were chopped off the original. Because of the success of *Survival* and her status as a media personality, Atwood's literary criticism is decidedly better known than Dudek's, though there can surely be no question as to the superiority of the latter. Those who accept the responsibility of reviewing and critical commentary should get their priorities straight. In this review I tried to make the necessary discriminations, praising what deserved praise but protesting against all that seemed below Atwood's best standard – and, most important, giving my reasons. Evaluative criticism once again.

IF I WERE ASKED to write a seventeen-word review of this book, I would have no difficulty: when it is good it is very very good, and when it is bad it is horrid. But I cannot, of course, stop there. I must explain what I consider good and what horrid, and I would like to set the book firmly into a general critical context, though to do so with any thoroughness would require far more space than I am allowed. Part of the difficulty arises from the fact that these reviews, speeches, and articles would never have been collected and republished had they not been written by Margaret Atwood, poet, novelist, and author of *Survival* (not to mention media personality). Readers will consult *Second Words* not so much to learn about the books and issues discussed as to explore and savour Atwood's responses to them. Inevitably, the spectre of *Survival* haunts this book, and before I can adequately confront *Second Words* I must make my peace – if that's the right phrase – with the earlier volume. Because Atwood makes a number of remarks in the course of this book about academic reactions to *Survival,* I must as a responsible academic reviewer (while agreeing with Atwood that some are irresponsible or incompetent) define my own response to the earlier book.

While I consider Atwood a major Canadian poet and one of our most gifted and intelligent contemporary novelists, I have to say that I found *Survival* infuriating and this book scarcely less so. In *Second Words* Atwood writes of *Survival*: 'most self-respecting professors of Canlit begin their courses, I'm told, with a sort of ritual sneer at it. It's true it has no footnotes: the intended audience was not the footnote crowd' (105). This is typical of Atwood's strategy. I have to plead guilty to the charge, but my reasons for warning students against *Survival* have nothing to do with footnotes, and I've never heard anyone criticize the book for that silly reason. (Footnotes, by the way, are not just academic frippery; they enable readers to check up on the writer – which is why I include page-references in this review. They facilitate access to truth, and this is surely no bad thing, even when *Survival* is in question.)

My own reasons are as follows:

1. As the subtitle ('A Thematic Guide to Canadian Literature') indicates, this is an example of thematic criticism, and I was just as suspicious of this approach in 1972, when *Survival* appeared and everyone was obsessed with themes, as I am now when thematic criticism is decidedly less popular.
2. It is frequently distorting and sometimes incorrect. Let us take, for example, some of her remarks about Margaret Laurence. First, in offering 'a few capsule Canadian plots', she produces the following travesty of *The Stone Angel*: 'Old woman hangs on grimly to life and dies at the end' (33-34). This is intended to back up a thesis about the difficulty of survival, but (apart from the absurd inadequacy of such a summary) Atwood's selective distortion becomes clear as soon as we realize that Hagar is the only heroine to die in the whole Manawaka series. Later, Atwood describes Nick Kazlik in *A Jest of God* as 'a visiting trifler, and a married one at that' (209). Now a main point about the plot of *A Jest of God*

is that Nick is *not* married. I am forced to quote Atwood against herself: 'Let us begin, please, by trying to tell the truth about the books we are reading' (*Second Words* 140). Thematic criticism has severe limitations at the best of times, but a thematic criticism that cannot even get the themes right is indefensible.

3. Atwood never makes up her mind whether *Survival* is an 'introductory guide' to Canadian literature (which is what she calls it in *Second Words* (385)) or 'a book of patterns' (*Survival* 11). If it is the latter, I'm just not very interested; if the former, then Robin Mathews (whom she takes to task in *Second Words*) is absolutely right in complaining about the omissions, though my own list would differ somewhat from his. There is something radically wrong about an 'introductory guide' that never so much as mentions T.C. Haliburton, Sara Jeannette Duncan, Stephen Leacock, Robertson Davies, Robert Kroetsch, Rudy Wiebe, and Hugh Hood (the last three, in case anyone wonders, had all published important work by 1972). If these writers had been included, Atwood could hardly have asserted that 'a reader must face the fact that Canadian literature is undeniably [*sic*!] sombre and negative' (*Survival* 245).
4. A curious feature of *Survival* (and, indeed, of *Second Words*) is that when Atwood has something subtle and particularly thoughtful to say, she writes precisely and well; but when she finds herself on shaky ground or wants (to change metaphors) to pull the wool over our eyes for some reason or other, she flounders on with slang and a joke. Unfortunately, I have no space to go into details, but the interested reader is welcome to test this opinion against the text, and some of my later quotations from *Second Words* will, I hope, illustrate the point.
5. Although this may well reveal all sorts of dire things about my own subconscious, I have to admit that I find the now famous 'basic victim positions' (36-39) irresistibly funny, and have never been able to keep them straight. In any case, they work on the heads-I-win-tails-you-lose principle (if you claim not

> to be a victim, you're basic position one), so argument is impossible. Atwood has hermetically sealed herself from challenge.

These are just some of my objections. Of course, there are lots of very sensible observations in *Survival* (as one would expect from a book written by someone with Atwood's intellectual sharpness), but its faults can lead the unwary into sloppy critical habits. Because I want my students to transcend thematic criticism, get their facts right, obtain a broad rather than a narrow view of Canadian literature, realize the importance of clarity and precision in writing critical prose, and concern themselves with more important things than 'basic victim positions', I feel bound to issue a public-health warning about *Survival* from the outset. When I do this, some students are shocked, some stimulated; some (Atwood may be interested to know) even find it liberating.

And so, at long last, to *Second Words.* This collection contains material spread over more than twenty years, extending back twelve years before *Survival* and ending at the moment of publication ten years after. Several of the items arise out of *Survival* itself, and it will be appropriate to start with these. Let me take 'What's So Funny? Notes on Canadian Humour' as a representative example. One of my complaints about *Survival* (related, of course, to the absence of Haliburton, Leacock, Davies, etc.) was the more or less total neglect of humour. Atwood admits rather ingenuously that the article contains 'material I would have included in *Survival,* had I thought of it at the time' (106). It eventually appeared two years later, in 1974, but it contains many of the same strategies – and inadequacies. She begins by isolating the characteristics of English, American, and Canadian humour, which she sums up at the end as follows:

> If laugher [i.e. writer] and audience in English humour are saying, 'I am not like them, I am a gentleman', and if their American counterparts are saying, 'I am not like them, I am not a dupe',

> Canadian laughers and audiences – or those examined here, at any rate – seem to be saying, 'I am not like them, I am not provincial, I am cosmopolitan.' (188)

Very neat – but it just doesn't fit the facts. Her generalization about English humour is based on (for goodness' sake!) 'the pages of the nineteenth-century *Punch*' (176) with a quick glance at Dickens. The only twentieth-century writer mentioned – with the exception of Shaw, who might reasonably protest that, if he can be classified as English, Atwood can be called a Yank – is (for goodness' sake again) P.G. Wodehouse! One can only assume that Atwood knows absolutely nothing about what has been going on in England for the past fifty years or more (where are the gentlemen of yesteryear? what about Lucky Jim?). The American section is (slightly) more up to date, though she implies that Faulkner and his readers have 'real admiration' for the Snopeses (179). She begins the Canadian account with *Sarah Binks,* but as no English or American versions of literary parody have been offered we can hardly draw any conclusions; and she misses an opportunity while discussing Richler of comparing his attitudes with those of the English 'angry young men' (by no stretch of the imagination 'gentlemen') who were prominent when he was establishing himself as a novelist. Atwood doesn't even begin to make her case. Admittedly, her observations are offered as 'notes', but in a country with a healthy critical tradition such preliminary jottings would not get published, let alone republished.

Of the fifty items collected here, thirty-two are reviews. The earliest, including a thoughtful and judicious treatment of Margaret Avison's *Winter Sun,* appeared in *Acta Victoriana* while she was still an undergraduate and offer dramatic evidence of her formidably precocious talent. Later reviews for, among others, the Toronto *Globe and Mail* and *The New York Times Book Review* concern themselves with non-Canadian poets like Adrienne Rich, Anne Sexton, and Erica Jong, and so (I risk being branded as an internationalist here, but so does Atwood) enable us to see her own poetry in a wider context than that provided by 'Canlit'. At the same time, unlike many poet critics, she has a wide range of appreciation for Canadian poetry that is often very different from her own. I am thinking in particular of reviews about George Johnston, Al Purdy, James Reaney, a beautifully controlled review-tribute to Pat Lowther and John Thompson who had both recently died, and a thoughtful article on John Newlove. She reviews a variety of fiction writers, including Marie-Claire Blais, Timothy Findley, Nadine Gordimer, Audrey Thomas, W.D. Valgardson, and if she displays a certain bias in favour of the Gothic, the macabre, and the grotesque, this suggests interesting links with parts of her own fiction. All in all, the reviews, though brief, are among the best things in the book.

Her articles and lectures tend to raise my hackles again. Here we find essays that range from popular pieces for *Maclean's* and *Saturday Night,* through contributions to books aimed at feminist readers, to papers delivered at universities and even addresses to Amnesty International and a Consortium on (wait for it) Inter-American Relations. As one reads these one after the other, one begins to detect a rather disturbing pattern not unrelated, I suspect, to the shifts in style and seriousness that I have commented on while discussing *Survival.* She will be flippant, jokey, brash, brassy, as slick as Trudeau and as slack as most of his Cabinet, and then, just as her audience has accustomed itself to some unliterary horsing around, she will slip in her serious 'message'. Now all teachers (and preachers) learn to play variants on this basic technique. As she observes in her introduction, 'what gets said, when you're making a speech, depends a lot on whom you're saying it to' (14). Agreed. If I were writing this review for the *University of Toronto Quarterly* instead of *Canadian Forum* I would write it more soberly and go into greater academic detail (I might even put in some footnotes). But (and this is important) I would basically be no more serious – though possibly a bit more solemn – than I'm being here. What disturbs me about Atwood's speeches is that all too often she gives the impression that she covertly despises her audience. I hear muted whispers in a sort of sub-text: 'I may be a poet, but I can get down to your level'; 'you never expected you'd hear a woman saying that in public, did you?'; 'all right, you thought I'd be outrageous but not in this way, so I've diddled you once again.' I feel rather mean in saying this – for all I know, it may be the result of nervousness or the pressures of being a public figure – but the impression is insistent and recurring.

Moreover, there are speeches where she makes surprisingly little effort to be careful about her facts. For instance, while addressing the Harvard Consortium on Inter-American Relations, she claims that in Canada in 1961 a 'novel that sold a thousand [copies] was a raving best-seller' (381). At this point I remembered something from Elspeth Cameron's *Hugh MacLennan: A Writer's Life,* and looked it up. In 1959 MacLennan (who was in a position to know) defined a best-seller as a book that sold '5,000 to 10,000 hard-back copies' and reported that in about eight months since its first publication *The Watch That Ends the Night* had sold 13,000 copies in Canada alone (298-99). Doesn't Atwood care about getting her facts right? I might add that, while she was an undergraduate at the University of Toronto, I was there as a graduate student just arrived from England and distressingly ignorant of Canadian literature. But I was well aware of its existence, began reading in the area on the advice of Canadian student-friends, and never encountered anything resembling the total hostility or indifference to Canadian literature that she claims to remember (see 381, 402, and elsewhere). Atwood didn't go to Victoria College for nothing; she is very good at constructing myths.

In numerous references to the critics of her books, she has story after story about the inept, the ignorant, and the contemptible, plus several of the to-be-expected sideswipes at academics, but I cannot recall her mentioning a single instance of the serious and respectful attention that her work has received from academic critics – some of it ponderous and misguided, to be sure, but much of it intelligent and informed. And, despite the impression that she gives here, a considerable percentage of it was written by male commentators. I'm not denying the truth of what she says – God knows, she's suffered from absurd notices in her time, but so have most writers, male or female. Hers is not, therefore, by any means the whole truth.

Atwood complains more than once, and very properly, about male assertions (intended as compliments) that she thinks like a man (193 etc.). I would never dream of saying anything so silly, but (and I think Atwood would accept this) I do believe that she thinks like a novelist – or, for that matter, like a poet. What I mean is that her thought is most probing and most profound when it displays itself in imaginative terms. For her insight into human relationships I shall return again and again to, say, *The Journals of Susanna Moodie* and *Life Before Man*; the Atwood who produced these books seems to me to be thinking far more deeply than the Atwood of *Survival* or *Second Words.* Furthermore, she has, I believe, far more of importance to say about the position of women in the modern world in *The Edible Woman* and *Surfacing* than in the articles reproduced here. I would not be so exasperated at the deficiencies of this book if I were not so conscious that sometimes she is writing far below the level of her best self. The two last items are perfect illustrations of my point. A review of *Poems Twice Told* is probably the best treatment of Jay Macpherson's poetry that I have ever read. But the final address, 'Writing the Male Character', originally delivered in a 'somewhat different version', whatever that means, at the University of Waterloo (436), might well have underestimated her audience even if she had been lecturing to the Shriners. The one is very good; the other is horrid. As a sincere, even devoted admirer of her poetry and her novels (and here it seems proper to mention *Lady Oracle* which, for all its wildly farcical elements, never loses its subtle poise). I am saddened by the 'horrid' instances that stick out, to discriminating readers, like the proverbial sore thumb. How could you, I want to say, how could you?

The Function of Canadian Criticism at the Present Time

'The Function of Canadian Criticism at the Present Time' began as a lecture delivered under the auspices of the Department of English at the University of Alberta and was later expanded as a contribution to the tenth anniversary issue of *Essays on Canadian Writing* (1984-85). It contains perhaps the most precise expression of my attitudes towards Canadian literature and Canadian criticism at that time. The intervening years have altered the situation in some respects – many of the promised editions, for instance, have now appeared. I believe, however, that my principal arguments are just as relevant now as they were then.

THIS WILL BE A VERY PERSONAL ARGUMENT, but I make no apology for that. After all, criticism is a very personal activity – which is not to say that anyone's preference is as good as anyone else's but that, at its bedrock, it is an art and not a science. It is possible to prove that the square on the hypotenuse of a right-angled triangle is equal to the sum of the squares on the other two sides; it is not possible to prove (though it may seem superficially even more obvious) that Hugh Hood is a better novelist than Ralph Connor. Words and images can paradoxically be more elusive than atoms and molecules. A correct scientific procedure for the analysis of a specimen can be established and followed; an appropriate literary procedure for the analysis of a work of art must be worked out anew every time. All this ought to be self-evident, but I fancy it isn't. I begin with it because I sense that a perennial problem in Canadian criticism has been a reluctance to face the facts of the discipline – or even, given the non-scientific nature of the enterprise, a reluctance to grant that any discipline exists.

What I offer in the next few pages is one man's report on the current state of literary criticism and scholarship as practised in this country. It is, I am convinced, a timely subject because I believe that we are now in a state of transition, that a period of retrenchment and consolidation is desirable if we are to develop the skills that our literature now demands of us. A recent article that I recommend for close attention (to be taken to heart, learnt from, and occasionally disagreed with) is John Moss's 'Bushed in the Sacred Wood', which begins as follows: 'The resources of English Canadian literary criticism are no longer adequate to the achievement of the literature' (161). I agree with that (though I would question the 'no longer'). There follows Moss's personal argument – I think, a valuable one. And hear also what uncomfortable words John Metcalf (no friend of Moss) writes in *Kicking Against the Pricks*: 'There is no critical consensus in Canada about Canadian writing and very little critical writing worth the paper it's printed on' (160). I agree with that too, and with most of Metcalf's contentious book (though there are details from which I firmly dissent). It is another personal argument. And here, for better or worse, is mine.

IN MY OPINION, then, the study of Canadian literature has recently come to the end of one phase and is in the process of entering another. It is no longer necessary, thank goodness, to argue for the subject itself. And here I remember a slogan from the past: 'Yes, there is a Canadian literature. It does exist.' That was Douglas Lochhead opening his general preface to the 'Literature of Canada: Poetry and Prose in Reprint' series which began to appear from the University of Toronto Press in 1972. I suspect that, even then, this opening gambit involved something of a rhetorical flourish, though a decade earlier it needed to be said. Now in 1984 it seems superfluous. We (at least those of us who are concerned with such matters) are much more solidly aware of a distinctive literary heritage; we do not have to be so defensive. Indeed (and I have *Kicking Against the Pricks* again in mind) the danger may well be, as Metcalf implies, that excessive adulation, the boosterism that goes along with aggressive publication and nationalistic propagandizing, can produce a backlash. We shall be wise to tread carefully. Where, it seems appropriate for us to ask, should Canadian criticism be going?

But to answer that question I must begin by looking at the immediate past, and by offering an embarrassing report from my own experience. I became a critic and scholar of Canadian literature – if, indeed, I can lay claim to those titles – after I had made a modest reputation for myself in another area of English studies. The same is true of a number of Canadianists, and all of those to whom I have spoken agree that they are conscious of a lowering of the intellectual temperature when they cross the boundary into Canadian studies. The standard of scholarship seems less rigorous, the level of criticism and commentary less disciplined and sophisticated; even the quality of writing appears slacker, less precise. Sad but, I am convinced, true – and I see no point in pretending that it isn't true. If the obvious response to my title is that the function of Canadian criticism at the present time is to foster excellence, then it would seem equally obvious that the first thing we need to do is to see that, as soon as possible, this lowering of the intellectual temperature will be no longer discernible. Whether we consider ourselves critics or scholars or editors, we need to set our sights higher.

Some specific examples – scholarly, critical, and editorial – may help. It is now comparatively well known that, unless we have access to a rare first edition, we are still reading John Richardson's *Wacousta* in a badly mangled text (even if we do not remain satisfied with the scandalously inadequate New Canadian Library edition, an abridgement of an abridgement). As a scholar I am outraged by the fact that a work of some historical importance in the development of nineteenth-century Canadian fiction is not available in the form in which it originally appeared (and I assume that this feeling would be shared by most readers of this article). As a critic, however, I have a rather different reaction. Granted, *Wacousta* should be available in a decent text in the way that, say, *Ralph Roister Doister* is available for those interested in early English drama. But let us not deceive ourselves (or our students) into thinking that *Wacousta* is anything more than a third-rate work, a lively but tawdry exploiting of the taste for historical romance that had been given a fillip eighteen years earlier by Sir Walter Scott and grafted onto the sensationalist Gothic tradition of Mrs Radcliffe. Yes, we want reliable, properly edited texts, and it is disgraceful that we do not yet have them; but we also want some critical standards that will discriminate between what is a historical landmark (because, like Everest, it's there) and what is a literary achievement of permanent interest.

Textually, *Wacousta* is an extreme but by no means unique example. Turning for a moment from older fiction to modern poetry, how many reliable texts do we have of Canada's leading poets, living or dead? Where can we turn for decent – not full-scale critical editions on the level of the Arden Shakespeares, but reliable, decent – texts for our university courses in Canadian poetry? And here I must begin to name names; I do so reluctantly, but I can see no alternative. And my first names are, in a perverse sort of way, appropriate (they are at least proof that I'm speaking out independently, not even sparing Jack David and Robert Lecker, the editors who invited the present article). Poetic texts are in my mind because I recently finished writing a long review for *Canadian Poetry*, 'Editors and Texts: Reflections on Some Recent Anthologies of Canadian Poetry', which included consideration of the David and Lecker two-volume set, also called *Canadian Poetry*. Interested persons may turn to that review for details. Suffice it to say here that there are more misprints than we can charitably excuse (including, on at least two occasions, poems cut off before the end) and no clear indication of editorial principles. Students (and teachers) using this anthology are not told where and when an individual poem first appeared, and are given no indication of what text is being reproduced. David and Lecker will bear the blame for this, since they are immediately responsible, but the fault, I suspect, lies with us all. They do not offer what seems to me an obvious and essential critical apparatus because they were not expected to do so. There is no effective pressure from critics and teachers to assure that we get reliable texts. But I for one am no longer prepared to be grateful just because an anthology, however imperfect, has been made available. I ask: where else is a country's poetic heritage treated so casually, so cavalierly?

Why, I ask again (turning back to prose) should we not have a series in Canada equivalent in quality to the Penguin English Library? Textual scholars (I claim no competence in this area) may find aspects of that library less than perfect, but at least the volumes are edited, a specific text is chosen, defended, and followed, and useful notes are provided. The New Canadian Library (for which I know we should all feel grateful) comes nowhere near that scholarly standard. Some examples follow. The introduction (dated 1965) to Catharine Parr Traill's *The Backwoods of Canada* (another unforgivably abridged text) informs us in a single sentence that Mrs Traill was the youngest of the Strickland sisters and that she grew up in Sussex. Neither of these facts is true (they seem to have been taken over without checking from R.P. Baker's *History of English-Canadian Literature to the Confederation* (1920) and an earlier edition of *The Backwoods* dating from the same decade); but the introduction remains unchanged after nineteen years. Again, the standard biographical note on Frederick Philip Grove in several New Canadian Library editions begins with four lines that do not contain a single fact that is true. The real facts have been available since Douglas O. Spettigue published them ten years ago, but no one has thought it worthwhile to substitute a corrected note. (It still appears, for example, in the most recent reprint of *Settlers of the Marsh*.) I suppose we get the scholarship, like the politicians, that we deserve.

For my other examples, I will let the New Canadian Library off the hook and go elsewhere. One of the best-known single critical studies of Canadian fictional texts (for reasons not at all clear to me) is Warren Tallman's 'Wolf in the Snow', which first appeared in *Canadian Literature* in 1960. In the section on *The Apprenticeship of Duddy Kravitz* Tallman makes reference to 'the sequence in which the documentary film director Friar produces a wedding ceremony masterpiece' (6: 46). Now we may wonder whether someone who confuses a wedding with a bar-mitzvah is ideally qualified to comment on Richler's novel, and we may also question the word 'masterpiece' – Richler's treatment of the scene may deserve such praise but the film itself, as described by Richler, most assuredly does not. All right, Homer nods and we all make mistakes (I must plead guilty to a goodly number myself). But I do not raise the matter merely to score an easy debating-point off Tallman. More important is the fact that this essay has been reprinted frequently – in, for example, George Woodcock's *A Choice of Critics* (1966), Eli Mandel's *Contexts of Canadian Criticism* (1971), Gregory M. Cook's *Ernest Buckler* in the Critical Views of Canadian Writers series (1972), even in G.D. Sheps's volume on Richler in the same series (1971). *And in none of these reprints has a correction been made.* More in sorrow than in anger I must ask: did none of these editors notice? or didn't they care?

Nor is this an isolated instance. In 1971 George Bowering published an otherwise admirable article on Margaret Laurence's *A Jest of God* in *Canadian Literature.* In it he refers to a passage where, as he states, Rachel Cameron describes herself as a 'tin giant'. This seemed odd to me when I first encountered it, so I made the obvious check. The actual phrase is 'thin giant', introducing a series of references to Rachel's thinness that recur throughout the book. This is not a typographical error; Bowering repeats the phrase later in a discussion of metallic imagery (43, 49). And again the article is repeated without change in Donald Stephens's *Writers of the Prairies* (1973), Woodcock's *The Canadian Novel in the Twentieth Century* (1975), and W.H. New's *Margaret Laurence: The Writer and Her Critics* (1977).[1]

---

1 I should add, however, that since this article was written Bowering's study has been reprinted yet again in *A Place To Stand On: Essays by and about Margaret Laurence,* ed. George Woodcock (Edmonton: NeWest, 1983), and that there the error has been corrected – a sign, one hopes, that scholars and editors are becoming more careful in these matters.

The writer and the critics indeed!

I could go on and on, but enough of washing dirty linen in public. I have had these (and other) instances at the back of my mind for some time – and have pointed them out to my students when it seemed necessary to do so. I repeat, it grieves me to say all this publicly, but the subject is so important that I cannot remain silent. We have a right to expect a better standard – all the more so since we are beginning to get the basic scholarly tools we need. When *The Letters of Frederick Philip Grove* appeared (as recently as 1976), it was 'the first complete scholarly edition of the letters of any Canadian author' (I quote the dust jacket which was, for once, accurate, though a few other letters have come to light since). Elspeth Cameron's 'writer's life' of Hugh MacLennan sets a new standard in Canadian literary biography, and the recently launched collected works of A.M. Klein and E.J. Pratt promise to give us two model critical editions. (We are even promised a scholarly edition of *Wacousta* from the Centre for the Editing of Early Canadian Texts at Carleton.) I should also mention the heartening number of critical outlets for literary discussion that now exist (including the development of *Essays on Canadian Writing* from a somewhat uncertain start to one of the best critical journals in the country). These are all healthy signs. It is also true, I think, that more good critical articles have appeared in recent years, even if the dross remains heavy and disappointing. But there is ample room for improvement. We must resolutely discourage the sloppy ways that, up until now, have been tacitly accepted even when they were not, in the best sense, acceptable.

SO MUCH FOR CRITICAL STANDARDS; what about critical approaches?

I do not intend to say very much at this time on the subject of thematic criticism. I have already had my say on this topic, and the approach is neither so prominent nor so dominating as it once was. Indeed, one of the remarkable trends of the late seventies was the way in which individual critics writing independently – including Frank Davey, Russell Brown, Barry Cameron and Michael Dixon, myself, and most recently a notable convert, John Moss – have firmly questioned the overwhelming critical assumptions of the previous decade.[2] Very simply, it is now generally recognized that an extremely important theme can be treated in a distressingly bad work of art. Thematic criticism belongs ultimately to the sociology of culture – which may be a legitimate object of study in itself but is no substitute for genuine literary criticism.

Nonetheless, if thematic criticism is less strong than it once was, other sanctioned critical generalizations about Canadian literature are frequently made despite the fact that they apply very uncertainly to the present-day situation. We need, I think, to question the slogans, phrases, and assumptions that we have inherited from the literary-critical past. Are they still adequate? Have recent developments rendered them obsolete? Can't we improve upon them? Too often we accept them as *données* without checking their credibility. Take, for example, the 'garrison culture' or 'garrison mentality' popularized by Northrop Frye. The term can be applied literally and usefully to the society portrayed by Frances Brooke's *The History of Emily Montague* or Richardson's *Wacousta,* but it has surely become at least partly metaphorical by the time of Susanna Moodie's *Roughing It in the Bush* and still more so by the time we come to Sinclair Ross's *As For Me and My House.* In 1984, when applied (say) to the cultural threat of the United States, I suspect it is more a psychological reaction than a literary description. There are several other such phrases, and I would like now to comment on the overuse of the adjectives 'colonial', 'puritan', and 'genteel'.

---

2 See Davey, 'Surviving the Paraphrase', Brown, 'Critic, Culture, Text: Beyond Thematics', Cameron and Dixon, 'Mandatory Subversive Manifesto: Canadian Criticism vs. Literary Criticism', Keith, 'The Thematic Approach to Canadian Fiction' (reproduced earlier in this volume), and Moss, 'Bushed in the Sacred Wood'.

I have long been uneasy with the use of the word 'colonial' in Canadian literary criticism, even from the pen of a critic as balanced and intelligent as A.J.M. Smith. At first I thought that, as an English immigrant, I was over-sensitive on the matter, but I have decided that this is not the case. The problem stems from the different implications of the term when employed in historical and literary contexts. When it is used in political history, we mean that one country is dominated by another through military force or economic influence or what we now call 'imperialism'. But even a brief look at the Canadian cultural situation should persuade us that the literary meaning must be very different. Thus the British made no attempt to force nineteenth-century Canadian literature into a British mould; if they were aware of its existence, they showed precious little interest in it. Their fault was neglect rather than interference. And much the same may be said of the current situation vis-à-vis the United States. I am not, I think, underestimating the insidious influence of media-control and dumping practices (paperback books rather than Japanese cars), but the fact remains that if nineteenth-century Canadian writers were 'colonial' in following British models and fashions, and their contemporary counterparts are 'colonial' in following American models and fashions (and more about that later), it is the Canadians who are primarily to blame.

Too often, in my experience, the term has the effect of disclaiming responsibility, of suggesting that Canadians have somehow been prevented from (or at least inhibited in) producing an authentic literature by the jealousy or evil-mindedness of dominating powers. This seems to me to border on paranoia (which may possibly, in one sense of the term, be a 'colonial' characteristic); but it fails to come even close to the facts. And again I offer a specific illustration involving the concept if not the word. At one point in *Survival* (a book I hope we have outgrown) Margaret Atwood has cause to mention turn-of-the-century Ireland and adds an almost Pavlovian appositional phrase, '*another* culturally unhealthy climate' (188; my emphasis). So unhealthy, I find myself adding, that it produced Yeats, Joyce, Shaw, Synge,

O'Casey, Beckett, etc., etc., a fantastically high percentage of the major figures of twentieth-century British literature. And the inferences I draw from that are: a) even oppressive political domination will not suppress a national literature if a strong creative impulse is present; and b) Canadian critics would do better if they thought through the logical consequences of their arguments more carefully. In short, the 'colonial' tag is used far too glibly and loosely as a classificatory and essentially evasive term in our literary-critical vocabulary. Even when used historically, it can be ambiguous, since the date when colonial status ended (in the strict sense) for individual provinces varies from 1867 to 1949. And even if used with a firm sense of historical accuracy, the word implies something different in Canada from the same usage in, for example, Caribbean countries. All things considered, we would be well advised to avoid it unless we define very clearly what we mean whenever we use it.

'Puritan' is (perhaps) more easily dealt with. One of those terms that survive despite the fact that history has long since passed them by, it has been seriously misused as anyone who studies the literary flowering in English or American literature can testify. But this is no place to argue the general problem; I content myself here with commenting on the pejorative use of the term that still occurs often enough in present-day Canada (either word or concept is prominent in the continuing controversy over sexism and pornography on pay TV). When in the late 1950s I first heard Irving Layton attacking the Toronto that was still – just! – 'Toronto the Good', the word still retained a comprehensible meaning. But a quarter of a century has passed since then, and the country's general attitudes and its literature have both changed drastically. It is worth remembering that eighteen years have now gone by since the publication of *Beautiful Losers* (I refer to this book as a phenomenon, not as a work of literary excellence). While there are certain individuals and even groups who would impose all sorts of censorship if they could, it seems to me absurd to suggest that the Canadian reading public, even in apocalyptic 1984, is so conservative as to be a stifling influence on creativity. Have the people who still consider Canada 'puritan' ever read Richler's *Cocksure* or Kroetsch's *What the Crow Said*? How do they explain the publication of books by (and again I imply no value-judgement) Martin Myers or Ray Smith? 'Puritanism' may well be used in a historical context – to explain the traditions and instincts behind the motivations of characters in Margaret Laurence's novels, for instance – but it makes no sense at all when used as a general classification for contemporary culture.

And now, 'genteel'. If there is a 'genteel' tradition in Canadian literature (and I'm not wholly convinced that there is) it has been healthily challenged ever since Haliburton's Sam Slick. And the idea that such a concern with gentility is characteristically British or English has always puzzled me, not only because it seems basically simplistic (think of the coarseness that complemented the glitter of the English eighteenth century) but also because I first came to 'Toronto the Good' at the time of John Osborne and the 'angry young men' – and the Canadian pseudo-gentility of that time did not seem English to me. The whole concept presupposes an assumption about the social realities of modern Britain that was always challengeable and has been hopelessly out of date since at least 1914. But this confusion has, I suspect, more serious literary consequences, especially when it appears in the form of the 'crude/fine' distinction popularized by Warren Tallman two decades ago. Again an oversimplification is involved, since insufficient distinction is made between crudity of subject matter and crudity of execution. Some of Irving Layton's poems, for example, employ a 'fine' rhetoric to communicate 'crude' material, while some are crude in both senses; on the other hand, much of the more tedious literary bric-à-brac of the Canadian nineteenth century was 'fine' in its aspiration and crude in its technique. Moreover, I have a suspicion that the word 'genteel' may extend in some minds to include a resistance to the style, poise, and polish characteristic of the work of, say, Ethel Wilson or Mavis Gallant. If so, I can only retort that, according to this sense of the term, one could well have more rather than less. Of course, there is a basic sense in which 'genteel' means excessively fastidious, and I make no objection to this legitimate, albeit pejorative usage. But once again contemporary usage is both loose and inadequate. All these words tend to be employed (and this is my main point) as literary-critical stock-responses. They are getting out of date and rough at the edges. We would do better to retire them.

I am concerned here with critical approaches, and no discussion of the topic would be complete without some comment on the current interest in structuralist, deconstructionist, and post-modernist criticisms (with all the fashionable permutations thereof). Here I write with some diffidence since I cannot claim to have made a special study of the subject. But I have observed some of its effects on Canadian criticism and am concerned about possible extensions of these approaches in the future.

A useful starting-point is a comparatively recent article by Stan Fogel, 'Lost in the Canadian Funhouse', that has provoked a good deal of discussion since its appearance in *Queen's Quarterly* in 1981. It illustrates very clearly the dangers of an urge to be up to date at all costs. Briefly, Fogel thinks that Canadian writers should endeavour to keep up with the Yankee Joneses by becoming as post-modernist, self-reflexive, and metafictive as possible – and as soon as possible. 'The Canadian novel', he writes, 'seems reactionary not only in its deference to social authority but in its assimilation of literary authority in the guise of the traditional novel and its ideological baggage' (705). Why literary authority in the guise of the post-modernist novel and all its baggage should be desirable is by no means clear to me. I am tempted to say: better 'where is here' than 'where it's at'. Fogel's article has some provocative force but many of its assumptions need to be countered. He never considers the possibility that current United States literature might have much to learn from us, nor that the difference in the make-up and general attitudes of our country may explain, justify, even require a 'traditionalist' stance. 'Californians', he notes with approval, 'are not concerned with national identity' (704). The difference between a united state and a culturally defensive would-be-independent country is never admitted. In its unquestioned assumption that the American latest is obviously the best, it is an article that might well qualify for the 'colonial' designation if I had not already cautioned against this.

Curiously enough, Fogel barely acknowledges the extent to which many Canadian writers have already adopted certain post-modernist techniques. He mentions Ray Smith and a few others but is oddly silent on such writers as Hodgins and Ondaatje (or, if French-Canadian literature is to be considered, Hubert Aquin). Stranger still, Robert Kroetsch gets no more than a passing mention, yet he has been arguing a Canadian version of deconstruction for years and the discussions recently brought together by Shirley Neuman and Robert Wilson in *Labyrinths of Voice* (though Fogel was not in a position to comment on these) constitute the most detailed Canadian consideration of post-modernist possibilities.[3] *Labyrinths of Voice* seems to me of particular interest for two reasons. First, Kroetsch discusses the subject not as a critic but as a writer. Robert Lecker (who knows far more about these matters than I do) tells me that Kroetsch says nothing here that cannot be traced back to statements by earlier theorists. That may well be so, but I still think that the novelist's viewpoint – the way we hear how new ideas and theories stimulate his creative art – makes a significant difference. Second, the Kroetsch interviews are interspersed with disembodied quotations from (mainly) structuralist and post-modernist critics. Kroetsch's discussion of these matters may not be original, but it is for the most part refreshingly free from the awkward and insensitive jargon that obscures so many of the

3 It is only fair to point out that in his later expansion of this subject, *A Tale of Two Countries* (1984), Fogel includes a chapter on Kroetsch; however, he still has little or nothing to say about other Canadian writers who identify with 'post-modernist' aims and attitudes. [1989]

interpolated critical voices. That Kroetsch is a creative artist *need* not explain this, but I suspect that it does.

Despite all this, however, the book provokes some unease. The editors rightly state in their 'entrance' that Kroetsch was 'the appropriate *magister labyrinthorum,* an author who continually re/reads his own writing in the context of his current thinking' (xi). Not merely 'the appropriate *magister*', I suggest, but perhaps the only one. *Labyrinths of Voice* is an excellent secondary source for those interested in modern critical theory in general and in Kroetsch's novels in particular. But the possibility of the method's being extended to other Canadian writers fills me with concern. Characteristically, and I think properly, Canadian writers have approached these new ideas circumspectly, prepared to adapt and experiment but bending the method to their own requirements rather than vice versa. The same is true of Kroetsch himself, though he has gone further than the others because it is an artistic procedure peculiarly suited to his somewhat eccentric talents. But the pressures of fashion are considerable; and, although some useful critical work is currently being done from a post-modernist perspective on such writers as Hodgins, Wiebe, and Munro, I shudder to think of the distortions that would result if the work of less suitable Canadian writers were subjected to the critical presuppositions that worked so well in the case of Kroetsch. Fogel apparently wants Canadian novelists to jump on an American fictional band-wagon; let us not have our academic commentators jump too eagerly on a literary-critical equivalent.

IN CONCLUSION, there is another, more pressing – even, perhaps, more nationalistic – reason why any full-scale concentration on post-modernist criticism in Canada needs to be resisted. I have already said that we are now much more solidly aware of a distinctive literary heritage. That is true of specialists, of likely readers of *Essays on Canadian Writing,* but the general reading public, though more aware than it used to be of 'home-grown'

Canadian writers, is not yet familiar with the idea of a historical Canadian tradition. Not the least of the limitations of thematic criticism was its neglect of *historical* continuities. Readers were invited to move spatially from one manifestation of a theme to another without noticing any ordered progression or temporal development in the literature. Similarly, approaches that emphasize the autonomy of the text are likely to be a-historical or even anti-historical in their general assumptions (as Fogel's article makes clear). But only countries that are fully conscious of their history and have fully absorbed their heritage can afford to neglect it. Canada is in the process of discovering (or in some cases rediscovering) her past, her lines of continuity. It is essential that this process be not only maintained but extended.

A main function of Canadian criticism at the present time is to address this problem. We cannot afford to lose either our newly gained awareness of our past or the all-important contact with our living culture. Our literary criticism must not retreat into an intense inane of abstract theorizing ('the great safeguard is never to let oneself become abstract', wrote Matthew Arnold in the essay whose title I have appropriated (257)); we must avoid at all costs a mandarin isolation in which experts communicate only with each other. I am constantly being asked by interested readers (from outside the academies): what should I read in Canadian literature? where should I start? One can recommend anthologies or compile lists of congenial titles, but something more is needed. Where does one turn, for example, for a reliable and straightforward introduction to Canadian literature? We have numerous studies of individual authors and of special topics (thematic or otherwise), but we are extraordinarily deficient in critically sophisticated studies of individual genres or historical accounts of the whole subject (the *Literary History of Canada* itself is more an encyclopaedic survey than a literary history proper). We badly need introductory handbooks that provide information and a firm sense of cultural context. Our library stacks readily reveal titles like *A History of the American Novel* or

English Poetry in the Nineteenth Century, but where are their Canadian equivalents?

Unfortunately, the flourishing of Canadian literature occurred at a time when popular cultural standards were fast becoming vulgarized. Louis Dudek, who has himself produced some of the most significant Canadian literary criticism of our time, has noted the distressing way in which the book-pages of our daily newspapers have been subsumed into a (minor) part of the 'entertainment section', how the standards of the CBC have declined, how 'in every area of art and culture there has been a deplorable regression' (*Technology* 39). It is against this subcultural background that our students grow up, and it is scarcely surprising that they are worse prepared than they have ever been for the serious (not pompous or pedantic but *serious*) study of literature. Too often they have been prepared (if that's the word) by teachers who lean on *Survival* as a combination of bible and crutch, or by those tiresome popularizers who try to interest them in poetry via pop records. They are the prisoners of TV and rock 'n' roll. The more intelligent of them, like the more intelligent members of the general public, know that these standards are inadequate but they do not know where to find alternatives.

For all these reasons, the art of reviewing needs to be taken far more seriously. The current standard of reviewing, whether in newspapers or the so-called learned journals, seems to me – with some notable exceptions – poor. The needs of particular readers are often ignored; important issues are not raised; chitchat about books replaces 'literary criticism'. For some (including university promotion committees) reviewing is considered less important than the writing of erudite articles. I disagree profoundly. Literary critics should see themselves as much-needed mediators between writer and reader, who explain trends, discuss intentions, transmit relevant information, clarify difficulties, and, yes, offer considered value-judgements. This is not the time to be talking about interesting patterns or semiotic subtleties. Nor is it the time to advocate one single critical approach. When we are fortunate enough to have writers as diverse as Margaret Atwood, Mavis Gallant, Jack Hodgins, Hugh Hood, Margaret Laurence, and Rudy Wiebe (to name only authors of fiction), we need a balancing flexibility. We must insist on clarity, precision, accuracy, good sense in our criticism. We must see that the best texts are readily accessible in decent editions, that they are intelligently introduced and helpfully annotated. We must provide background studies that are at one and the same time accurate in their information, cogent in their interpretations, brightly and elegantly written. We still have a mission: to have our literature recognized as an essential reflection of our national life. This is what I mean by retrenchment and consolidation. Literature can survive without literary criticism but it cannot survive if it is unknown and unread. It is criticism's prime function at the present time to see that it is both known and read with that mature enjoyment which is a combination of emotional sensitivity and humane intelligence. As critics, scholars, editors, we shall not be fulfilling our responsibilities or justifying our existence if we attempt anything less.

The Quest for the (Instant) Canadian Classic

John Metcalf commissioned an article on this general topic for *The Bumper Book,* published by ECW Press in 1986. It seemed a good opportunity to tell the inside story of the Calgary Conference and the paper I gave there (reproduced earlier in this volume), and offer an account of the New Canadian Library Classics committee, about which rumours had circulated. All of this is, to some extent, more literary politics than literary criticism, but at the present time the relation between these two is of considerable significance.

IN 1978 I WAS A SPEAKER at what is now sometimes referred to as the 'infamous' Calgary Conference on the Canadian Novel. In 1981-82 I served as a member of the advisory committee for the McClelland and Stewart 'New Canadian Library Classics', which has also – and for similar reasons – been the subject of critical comment. Why, I sometimes ask myself, do I get attached to such supposedly dubious enterprises? One reason is probably my congenital incapacity to say no – which may explain why I agreed to write this article. But when John Metcalf solicited a short piece on this subject, I felt obliged to take up the challenge and put the deeper reasons on record. They relate to the much larger and important issue of how a teacher and critic responds to the contemporary development of a young literature.

But first, since I am in the mood of memoir, an earlier but relevant recollection. It was in 1974 that I had first been asked by my Department to teach a course in Canadian literature – on the Canadian novel (I had volunteered several years earlier, but I suspect that my English accent was against me). One day, in the vicinity of Queen's Park, I met a colleague who had taught a section of the course for some years, so I thought it proper to ask for some advice on the matter. I forget the immediate details, but the main part of the conversation went something like this:

Colleague: What are you using as an organizational structure?
Self: Er ... what?
Colleague: An organizational structure, a unifying theme.
Self (gulping): Well, I don't have one, actually. I just made a list of the fifteen Canadian novels I liked best and arranged them in chronological order.
Colleague (dauntingly, and about to change the subject): Oh!

A dozen years (and, I hope, a good deal of experience) later, I am unrepentant. I still have no organizational structure. I still teach the novels I like best – or, since so much of interest has been written since, a selection of the novels I like best. I try to convey to my students something of the variety (*not* unity) that characterizes Canadian fiction in this century, and offer them suggestions about the appropriate, differing emphases that sensitive readers should bring to each book. Whatever else would one do?

I gatecrashed – stumblingly and perhaps arrogantly – the teaching of Canadian literature because my own attempts to educate myself in the subject had not been assisted as they ought to have been by the criticism at that time available. I had looked for guidance in reading the best Canadian literature but had encountered reluctance on the part of the critics and literary scholars to tell me what, in their opinion, the best was. This puzzled me. I had come from a Cambridge undergraduate experience where evaluation was assumed as a natural outcome of reading and thinking. I knew, however, that such a response was a comparatively recent development at the older English universities. I had read Robert Graves's *Goodbye to All That,* and was amused by the shocked response of a member of his Oxford college board when he was an undergraduate just after the First World War: 'I understand, Mr Graves, that the essays which you write for your English tutor are, shall I say, a trifle temperamental. It appears, indeed, that you prefer some authors to others' (259). I was later to discover, with delight, that F.R. Leavis had used the same anecdote as one of the epigraphs for *The Common Pursuit.* And mention of Leavis – who, I should say at once, remains for me the greatest English literary critic of this century – reminds me of that (nowadays, perhaps, also 'infamous') opening to *The Great Tradition*: 'The great English novelists are Jane Austen, George Eliot, Henry James and Joseph Conrad....' In other words, they are the classics – or, at the very least, among the classics.

Those were, as it happens, the first quoted words at the opening session of the Calgary Conference. Robert Kroetsch was the speaker, and he went on immediately to make some remarks that will perhaps surprise anyone who did not attend that conference or has not read its proceedings:

> Literature and literary values have undergone enormous changes in the twenty-five years since Leavis collected his controversial essays. The very idea of 'canon' has come into question. What a novel is, is open to debate. The idea of evaluating at all is dismissed by some distinguished critics. There are even those who ask what an author is or what he does. And yet, over the past few weeks, I've found myself going back to Leavis' book – if only to see how he could be so confident.
>
> This paper is a record of my reluctance – and of my need – to locate/discriminate the canon of Canadian fiction. (Steele 9)

That doubleness – reluctance and need – set the tone for the whole conference.

My own part in the event was a curious one. I was the dark horse among otherwise distinguished main speakers, since I had published little on Canadian criticism at that time and few of those present knew who I was or what I thought. The convenors certainly didn't. I well remember receiving the invitation 'out of the blue'. I was asked to speak on 'Themes in Canadian Fiction'; the names of the other speakers were listed; I was asked to telephone collect as soon as I had made up my mind; clearly, I was a crisis choice and they were scraping the bottom of the barrel. I contacted them in order to decline, saying that I disapproved of the very concept of thematic criticism and would only end by attacking the whole silly business. When the voice at the other end of the telephone encouraged me to come and do exactly what I had described, I couldn't resist the temptation to ride my hobby-horse before a captive audience, so I agreed – but was somewhat taken aback to discover later that the panel discussion to follow included some of the best-known thematic critics. So the cat was among the pigeons – or, rather, I was the pigeon surrounded by the cats.

As it turned out, the confrontation was good-humoured; I enjoyed it, and even made new friends. Looking back on it, one can now see it as part of the shift towards other literary-critical possibilities beyond the thematic, a shift that had been prepared for by others, including Frank Davey, Barry Cameron and Michael Dixon, and Russell Brown. More important, the whole conference was marked by a raising of essential issues concerning the position of the Canadian novel and the adequacy of its criticism, evaluative or otherwise. Unfortunately, the media (as might have been anticipated) placed more emphasis on the 'hundred best novels' tag and the awkwardnesses and absurdities involved in the ballot. I believe, however, that if interested readers would turn to *Taking Stock,* Charles Steele's edition of the conference papers, they would find some of the widest-ranging and most important discussions surrounding the criticism of Canadian fiction.

But the ballot? Surely you don't defend the ballot? No, there were a lot of misjudgements connected with that. It represented an uneasy compromise between the desire of the conference organizers, in Steele's words, 'to define a more specific and wider *corpus* of novels than the individual delimitation of theme papers could provide' and Malcolm Ross's interest in discovering 'the efficacy and utility of the implicit canon of Canadian fiction established by his New Canadian Library series' (155). Ross insisted that he 'asked for a choice of one hundred titles and a short list of ten novels which seemed most important – not great, mind you, *important*' (137). But the letter accompanying the ballot asked for one's choice of the ten 'best Canadian novels yet written' (159). The confusion arose, presumably, across the distance between Ross's Halifax and the organizers' Calgary. But there were a number of additional and bothersome factors. Ross's association with the McClelland and Stewart series, together with Jack McClelland's conspicuous presence at the conference, suggested a publishers' propaganda campaign. The printed list – perhaps inevitably – contained a high proportion of NCL titles. Write-in titles were invited, but the chances of such books appearing on the resulting lists were minimal. French-Canadian literature was poorly represented, and only in translation. (I dissociated myself from that error at the conference itself (146).) The process that led to the selection of pollsters was never made sufficiently clear.

The organization may, therefore, have been clumsy – perhaps inept – but surely it represented little more than a foreshortened version of the process of acceptance that is taking place at all times. What surprised a number of people about the conference was the idea that, whether the words 'best' or 'important' or merely 'useful' were employed, discrimination among books and authors was being attempted. In other words, we were preferring some authors – some *Canadian* authors – to others. Why should this, in itself, be controversial? Of all the academic oddities, the pretence to some kind of objective, scientific, 'value-free' treatment of literature has always seemed to me the most ridiculous. I have stated the obvious on several occasions, but it needs to be repeated: when a teacher draws up a syllabus and selects one text rather than another, acts of evaluation and discrimination are involved. When I decide to introduce my students to Margaret Laurence rather than Marian Engel, to Jack Hodgins rather than Matt Cohen, I am (rightly or wrongly) making an indirect value-judgement. I could not help it even if I wanted to, and I see no reason for trying to disguise the fact. When the Calgary Conference polled their selection of teachers, they found out which were the choices that were being made at that particular time. This had statistical and informative value. The results as printed in *Taking Stock* (which, through an unfortunate typographical error, omits *The Stone Angel* which headed List A) contains some oddities, but anyone who studiously read through the hundred would obtain an excellent grasp of the mainstream of Canadian fiction. I wish I had had such a list to guide my reading a decade earlier.

Turning to the 'top ten' list, which I consider decidedly problematic, one nonetheless discovers with interest that only three were winners of the Governor General's Award. If a list is substituted of the G. G. winners for the years concerned (though the process is complicated by some overlapping of dates), a notably inferior list will result. And that, surely, is how 'consensus' works. In the intervening years between publication and 1978, discriminations had quietly been made. *As For Me and My House* was found to be more rewarding than Alan Sullivan's *Three Came to Ville Marie*; *The Mountain and the Valley* has outlasted David Walker's *The Pillar.* If a similar group of persons were polled in 1986, the list would doubtless be different (as I pointed out at the time, 'the top ten never stays the top ten for very long' (146)); and, so far as later titles are concerned, I would be prepared to bet that the list would have become further refined. Yes, the mechanism was crude, and there were a number of undiplomatic and maladroit factors that marred the project, but that is easy to say with the gift of hindsight. Among the positives was the fact that various books were publicized because of their merits, and sometimes for the very reason that their qualities were not adequately reflected in the tabulations. For instance, in my own paper I put forward high claims for Ethel Wilson's *Swamp Angel* (which ranked a gratifying and surprisingly high twenty-eighth on the poll, though I didn't know that at the time) and Jack Hodgins's *The Invention of the World* (which had only been published the year before and did not show up on the ballot-results). Several people came up to me afterwards and said that my remarks had aroused their interest and that they would read the novels at the first opportunity. Such responses must surely have multiplied many times in the course of the conference. I doubt if any of the delegates left without having learned a good deal about the complex and contentious issues involved. Even the distorted (because sensationalized) accounts in the national media must have had the indirect but happy result of alerting some people to the existence of literary material that was worth arguing about. No, I do not regret taking part. I stated my reservations at the time, but said that the larger list was useful 'as long as you don't take it too seriously' (146). Reading over my remarks eight years later, I am glad to say that I still stand by all of them.

THREE YEARS AFTER the Calgary Conference, the Canadian Classics Committee was formed by Jack McClelland. I was involved for about eighteen months, and then withdrew for reasons which I shall attempt to make clear. I approach this topic with a certain reluctance of the let-sleeping-dogs-lie variety, but the matters involved are of great importance, and I have not seen any clear public statement of what went on. I must stress that I am telling the story of my own association with the project. I will describe events as accurately as I can, but my opinions are not necessarily shared by others. I don't think I am betraying any confidences in relating my own experience at this time. My position on the original committee has caused raised eyebrows on more than one occasion: I have a right to defend myself.

Before embarking upon the details, I want to begin by acknowledging the immense debt that we owe to the New Canadian Library, to its publisher and its first general editor. It is not exaggerating to say that the serious study of Canadian literature at school and university only became possible with the inauguration of the series. A national literature cannot be said to exist if the main texts are not readily accessible. You can't teach a course in Canadian fiction if the important books are out of print, and one of the significant features in the instituting of the series was the publishers' pledge to keep the titles in print. The ease with which McClelland and Stewart were able, in the early days, to secure paperback rights from other publishers attests to the extent to which publisher and editor were in advance of their time in anticipating a growth of interest in Canadian literature. For years only Macmillan's Laurentian Library came close to being a rival. Awareness of the debt we all owe to NCL played some part in my agreeing to serve on the committee.

The members were drawn from a wide geographical range – from sea to sea, as they say – with university, college of education, and high school representation. Bibliographers, editors, thematic critics, and value-judgement people like myself were all invited to participate. We were asked to advise on the future of the series that was clearly at a crucial stage in its development. It had grown dramatically at a time of economic expansion, and was facing problems in an age of cutbacks and retrenchment. The early volumes had introductions that were now out of date. Thus Roy Daniells was still telling us, in the introduction to *As For Me and My House* (No. 4 in the series, 1957), that it was 'a book ... unfamiliar to the Canadian public'. The publisher, in the interests of commercial distribution, clearly wanted to add to the series titles that were less 'intellectual' in tone and quality than had originally been envisaged. What was to be done? One possible solution was a two-tiered strategy in which more popular books were to be reprinted without introductions while the more traditional titles – those considered important for school and college teaching – would continue to be graced (if that's the word) with scholarly introductions and given a distinguishing designation as 'classics'.

I was primarily interested because, at that time, I was becoming increasingly concerned with the general sloppiness of student texts in Canadian literature courses. There are virtually no annotated editions – certainly none of modern fiction texts that tend to loom large in classroom teaching. Typographical – even grammatical – errors abound. In some cases, complicated textual matters – cuts, revisions, etc. – are involved. My main motive for agreeing to serve on the committee was the hope that I might be able to draw attention to such matters.

At the first meeting, after a welcome and an explanation of plans and problems, Jack McClelland withdrew and left the committee to its deliberations. The group's independence was acknowledged and respected. I am relying on memory here (I rather foolishly threw out my files after withdrawing from the committee), but the following – though not necessarily in this order – were among the suggestions and recommendations: a) that any 'classic' designation should be made regardless of whether McClelland and Stewart held the copyright; b) that, if considered necessary, introductions to existing NCL editions should be rewritten and updated; c) that no 'classic' should be reprinted in abridged form; d) that a qualified person should scrutinize the text and see that a correct and accurate text was reproduced; e) that notes (on such matters as historical references and the identifying of quotations) should be provided when necessary; f) that the series should not be confined to fiction. There were probably others which I have forgotten. I remember myself advocating that what was needed was the kind of text and apparatus provided by the Penguin English Library. A short list of what seemed obvious titles – a first step in no way considered final or limiting – was also drawn up. At this point, McClelland and Stewart responded, agreeing with only minor reservations to the general principles. All in all, I considered it a very heartening session. For a short period, it really seemed as if some important developments, along lines that appeared to be genuinely progressive, were about to be made. Unfortunately, the impetus did not last for very long.

By an unhappy stroke of fate I was prevented (by jury duty) from attending the second working session some months later. The accounts I received of that meeting were disappointing. Some of the potential classics now proposed seemed to me unworthy; at least one of them (could it have been *The Man from Glengarry*? or *Wacousta*? or even *Bear*?) was a work which, I thought, could only bring discredit to the credentials of any 'classic-making' group, and I had no wish to have my name attached to such an edition – especially when I hadn't been present to argue the point. More significantly, I got the impression that the publishers were backing off from some of the principles that meant most to me. Textual alterations were expensive; perhaps unabridged texts of in-print volumes could wait awhile; and so on. Announcements were also made to the press which suggested that the committee was less independent of the publishers than I for one had considered us to be. I suspected that, willy-nilly and no doubt unintentionally, we were being pushed into a position very different from the one that had originally been envisaged. At about this time changes were also announced in the management of the company that would inevitably mean renegotiation of previous agreements. Above all, the general economic climate for improvements appeared bleak. I felt that what I had argued for was not going to come to pass and that my name would be associated with decisions of which I disapproved. I therefore wrote to the publishers politely but firmly announcing my withdrawal; so far as I know, we parted amicably. What happened to the committee after that is unknown to me. I was disappointed that the process had not yielded the results I had hoped for; on the other hand, I can never regret making the attempt.

My reasons, then, had comparatively little to do with the concept of a canon of 'classics'. Indeed, I had not anticipated that the use of that word would be anathema in some quarters. I had grown up in a society where the Oxford University Press's 'World's Classics' editions were accepted parts of a literary bookshelf, despite the fact that the series contained some recent, obscure, even provincial titles. (Turning to my English rural shelf, I notice with interest that Constance Holme's *The Old Road from Spain*, published in 1916, took its bow in the 'World's Classics' in 1932.) Moreover, it did not strike me as in any way odd that certain Canadian texts should be considered worthy of classic status. While I was still a member of the committee, indeed, General Publishing announced its 'New Press Canadian Classics' series. Was this an independent development or a rival publishing ploy? I have no idea. Some of their titles seem to me challengeable, but the main point is that some fine fiction – by Mavis Gallant, Michael Ondaatje, Margaret Atwood, and Antonine Maillet, among others – has become available to a wider range of readers. That is surely more important than the purity of an already somewhat debased word.

At this point I am reminded of the fact that, when I quoted the opening sentence of Leavis's *The Great Tradition,* I left off where Robert Kroetsch left off at Calgary. Let me now quote the sentence in full: 'The great English novelists are Jane Austen, George Eliot, Henry James and Joseph Conrad – *to stop for the moment at that comparatively safe point in history*' (my emphasis). Aye, there's the rub: how classic is classic? Or, as Hugh Hood asks in *A New Athens,* 'How much past is past?' (11). This was a problem that had properly bothered the Canadian Classics Committee. As I recall, we agreed, at least initially, to keep at least a ten-year gap between publication and designation as a 'classic'. A mere decade may seem ridiculous to the purist, and I sympathize with this view, but it is worth pointing out that this modest decision implied a restraint unrecognized by those responsible for the New Press Canadian Classics. And even the traditional British have their 'Penguin Modern Classics'. How classic is modern? How modern is classic?

Yes, of course, one risks absurdity in making high claims for contemporary work. Henry Kreisel, at the Calgary Conference, wisely reminded us of the long and justly forgotten first winner of the Nobel Prize for literature (Steele 142). Similarly, a list of the British poets laureate makes depressing and humbling reading. But I cannot help suspecting that some of the people who laugh heartily at the idea of an 'instant' or even recent Canadian classic see nothing odd in speaking condescendingly of the old fogeys of the 1930s who hadn't yet recognized Eliot or Joyce as 'modern classics'. And reliance on the accepted successes of a more distant past does not guarantee respectability. I may possibly be premature in requiring my students to read a novel as recent as *The Invention of the World,* but at least I am not, like one of my colleagues, still insisting that they read *Jalna.*

Ideally, of course, the attaining of classic status should come gradually – as naturally as, and much more slowly than, leaves on a tree. But we do not live in an ideal world, and a literature as young as Canada's needs – and, I am certain, deserves – help. It is a duty that should not be evaded. Ivory-tower academics who never get their hands dirty are, in my opinion, abrogating their responsibilities in the modern world. I am unimpressed by those who wait until the dust has settled before admitting a work into the category of 'classic' literature and then blandly telling us about its already established virtues. If all academics took this view, who would decide the question of what is a permanent part of our literature and what isn't: the publishers? the booksellers (including those who control the chain book stores)? the popular reviewers? the writers of literary gossip-columns in our newspapers? The prospect is disturbing.

That there is a danger of eulogistic inflation is undeniable. Undeserved reputations should certainly be questioned. I agree that the time has come for a more rigorous scrutiny of the Canadian literary achievement; some apparently established titles may well be ripe for toppling. But this is not a conspicuously Canadian scandal. It is a recurring cultural phenomenon (remember Pope's *Dunciad*) by no means confined to the Canadian situation. In the early 1960s Britain needed its ungentlemanly Leavis to attest that C.P. Snow was *not* a contemporary classic. By the same token, other articles in *The Bumper Book* contain similar challenges to present-day Canadian opinion.[1] But we need some yea-sayers as well. The Leavis who said no to Snow had previously said yes to D.H. Lawrence. Discrimination can and should be positive as well as negative. True, there is too much puffery for nationalistic rather than literary reasons, and a good deal of it is ill-advised and distasteful. However, the insensitively dismissive review is at least as damaging as unmerited praise. There is no need to elevate the indefensible, but reasonable claims deserve to be articulated. We cannot afford to wait until all the

1 These included articles querying the 'classic' status of Ross's *As For Me and My House* and Buckler's *The Mountain and the Valley*. [1989]

academics are convinced of the existence of a Canadian *Middlemarch*.

Another point. If students are not to be introduced to contemporary and so possibly suspect texts, then most of what seems most interesting and worthwhile about Canadian literature would never get taught. We will not further Canadian writing by limiting our teaching to Haliburton, Richardson, Moodie and Traill, plus (daringly) Leacock. It is worth remembering that as recently as twenty-five years ago Margaret Laurence was unknown. It is fatal to apply the cautious procedures appropriate for a venerable literature to a vigorously youthful one.

For my part, I am not content to remain aloof. A passage in one of D.H. Lawrence's letters comes to mind:

> A book should be either a bandit or a rebel or a man in a crowd. People should either run for their lives, or come under the colours, or say *how do you do?*... An author should be in among the crowd, kicking their shins or cheering on to some mischief or merriment. That rather cheap seat in the gods where one sits with fellows like Anatole France and benignly looks down on the foibles, follies, and frenzies of so-called fellow-men, just annoys me. (2: 827)

Much the same applies to literary criticism. It may involve associating with the barbarous crowd, but degrees of dignity are still possible. (One needn't descend to the vulgarities of *Books in Canada* or the CBC 'State of the Arts'.) Sensationalism is undesirable, but in our world a literature unpublicized is a literature unread. In a healthy situation, the yea-sayers will be challenged and kept in check by the nay-sayers, and vice versa. 'This is so, isn't it?' 'Yes, but ...' or 'No, not at all' (Leavis again). Both viewpoints are necessary; both sides need to speak out. The yea-sayers are not the only group who can be charged with excess. In the final analysis doesn't even *The Bumper Book*, in its snook-cocking and cheeky iconoclasm, belong to the same hoop-la?

The Post-Modernist Phenomenon and Canadian Literature

Early in 1987, University College in the University of Toronto (my own college) devoted its annual symposium to 'Our Post-Modernist Heritage'. The symposium was interdisciplinary, and the literary papers covered several literatures in several languages. The occasion stimulated my own thinking on the relation of the topic to Canadian literature in English, so I offered the following paper. I make no claims to particular expertise in the area of post-modernism; I merely attempt to assess the effects of a contemporary movement on my own field of special interest. The paper, which has not been published before, may be of interest in its presentation of some non-technical thoughts on a subject too often debated at an arcane level.

NOT LONG AGO, I attended a series of lectures at the Art Gallery of Ontario, in connection with the 'Vatican Splendour' exhibition, that examined 'baroque' as a term applied to the fine arts. One of the speakers began his paper by observing that, so far as he was concerned, 'baroque' was *almost* as useless a term as 'post-modernist'. Certainly, 'baroque' is a broad and often puzzling adjective; it is not uncommon, for instance, to meet intelligent and not notably inconsistent people who respond with enthusiasm to baroque music while remaining unmoved by baroque painting. But at least the term conveys a sense of the artistic activity, however varied, of a particular period in time – roughly, between 1550 and 1700. How can one respond, however, to a term that merely insists that it comes *after* another period whose boundaries are themselves indeterminate? Moreover, if that does not involve difficulties enough, there is a strand of post-modernist thinking – one for which I have a good deal of sympathy, as we shall see – that refuses to be bound by chronology at all, and insists upon pushing its origins back into the *pre*-modernist past.

Let us now look at the make-up of the term a little more closely. I find it convenient to begin with the root-word 'modern'. This is, it would seem, a relatively innocent term indicating an emphasis on the practices of the present day in contrast to those of the past. But, by definition, it is a slippery term that inevitably changes in meaning as the years go by, and experience shows that it is unwise to introduce it into a title. Ruskin's *Modern Painters* is not concerned with what we would call Modern Art; Meredith's *Modern Love* is now a Victorian period-piece; Alfred North Whitehead's Science is not that of *our* 'Modern World'. Or, if you want some Canadian examples, in 1896 a woman by the name of Carrie Jenkins Harris published a fictional romance entitled *A Modern Evangeline.* I confess that I haven't yet got round to reading it, but I very much doubt if it would seem modern to us. And Sir John William Dawson, the late nineteenth-century Principal of McGill, has among his many publications *Modern Science in Bible Lands* (1888) and *Modern Ideas of Evolution as related to Revelation and Science* (1890). Proof, surely, that the word 'modern' is a classic guarantee of built-in obsolescence.

This being so, the inventors of the term 'modernism', whoever they were, seem to be responsible for our present dilemma. According to my dictionary, the term emerged out of theology, and this may explain why popular definitions of literary modernism tend to emphasize 'nihilism' and 'alienation' as modernist characteristics. The difficulty here is that they usually go on to name T.S. Eliot as a prominent modernist, and these characteristics do not immediately spring to mind after a reading of *Four Quartets.* What has happened, it seems, is that, while Eliot himself emerged out of the waste land, definitions of modernism remained lost in the desert. As we look back, the modernist period, which ought surely (for literary purposes, at any rate) to be rechristened 'early twentieth-century', is characterized more by experiments in technique, approach, or language than by any common philosophical beliefs – or lack of them.

And so we come at last to 'post-modernist', which has chosen to distinguish itself as merely coming after a period that is known for its lack of cohesion if not of coherence. Here, so far as my own discipline is concerned, we encounter another split. 'Post-modernism' in literary studies tends to divide into two strands which, though by no means unconnected, should not be equated. In one sense of the word, we refer to literary works written in the last twenty years or so that share certain attitudes and assumptions; but we also use 'post-modernist' to denote an increased emphasis on the importance of literary theory. I find it necessary for my purpose to consider this last matter, the preoccupation with theory, before zeroing in on my announced topic.

Here I must admit to – not, I hope, a prejudice in the narrow sense of the term, but at least a temperamental bias or partiality. I have always been uneasy about theory, and 'post-modernist' theory has done nothing to alleviate my doubts. I am, indeed, especially suspicious of 'post-modernism' because of the apparent ease with which its practitioners have accepted a descriptive term that seems so inadequate theoretically. It seems to me inconceivable that the term 'post-modernist' (as distinct from its characteristics) can last for very long. Where do we go from here? 'Post-post-modernist'? Or perhaps 'post-contemporary'? That may sound like a contradiction (which it is) but that is because we have not yet grown accustomed to it. Is it any more contradictory (if you can have degrees of contradiction) than 'post-modernist' itself? I see that a contemporary – but not post-modernist – Canadian poet, George Johnston, has recently parodied the whole terminology by describing a traditionalist as 'most ante post-post-modernist' (106).

But my doubts about post-modernism go deeper than that. I am profoundly troubled by recent tendencies in literary studies because I see the emergence of more and more literary students who have been pumped full of up-to-date literary theory (which will not remain up to date for very long) but who lack a sufficient breadth of reading, an adequate experience of literature, to be able to test the validity of the theory. I am not, of course, naïve enough to believe that anyone can read a literary text without bringing to it some prior theoretical assumptions; I realize that I am doubtless reflecting an unarticulated theory by beginning with a suspicion of theory. But that kind of argument can cut two ways. If Blake was generalizing when he announced, 'To generalize is to be an idiot', so Derrida, with his apothegm now quoted increasingly as a sort of post-modernist catchphrase – '*il n'y a pas de hors-texte*' – is making a statement (deliberately, of course) that is located within his own text but outside all others and therefore imposed upon them and possibly irrelevant to them.

My reservations about 'post-modernist' theory are basically threefold. First – and it is no less genuine for being a widespread complaint – I object to the opaque language in which so much literary theory is written. It is odd that a movement that claims to be preoccupied with language should be so inept in its use. (And here I must insert a digressive comment. I have noticed recently that some post-modernist theorists have tried to brush off this charge with the assertion that they are merely employing terminology of which their critics are ignorant. This is not acceptable. A proper definition of jargon might well be: 'an excessive concentration on abstract terms [or 'terminology'] that results in the obfuscation of meaning.' On these grounds, the *extremes* of post-modernist writing are stylistically indefensible.) Second, the emphasis on labels and categories tends, in my view, to result too often in a clumsy inflexibility. While I am in favour of precision, I am also aware of the subtler nuances that elude the over-emphatic pigeon-holer. The cataloguing of effects into pre-established, cut-and-dried divisions that offer the illusion of scientific nomenclature ignores the tonal variety, the unique particular achievements that lie at the heart of literary creation. A recent epigram by Louis Dudek on Northrop Frye's approach could, I suspect, be applied to most literary theory: 'What Frye's theory cannot explain is how the transposition of a single word can change a piece of tripe into a line of poetry' ('Can Lit' 40). Third, I am troubled by the pedantic over-intellectualism that too often pervades the whole enterprise – the theorizing that so rarely gets down to the consideration of actual texts and proves notably helpless when it does. Such rarefied thought has, no doubt, a legitimate place in specialist aesthetics, but does little or nothing to foster a sensitive critical faculty. It may or may not produce canny philosophers – that is not for me to judge – but it does not, in my experience, encourage careful and skilled *readers*.

But all this applies, let me insist, only to the wilder extremes of the movement. On the other hand, I am perfectly willing to admit that I have benefited greatly from the insights of a number of post-modernist critics. In such cases, however, I have almost invariably found that these insights were not dependent upon any radically new theory (and were often obscured by the new terminology) but were the result of intelligent and perceptive human beings communicating their shrewd responses to a literary text. That is, I think, what all literary critics should be doing.

Let me turn now to post-modernist *literature*. The distinguishing features of this literature appear to me to be as follows:

1. Notably in fiction, a transcending of the boundaries of traditional realism;
2. An emphasis on the supremacy of artifice, what is *made* – in fiction, a preoccupation with story;
3. An insistence on the visibility of the artist within and behind the work of art;
4. A playing with – often a deliberate confusion of – such sanctioned opposites as fact and fiction, truth and falsehood, history and myth;
5. An urging that the reader become an active participant within the imaginative and creative process.

These qualities are all, of course, discussed at length by the theorists, but my point is, once again, that they are all obvious enough to anyone who makes direct contact with the texts. At this stage, however, I must revert to an aside I made earlier. The more historically-minded post-modernist critics have acknowledged – as they must – that all these characteristics have been common enough in the literature of the past. In some respects,

Lawrence Sterne's *Tristram Shandy* is the post-modernist novel *par excellence* – but it was published in the 1760s. Thackeray's *Vanity Fair* (1847-48) gives second place to none in involving reader with author in discussion of its puppet-characters. Such well-known works as *Gulliver's Travels* and *Alice in Wonderland* respond to an application of so-called post-modernist principles that might have puzzled their authors, and works of the past that have hitherto seemed idiosyncratic, like James Hogg's *Confessions of a Justified Sinner* and George Borrow's *Lavengro,* now fit more comfortably into our literary heritage. Even a text as seemingly innocent as *Jane Eyre* contributes to post-modernist debate when we remember that it was originally offered (albeit, perhaps, half-heartedly) as if it were a genuine autobiography, 'Edited by Currer Bell'.

All of this suggests, then, that the post-modernist movement in literature represents not so much a discovery of new methods and approaches as a re-exploration – even re-colonization – of terrain that had been identified and roughly charted long ago. The modern emphasis on fiction has complicated the issue since the novel has, until recently, been going through an exaggeratedly realistic phase for the best part of a century, and in consequence has neglected the subject matter, technique, and imaginative possibilities that have been re-explored (and re-exploited) in recent years. Poetry has always been more conducive to worlds of wonder and elaborate linguistic play; and drama, because of its obvious visible artifice, has accommodated radical experiments far more easily (think of Strindberg, Pirandello, and even the non-realistic side of Ibsen). And after all that – and my apologies for the (necessary) delay – let us consider Canadian literature in relation to this complex and tortured intellectual issue.

WHEN DOUGLAS FREAKE began to recruit volunteers for this symposium, he circulated to potential contributors what might be called a springboard definition of literary post-modernism from Frye, Baker, and Perkins's *Harper Handbook to Literature.* It reads as follows:

> Post-modern period (1965-) The period, after a post-war lull from 1945-65, in which a new generation of talented writers have explored the modern dilemma of self and meaning. (363)

When I started to think about the possibility of offering this paper, I found myself returning to that passage and asking: why 1965? I assume, because that year saw the death of T.S. Eliot, the last of the major modernists (that is, if we discount Ezra Pound, who had returned to Italy and silence in 1958, his last work of any consequence being the collected *Cantos* of (significantly) 1964). The most prominent English modernists – Lawrence, Ford Madox Ford, Yeats, Joyce, and Virginia Woolf – had died earlier, in the thirties and early forties; of the Americans, Gertrude Stein died in 1946, Wallace Stevens in 1955, and then, one after the other, Hemingway in 1961, Faulkner in 1962, William Carlos Williams in 1963. Eliot's death in 1965 marked, from one point of view, the end of an era.

But that point of view is decidedly Anglo-American. It reflects a centralist hegemony that could reasonably be accepted as representing the facts of the literary situation up to the Second World War. But the period since then has been remarkable for the emergence of important new writers in other parts of the English-speaking world. If the sun set on the British Empire at mid-century, it rose on an astonishing upsurge of literary activity within the Commonwealth, and in other ex-colonies that continued to use the English language. The names of Chinua Achebe, Nadine Gordimer, Doris Lessing, V.S. Naipaul, Wole Soyinka, Derek Walcott, Patrick White, and many others attest to this fact. And all of them came into prominence – for anyone who was listening – in that so-called 'post-war lull from 1945-65'. Moreover, a gratifying number of Canadian writers appeared as well, many of them currently enjoying international reputations.

Now in English-speaking Canada no comparable pattern of lull followed by new start is evident in or around 1965, and there is no reason, other than the dictates of a palpable but doubtless unconscious cultural imperialism, why there should be. Modernism had perhaps played itself out in the United Kingdom and the United States. But we are all aware of a phenomenon known as 'cultural lag'. Canada, to be sure, took a long time to accustom itself to modernism. As Charles G.D. Roberts shrewdly remarked in 1930, 'to Canada modernism came more slowly and less violently than elsewhere.... Modernism has come softly into the poetry of Canada, by peaceful penetration rather than by rude assault' (298, 299). And the same, he goes on to assert, applies to prose fiction. It could be argued, indeed, that in the novel the process had barely got under way by 1930. At all events, by the time modernism became respectable in Canada, it had passed its prime elsewhere.

This has often been said before, and Canadian commentators are fond of mentioning it with what I can only describe as a complacent masochistic shame. But there is a positive side to the matter. When modernism had run its course elsewhere, when the vein was running thin in Britain and the States, its tide (to mix metaphors shamelessly) was still in full flood in Canada – indeed, I believe it still is. Some people have argued recently that Canada has been or is being equally slow in embracing 'post-modernism'. There is *some* truth in this, though I shall have a few things to say about that in a moment. But it is false, I believe, to draw simple parallels between the modernist challenge of the 1920s and the post-modernist challenge (even, to quote the title of this symposium, 'post-modernist heritage'!) of the 1980s. Canadian literature was decidedly in the doldrums in the years immediately following the First World War. The process of recovery began in poetry idiosyncratically with E.J. Pratt in 1923 and in the novel stolidly – even lumberingly – with Frederick Philip Grove shortly thereafter. Until they emerged, the poetic language and rhythms and the narrative techniques remained those of the 1880s and 1890s, and after Sara Jeannette Duncan's departure for India, only Stephen Leacock had been using prose with any notable (if fitful) originality. Modernism (or some other equally challenging movement) was desperately needed. But in the mid-sixties, Canadian writing was in a mood of youthful exhilaration and ambition. Robertson Davies had already established himself as an all-round man of letters and was preparing, in the *reculer pour mieux sauter* tradition, for a new step forward; Margaret Atwood burst on to the poetry scene in 1966; Hugh Hood was gathering strength; Alice Munro's short stories were beginning to attract attention; Mordecai Richler had already arrived; and so on. There was no need of a 'new movement'; Canadians were in the process of rediscovering their history and establishing their own literary tradition that answered their own needs, and not the dictates of fashion-brokers or pace-setters in New York or London or anywhere else. In terms of Canadian literature, it is palpably false to say that the modernist movement faded away in the mid-sixties or was in need of drastic recharging.

But let me now turn to Canadian literary history as it looks (or so it seems to me) from a 'post-modernist' perspective. If we look in Canadian literature for the post-modernist qualities that I identified a few minutes ago (transcending realism, glory in artifice, subverting of rigid categories, etc.), where and when do we find them? It is still fairly standard, even among old-fashioned modernists (let alone post-modernists), to see Grove as a bumbling, Cro-Magnon realist-cum-naturalist. But if we read *A Search for America* (published, please note, in 1927) with care, we shall find a writer preoccupied with blurring the distinction between fact and fiction, an inveterate role-player delighting in complex artifice, and (yes) a master of intertextuality. Realism is undermined continually; the author is adept at raising and lowering a variety of masks. *A Search for America* is an elusive, playful text, product of the artist as trickster, that, while containing other elements to be sure, has much to say to the developing tastes of the 1980s.

But even if we ignore Grove (whose more typical work belongs elsewhere), let us engage in another piece of literary-historical revisionism. It is customary to cite 1941 as an important year for fiction in English-speaking Canada, seeing as it did the publication of MacLennan's *Barometer Rising* and Sinclair Ross's *As For Me and My House.* Yes, indeed, but two years earlier, the unknown Howard O'Hagan had crept inconspicuously into print with his remarkable novel *Tay John.* A whole generation passed before the book became readily accessible in the New Canadian Library in 1974, and it is no coincidence that the first article to insist upon its importance was written by the at least semi-post-modernist poet Michael Ondaatje. *Tay John* is modernist in its debt to Joseph Conrad, but, in its exhilarating mixture of literary modes, its emphasis on the dramatic significance of 'story', it dramatically anticipates 'post-modernist' interests. And it first appeared, let me repeat, in 1939.

I do not have the time to pursue my historical revisionism very far, but it suggests that such labels as 'modernist' and 'post-modernist' are hopelessly inadequate categories in which to attempt to express the subtleties to be found in complex literary works. I doubt if anyone has got around to considering W.O. Mitchell's *Who Has Seen the Wind* (1947) as a post-modernist text, but its vigorous high spirits, its drawing on the historical Canadian tradition of the tall tale, its zestful flouting of literary decorum in juxtaposing the mundane and the apocalyptic, the deeply moving and the farcical, are continually threatening to break out of any 'realistic', modernist constraints. Robertson Davies is clearly not the kind of author whom passionate advocates of post-modernism have in mind, yet there is a curious Borgesian quality of serious playfulness about much of his work. And *Fifth Business* (1970), while positively old-fashioned in its 'well-madeness' and its adherence to the conventions of classic comedy, was in the vanguard of the new wave in its undercutting of sober realism by its emphasis on wonder, magic, and artifice – and not least in its historian narrator whose insistence on the interrelation of history and myth anticipates so much post-modernist debate on historicity and objectivity.

I suggest, therefore, that the setting up of 'post-modernism' against 'modernism' is an inadequate way of coming to terms with the development in literary achievement – and especially in Canadian literary achievement – in the last twenty years or so. To talk of 'the death of modernism' or 'the death of the novel' is to posit a totally false scenario. To claim, when making a case for non-realistic elements within the new literature, that the literature of the past was trapped within the confines of a naïvely 'photographic' realism; to suggest that the fictional creation of imaginative worlds transcending the limitations of ordinary 'reality' is somehow uniquely contemporary; to argue that literature has only recently begun to concern itself with the literary process as process; to posit an earlier literary model which asserted an eternally fixed system of values to the neglect of process, organicism, and discontinuity; to imply that exploring 'the modern dilemma of self and meaning' (to quote the handbook definition again) was an original breakthrough of the 1960s: all this runs so plainly against the demonstrable historical facts that a counter-argument is hardly necessary. I want, therefore, to devote the rest of my time to commenting very briefly on certain Canadian products of 'post-modernism' and to show how they do not represent any dramatic break from earlier 'modernist' traditions.

Jack Hodgins's novel *The Invention of the World* was published in 1977. It begins with the miraculous birth of a demonic Irish anti-hero at the top of a mountain, the child having (according to one 'invention') been fathered on a poor Irish peasant-girl 'by a bull-god from the sky' (69). It is chock-full of parodies, absurdities, philosophical jokes on the impossibility of accurate communication, and, moreover, contains a host of unlikely and irrepressible eccentrics to delight anyone with non-realist predilections. Narration is split between parody-omniscience and a string of unreliable (indeed, contradictory) narrators. And it ends with a mock epic to balance the earlier mock myth, a tall tale of a wedding-brawl to end all tall tales. It sounds unabashedly 'post-modernist', and in a sense it is. But there are difficulties. Hodgins continually insists on the authenticity of his apparently fantastic characters, remarking that the inhabitants of northern Vancouver Island are in fact 'like that'. 'What I write is to me "realistic"', he stresses in the interview with Geoff Hancock, and casts scorn on 'those writers who are interested in nothing but playing games with language' (63, 57). And this is clearly no sophisticated 'con' on Hodgins's part as it might be on, say, Leonard Cohen's.

Hodgins has acknowledged a 'post-modernist' debt to the South American school of 'magic realism' associated with Gabriel García Márquez and *One Hundred Years of Solitude,* but lays as much emphasis on the realism as on the magic (Hancock 56, 71). And he made an important and often neglected geographical point when he remarked to another interviewer: 'The coastline that runs past me here goes all the way down non-stop past Gabriel García Márquez's house. Surely that's as legitimate a connection as the 49th parallel to Toronto' (Ohm 4). Yes, indeed. And if we read Hodgins in the historical-geographical context of Western writing, alongside Howard O'Hagan, Ethel Wilson, Emily Carr, and the Western squatter Malcolm Lowry, he appears decidedly less *avant-garde* and notably more 'traditional'.

The norms of Toronto, as I have frequently felt the need to point out, are not necessarily the norms of the rest of Canada. The answer to the question 'Where is here?' may still be in doubt, but it certainly isn't within a few kilometres of Bloor and Yonge. But let us turn for a few moments to a writer centrally associated with Toronto, Margaret Atwood, and another deeply rooted in Ontario, Alice Munro. In Atwood we find a writer whose work explores both the minuscule realistic details of Toronto living ('... and partly living'!) and the emotional landscape of irrationality, terror, and paranoia. 'Post-modernists', so far as I can see, are a little uneasy about this – and well they might be. Here the crucial text, I believe, is *Lady Oracle,* a book that, on the surface, caters to all the requirements of traditional and even popular fiction – a strong plot, a series of memorable, almost Dickensian characters, and a vivid, iconoclastic presentation of current fads. But the satire goes much deeper than that. Below the surface, *Lady Oracle* is an exhilarating parody – a deconstruction – of virtually everything, including Atwood herself *and* post-modernism. The novel uses the techniques of post-modernism to undercut the pretensions of post-modernism itself. It parodies realism and the cult of fantasy, traditional critical approaches and contemporary metafiction, with equal zest. Atwood is mistress of the Swiftian satiric trap, yet she has quite properly acknowledged a debt to Jane Austen – not merely, I suspect, to *Northanger Abbey* but to the subtler ironies of the later Jane Austen as well. Once again, we find post-modernist preoccupations side by side with a profound traditionalism.

Alice Munro presents a rather different case. She consistently regards herself as 'old-fashioned' in her literary approach. 'I see my technique', Munro stated at the beginning of the seventies, 'as being very traditional, very conventional' (Gibson 256). It could be argued, perhaps, that in her work we see a contemporary sensibility, presented in all its psychological 'modernist' subtlety, in the process of painfully breaking out of a constricting traditional society. At the same time, we can see a fascinating development in her work, technically, as it emerges from the sixties and continues through the eighties. In her early work, as she has confessed often enough, a concluding paragraph almost invariably rounds off the story by summing up its central preoccupation and as it were manipulating the reader into an understanding and acceptance of the author's meaning and viewpoint. This seems to have originated in part from a concern to sell stories to popular (and paying) magazines. But it is also a reflection of an unquestioned assumption, in the literary air at that time, about how stories should be written. Munro was, then, working within an accepted convention. In the seventies, however, fashions changed somewhat, and Munro experienced what might be called a reaction against the neat ending, against the tyranny of closure. In some well-known stories of this period – notably 'The Ottawa Valley' and 'Home' – she deconstructs the story she appears to be creating, refuses to provide a neat ending, commenting instead on the unreality of story in the best 'post-modern' way. *But,* and here the crunch comes, this inevitably evolves into a new convention. These stories have been much admired by critics eager to haul Munro into the post-modernist camp by her bootstraps; but Munro herself has begun to have second thoughts. In a recent interview she rejected the technical innovations of 'backing off and reflecting on the story' as 'a kind of trick I wouldn't use now' (Connolly n.pag.). Can this mean, I wonder, that Munro is now '*post*-post-modernist'?

Perhaps. More to the point, though, it suggests the ultimate irrelevance of trying to fit writers into rigid categories, to put constraining and often inappropriate labels upon them. That the 'post-modernist' characteristics I have isolated are important and stimulating to many contemporary writers, in Canada and elsewhere, no one in their senses would deny. But to argue that these are the only viable literary attitudes and approaches in our time is ridiculous – as ridiculous, I believe, as the neat Anglo-American dating-scheme that I objected to earlier. Let me take one more Canadian example I haven't yet mentioned: Mavis Gallant. To stick a 'post-modernist' label upon her would surely be grotesque. The only comment that I have come across in which she would seem to refer to this matter herself occurs in a well-known interview with Geoff Hancock in which she remarked, in a way that seemed to render any further discussion unnecessary: 'I find Robbe-Grillet very boring, don't you?' (102). I quote this not to defend or uphold Gallant's adverse judgement, but merely to point out that, in the real world of writing, totally different interests and attitudes can co-exist within a cross-section of major writers at any given moment in historical time. Gallant cannot, I think, be properly categorized as post-modernist because, though she explores the contemporary concern about difficulties of communication, notably in *A Fairly Good Time* and the short stories 'Jorinda and Jorindel' and 'Orphans' Progress' in *Home Truths,* she never loses faith in the adequacy of language itself. But this does not mean that Gallant is old-fashioned or inadequate or somehow out of touch; rather, it suggests that 'post-modernism' is too narrow a term to encompass the variety possible within contemporary writing.

I end, then, where I began (a non-post-modernist trait, I suspect, but that doesn't worry me). As a *term* 'post-modernist' is inadequate as a general description and needs to be scrapped. If we want a phrase to describe the literature of the last generation or so (which would certainly contain a post-modernist element), 'late twentieth-century' will do as well as any. And when the history of 'late twentieth-century' literature in English comes to be written, the qualities I have identified as 'post-modernist' will be seen, I am convinced, to have made an important but not exclusive contribution to the whole. Similarly, I am prepared to forecast that the characteristic features will reveal as much a continuity with 'early twentieth-century' traditions ('modernist', if you will) as a radical break from them. The major figures will be the most skilful, the most intelligent, the most profound *writers* irrespective of their practical or theoretical connections with what we now call 'post-modernism'. Munro and Gallant (and other contemporary writers, Canadian or non-Canadian) are no less central to our literary-historical period for not doing, in Munro's words, 'the current thing'. So far as Canadian writers are concerned, critical emphasis will be somewhat different if they are seen within the narrower national context or in the wider 'cosmopolitan' scene. But I am sure that they will form a significant part of that scene. Moreover, and in conclusion, the precise nature of that 'scene', late twentieth-century literature in English, will undoubtedly be affected by the most distinguished Canadian writers who, whether 'post-modernist' or not, will by that time have taken their deserved place within it.

'Criticism in Practice': John Metcalf's Private Part

This address was delivered in November 1988 at a four-day conference held at the University of Guelph, organized by J.R. (Tim) Struthers, and entitled: 'Coming of Age: John Metcalf and the Canadian Short Story'. The immediate occasion celebrated Metcalf's fiftieth birthday (which coincided with the final day of the conference), an opportunity to pay tribute to his unstinting encouragement of good Canadian writing, especially short fiction, over the previous two decades. His latest critical book, *What Is A Canadian Literature?*, was also launched at this time. The address, at which Metcalf was present, combined assessment of his literary criticism with a personal tribute. It is scheduled for publication in the conference proceedings, but finds an appropriate place here since, though we differ (sometimes quite vehemently) on certain issues, our basic attitudes contain, I like to think, some striking similarities.

THIS IS NOT going to be an academic lecture. (Nor, I'd better add in parenthesis for those who respond to the second part of my title with a strong visual imagination, will it be an illustrated one.) When I first undertook the assignment, I must confess, I began with the idea of a standard, conventionally organized scholarly paper. But I soon realized that this would not be the appropriate form. Metcalf is not an academic, and the value of his criticism, which I hope to define in the next few minutes, is important as a much-needed challenge to the entrenched academy. Some different method of inquiry needs to be found. What I propose to do is to engage in a succession of exploratory forays – not unlike McLuhanesque probes, though I'm not at all happy with the association – forays undertaken in an endeavour to establish bearings.

PROBE 1: Let's start with a foray close to home. The blurb on the back cover of the Red Kite edition of *Kicking Against the Pricks* begins: 'Since its first publication by ECW PRESS in 1982, this volume has won a place as a major work of Canadian cultural criticism – as a writer's, an editor's, and a teacher's Bible.' 'Well, no' (as Metcalf would say). It is, to be sure, in a good cause, but that is the kind of exaggerated puffery that Metcalf has consistently lamented. Besides, I note with interest how the last page of the printed text informs us that the book has been reissued 'in an edition of 620 copies' – which suggests to me, and doubtless to Metcalf, that the literary and academic Gideons have not yet latched on to it. No, 'Bible' isn't the right word for either its message or its effect. Perhaps 'underground protest' or 'guerrilla warfare' would be more accurate.

PROBE 2: My next foray takes the form of a memory, but it is not in fact unrelated. Some eight months ago, before I was invited to give this address, I was talking with a graduate student whose doctoral thesis I am supervising. I happened to make a reference to something (I've forgotten what) that Metcalf had written in *Kicking Against the Pricks.* The student smiled, and said with apparent surprise: 'You think a lot of that book, don't you? You've mentioned it before.' After I'd been asked to come and speak with special reference to the book, I remembered the remark and thought I'd like to know more. So I phoned my student and asked him to elaborate. He replied that he was uneasy about Metcalf because he seemed 'too depreciatory'. Well (in this case), yes. Bible or not, the message – which I take to be the need for some honest depreciation – clearly hasn't yet got across. To imagine a non-depreciatory Metcalf would be rather like trying to visualize anti-matter.

PROBE 3: Let me change tack once again. Does my high rating of Metcalf's critical work stem from the fact that we share the same prejudices and that I therefore agree with everything he writes? By no means. To be sure, a lot of what he says sums up so perfectly what I've oft thought but ne'er so well expressed that

I'm frequently moved to place appreciative check-marks in the margins of my own copies. On the other hand, there are times when I disagree violently. As a devoted, even insatiable reader of Robertson Davies, for example, I resent Metcalf's observation, in the interview with Geoff Hancock that opens *Kicking Against the Pricks*: 'Surely people don't actually *read* Robertson Davies? They're the sort of books that people own to show they're "cultured"' (2). Witty, but way off the mark. And I've even written a few articles (here I begin to see Metcalf's head shaking sadly) to argue that there is even something to be said about the artistry (yes, artistry) of Frederick Philip Grove. I mention all this not to indulge in nit-picking reservations ('you're wrong *here,* John, and *here*') but to make what seems to me an important critical point that Academia invariably has difficulty in understanding. *The good critic is often one who provokes you into disagreeing.* The idea that criticism works like, say, the proving of a scientific proposition, that a demonstrably false step vitiates the whole endeavour, is one of the sillier assumptions of our time. What ultimately matters is the soundness (or otherwise) of a critic's *basic* approach. The details, especially the possibly vulnerable asides, are always open to challenge. Many of Metcalf's individual judgements both puzzle and irritate me – and I'm sure he can, and probably will, say the same about mine. (Now I come to think about it, he has.) As Alice Munro said about him in 'On John Metcalf: Taking Writing Seriously', 'he has a blind spot or two, like the rest of us' (7). But the important point – hopelessly unfashionable and sentimental as it may seem – is that his literary-critical heart is in the right place, that he knows where he stands, and that he sets out (provocatively) in the right direction.

PROBE 4: My next foray, longer and more complicated, will be seen by most of you (including, I suspect, Metcalf) as moving in a very doubtful direction, but it develops smoothly enough out of what I have just said. A few pages later, still in the Hancock interview, Metcalf makes a reference to 'Leavis and all those lugubrious people ...' (7), and in the immediately succeeding essay, while reminiscing about his undergraduate experience at the University of Bristol, he vaguely recalls 'a seminar of Leavisite persuasion that twittered on about Lawrence' (44). (There is also a reference in a somewhat sarcastic tone within the short story 'Beryl' (*Teeth* 116).) Here again, my hackles rise. I can reminisce too, and it so happens that I was an undergraduate at Cambridge when Dr Leavis was still lecturing there. I must repeat immediately what I've stated more than once elsewhere: that I consider Leavis the finest literary critic in English in this century. He is in no way 'lugubrious' (I cannot think of a more exhilarating literary commentator) and if that seminar really 'twittered', I can only say that it didn't deserve – what is in any case a dubious epithet – the 'Leavisite' tag.

Let me now reveal what many here may not know: that, although Leavis is generally associated with the phrase 'practical criticism', he disliked the term (probably because it had been coined, or at least popularized, by I.A. Richards), and himself favoured the phrase 'criticism in practice'. Hence my title. I get the impression (if he'll forgive me) that Metcalf's familiarity with Leavis's writings is fairly slight, and it may possibly surprise him to learn that I am constantly reminded of Leavis when reading Metcalf's work. (From what I have already said, I hope it is clear that this is intended as a high compliment.) Of course, there are obvious differences, most notably the fact that Leavis is an academic teacher and Metcalf is a writer-critic. Yet I am reminded of Leavis for two reasons: first, because of the similarity of their views about cultural decline; and second, because of the acerbity – even the invigorating acerbity – with which their points are made.

To establish my argument, let me now offer a series of quotations from *Kicking Against the Pricks* with the suggestion that, given a minimum of obvious alteration, they could have been written by Leavis:

1. '... it seems axiomatic to me that a mass readership and a literary writer are incompatible' (1). And, from a different

statement: 'What concerns me as a writer ... is what happens to the gifted and literate minority' (57). (One of Leavis's first publications was a pamphlet entitled *Mass Civilization and Minority Culture.*)

2. 'The quality of education has declined everywhere ...' (2).
3. A comment which even reproduces Leavis's idiom and speech-rhythms: 'Yes, I suppose I delude myself that there *are* values extant. And in literary terms, one writes against a background and tradition' (4-5).
4. '... I'm very much outside the system. I cannot conceive of anything more horrible than being inside' (8).
5. '... when I persuaded Michael Macklem of *Oberon* to change the title [from *New*] to *Best* [*Canadian Stories*], it was a conscious decision to attempt to improve standards' (9).
6. 'We will not have good teachers until we have teachers who love their subject.... Such love as I speak of is a matter of the whole man. It cannot be imparted in a three-credit course. It is the sum of what a man or woman *is.* ... literary taste cannot be separated from the minute and endless activities of our daily lives' (60-61).
7. 'If we cannot honestly evaluate the past, we cannot make intelligent judgements about the present' (150).
8. 'Our major story writers are Mavis Gallant, Norman Levine, Hugh Hood, Alice Munro, Leon Rooke, and Clark Blaise' (169). (Compare the opening sentence of Leavis's *The Great Tradition*: 'The great English novelists are Jane Austen, George Eliot, Henry James and Joseph Conrad....')
9. A remark described by Barry Cameron in his book on Metcalf as 'neo-Leavisite' (118): 'It is my quaint contention that writing is a moral act' (197).

You will notice the consistent preoccupations here: the need for an educated and cultured public; the quality of education; a concern for values and tradition; independence from 'the system' (which Leavis habitually called 'the literary racket'); the duty to improve standards; the intimate relation between literature and life; the supreme importance of evaluation; writing as a moral act. These form the staples of Metcalf's and Leavis's attitudes alike. I honour them both because, in their very different ways, they share these principles. And I needn't say here, I suppose, that such views are rarely upheld in fashionable academic circles at the present time.

The explanation for this similarity in their views is not in fact difficult to discover. I must speak again from my own experience. I am not a 'Leavisite' in the strict sense of having attended Downing College and having sat dutifully at the feet of the master. (That is itself, one suspects, an outsider's caricature.) On the contrary, I went to a college where the actual Master (capital M) was Leavis's arch-enemy, E.M.W. Tillyard. But by that time (the mid-1950s) Leavis's influence had been felt, unwillingly but palpably, in schools and universities throughout Britain – and not least (this is my main point) in places where the official 'line' was very different. Metcalf's teacher in his pre-university years at school, whom he describes as 'a serious man with a great love of literature' who 'concentrated on close reading of the texts' (41) may well have been a direct or indirect disciple. I would be very surprised indeed if Leavis's influence hadn't permeated the University of Bristol by the time Metcalf arrived – and not merely in L.C. Knights's seminars. This influence, everywhere, was almost invariably grudging, and was regularly denied by officialdom, but it was unquestionably there. Leavisite views are currently out of favour now that we are in danger of being inundated by what I find myself calling the intense inane or Higher Obscurantism of literary theory, but there is still a scattered remnant of people seriously interested in literature as a contemporary art dependent upon a living tradition. Metcalf is undoubtedly of that company, and, whether he knows it or not, and is prepared to acknowledge it or not, he owes an intellectual and cultural debt to F.R.L.

PROBE 5: At the opening of 'Editing the Best', Metcalf registers surprise that he is 'about to write something which can only be described as history' (143). Now that he is reaching the venerable age of fifty, he may be resigned to this. In any case, since he came to Canada at exactly the same age as I did, and only four years later than I did, and since I have already had occasion to refer to Metcalf's and my own reminiscences, I want now to continue that process in order to develop my general argument. What Metcalf experienced when he arrived in Canada was the phenomenon now generally known as culture shock. He was amazed to discover a country that didn't seem to be sure whether it had a literature or not, and anyhow didn't seem to care. He also encountered the Cro-Magnon beginnings of 1967 nationalism, which assumed (with a combination of arrogance and xenophobia) that immigrants, whether writers or critics, had nothing useful to contribute to an understanding and amelioration of whatever national literature existed.

My own academic culture shock had been similar, though in a sense even more emphatic. In the academic year 1957-58 I was attending Leavis's lectures at Cambridge; in the academic year 1958-59 I was enrolled in Northrop Frye's graduate seminar at Toronto. I enrolled in that course because I was aware of Frye's scholarly reputation. (The *Anatomy of Criticism* had appeared the previous year, and before that the traditionally xenophobic English had *not* taken the view that a Canadian had nothing to teach them about English Blake.) My first discovery in Toronto, however, was that, while in Britain Frye was by then quite well known in academic circles, in Canada Leavis was generally *persona incognita* – and, when known, decidedly *persona non grata.* I discovered to my amazement that the University of Toronto Library did not contain a run of the Leavisite periodical *Scrutiny* – undoubtedly the most influential literary-critical journal in mid-century England – and when I mentioned this *lacuna* to a senior Professor of English responsible for library acquisitions I found myself in the following eloquent dialogue:

Self: The University Library doesn't have a run of *Scrutiny*.
Professor: No.

The reason soon became clear to me. Leavis had expressed heretical views about Milton, and his journal, if not his books, was on an unofficial Index. It seemed a strange procedure for a department that claimed to be a model for the rest of Canada in the championing of humanistic studies.

You may think that I have ranged a long way from John Metcalf and his criticism, but my motive is to suggest: a) that Frye's pre-eminence has, over the years, created a Canadian literary-critical orthodoxy into which Metcalf doesn't fit ('... I'm very much outside the system. I cannot conceive of anything more horrible than being inside'); and b) that Metcalf brought with him, perhaps unwittingly, a number of Leavis-influenced assumptions and attitudes that proved to be unfamiliar and even offensive. There are, I believe, three main areas where Frye's principles come into conflict with Metcalf's. First, it will be remembered that Frye always keeps his Canadian criticism and that of the rest of the world in separate compartments. The *Anatomy of Criticism* doesn't contain a single reference to a Canadian work – for obvious reasons, both practical and strategic, that Metcalf could explain as well as – though far more forcefully than – anyone else I know. I am not criticizing Frye for this, but it has led – at least until very recently – to the hermetic sealing of Canadian literature in protective isolation, and this, as Metcalf has argued so well, has had deleterious effects upon what should have been its natural growth. Second, Frye is well-known for his dislike of evaluation – and for the devious lengths to which he will go to disguise the extent of his own inevitable value-judgements. This influence is receding as the literature has developed and at least some commentators have gained greater confidence, but the danger now is an immature evaluation without the literary-critical experience to justify it, the dismal effects of which are to be seen in the reviewing sections of virtually every newspaper, magazine, and academic journal in the country. As Metcalf put the matter so succinctly in the interview by Barry Cameron in 1975 (and the situation has probably deteriorated since then), 'reviewing in Canada is appalling' (407). Third, and perhaps most important, Frye is a generalizer. Even as a callow graduate student in 1958-59 I had noticed how, when discussing Romantic poetry, he managed to make Keats and Shelley sound virtually identical, since his highest common factor of theoretical Romanticism ignored the all-important differences of style and use of language to which I had been introduced in my Leavis-influenced past. Metcalf, on the other hand, is a confirmed particularizer. One of his essays that I most admire is 'Punctuation as Score', mainly because of its concentration on the minuscule but essential nuances that details of punctuation, paragraphing, italicization, etc. can contribute to the total effect of a piece of prose. I believe this offers an invaluable insight into what distinguishes permanent literature from dispensable literary chaff, a supreme demonstration of 'criticism in practice'. There is not, I believe, a single instance in the whole of Frye's critical *oeuvre* that shows any interest in such details – or even any indication that they exist.

PROBE 6: My next foray sets off on yet another tack. It so happens that I have been favoured, through the courtesy of Metcalf himself and Tim Struthers, with a sneak preview (as you might say) of *What Is A Canadian Literature?*, since it was thought that I might care to comment on it in this paper. I am indeed happy to do so. I am therefore going to whet your appetites – and, perhaps, your neuroses. This new book carries the argument of *Kicking Against the Pricks* one step further by casting doubt on the whole idea of a Canadian tradition, either as a historical entity or as a useful concept. Anyone who has written on the subject may expect to find himself or herself quoted and (to use the Leavisite word) 'scrutinized'. Now I calculate from what he says of myself that on the Metcalf scale I earn something around a C+; since for Metcalf this is a decidedly high grade, those of you who qualify to be named can look forward to measuring your own standing with eager anticipation.

This, then, is another literary-critical rough-house in which Metcalf is being even more controversial than usual. It provides, however, a useful way of testing the principle that I formulated earlier: the good critic is often the one who provokes you into disagreeing. In this case, though, it is not a simple matter of disagreement. Metcalf has here raised an issue (the phrase 'criticism in practice' is as apposite as ever) with which I have been personally concerned for many years: is there something that can usefully be called a Canadian literary tradition, and if so what is it? It's not so much that I disagree with Metcalf's stance – a lot of what he says seems to me unquestionably true – but rather that I believe there to be elements in the situation that he ignores. He has thrown down a challenge, and I am not at all sure that I am sufficiently well-equipped to take it up – or even that I want to. But because Metcalf and I have a certain amount in common – no, not creative genius, but closeness of age, experience as 'non-birthright' Canadians, and the broad lines of our upbringing, the kind of thing that earns us both honourable places in the black book of Robin Mathews (to whom, it will not surprise you, Metcalf assigns an F) – I find myself in a special position from which to comment.

Metcalf's argument goes, basically, as follows: virtually all Canadian literature written up to the middle of the twentieth century was rubbish, and the important date is 1962 – important not, as my ex-student, now friend and colleague Sam Solecki suggested wittily though a bit naughtily in *The Bumper Book*, because that was the year of Metcalf's own arrival on the Canadian scene (214), but because it was the year in which Hugh Hood published *Flying a Red Kite* and impelled Canadian writing into something called the international style. There is no Canadian literary tradition, Metcalf argues, because until recently what was written was third-rate and so could not qualify for the dignified status that a genuine tradition implies. Furthermore, because most of the writings from the Canadian literary past were not accessible except on dusty library-shelves in certain urban centres, potential writers couldn't look to Canada for a tradition even if they had wanted to and there was one to find. Willy-nilly, then, such young writers turned to the giants of international modernism, who for Metcalf represent the necessary and obvious source of stimulation anyway.

Thus far, Metcalf. Let me set against that my own attitude as it has developed over the years. My first venture into Canadian literary criticism was a short introductory book for students on Charles G.D. Roberts that assumed (it never occurred to me to question that assumption) that Roberts should be treated like any other writer in English publishing between 1880 and 1940. Very briefly, I found his poetry at best interesting in a rather minor sort of way and at worst embarrassing, his novels generally unsuccessful, though very occasionally showing hints of a somewhat eccentric originality; but then there were the 'stories of the wild' which, I argued, constituted his best work and opened up a literary area, admittedly limited but not to be despised, where a Canadian in Roberts's situation could use his experience to advantage. For that less-than-enthusiastic judgement – which still seems to me, by and large, accurate – I graduated (not *cum laude* but, I assume, *cum reprehensione*) on to Robin Mathews's hit-list.

In the course of the discussion, I tried to make a distinction (which no one seemed to understand) between what I called 'universal trends' and 'universal standards'. What I meant was that, ultimately, one judges against the standard of what Matthew Arnold called 'the best that has been thought and said in the world', but that this in no way implies that the content, the basic approach, the individual nuances, will not reflect a local (in this case, Canadian) situation. In other words, there is a basic standard of expertise, of technique, of literary accomplishment, against which all writing has to be measured (if Canadian athletes are not at least potentially world-class, they aren't selected for the Olympics; if Canadian musicians don't measure up, they aren't booked into Wigmore Hall or the Lincoln Center); at the same time, because literature has an intimate connection with human life and the details of living differ so dramatically in various parts of the world, an excellent Canadian novel (if you can find one) is going to produce a noticeably different flavour from an equally excellent novel from another part of the world, even if that novel is also written in the English language.

More recently, when invited to write my *Canadian Literature in English* volume, I was inevitably faced with the question of tradition, and was acutely aware of the difficulties Metcalf lists – the shortness of time for a tradition to develop, the doubtfulness of positing historical influence for works not widely known, and, above all, the embarrassingly poor quality of so much of the early material. (Yes, like Metcalf, though the wording is my own, I see no reason why a nineteenth-century Canadian should have felt obliged to read *Wacousta* or *Antoinette de Mirecourt* when *Great Expectations* or *Middlemarch* was available.) I eventually wrote in my preface as follows:

> ... the concept of a 'Canadian tradition' is not easily established. In literary terms it is, I believe, neither an abstraction like a sense of identity nor a theme like survival. It evolves gradually from the achieved literary works that have been written by its people.... Ultimately, I am convinced, it is the tradition established by the best that sets the standard. (x)

I also insisted that 'the concept of tradition is constantly revisionist' (x).

Let us now return to Metcalf. In *What Is A Canadian Literature?* his list of inescapable influences for a young writer in 1962 reads as follows: 'Joyce, Beckett, Faulkner, Hemingway, Eliot, Pound, Sartre, Céline, Camus, Kerouac, etc.' (35). Two Irishmen, five Americans, three French. No Canadians, of course, and – interestingly – no English. But the point I wish to make – and surely Metcalf realizes this, though only once does he give a hint of it – is: are not Joyce and Beckett recognizably Irish as well as international? Are not Sartre, Céline, Camus just as recognizably French? Moreover, surely it is not unreasonable to see Joyce and Beckett as culminations of a smaller but highly important Anglo-Irish tradition, and so on. I confess that Metcalf's list is just as puzzlingly diverse to me as any of the lists of people supposedly constituting a Canadian tradition that Metcalf quotes and derides. Yes, the overall standard of accomplishment is higher, but they are still a motley crew (Eliot and *Kerouac*?!). And I'd better say that, if a similar list were compiled from the 1980s, I see no reason why certain Canadians shouldn't be admitted. Metcalf and I could probably agree at least on Mavis Gallant – not, to be sure, because she's Canadian but on the basis of literary merit. At the same time, I would argue (though Metcalf would probably disagree) that this literary merit derives its special quality from her Canadian origins.

PROBE 7: We need a specific instance about which to argue at this point, and I am now going to produce a literary guinea-pig or early-morning rabbit out of my (Robertson-Davies-like?) magician's hat. I give you a writer who, it seems to me, is a living instance of the fact that an individual's output can change dramatically when he becomes assimilated into something that I shall call, for want of a better term, a Canadian tradition. His name (will it surprise you?) is – who else? – John Metcalf.

I welcome the opportunity because it allows me to remedy what I now see as the inadequate assessment that I provided of Metcalf's work in *Canadian Literature in English.* My difficulty with Metcalf in that book, however, is surprisingly germane to my present concern. Let me quote what I wrote then about his fiction:

> John Metcalf ... has produced a number of stories in which inspiration comes from his English childhood. Retrospection is a predominant subject in his work; the past always seems a better because more human place, and he has a sharp eye for the absurdities, even obscenities, of modern living (Evelyn Waugh is one of his culture-heroes). But although his satiric streak finds ample material within Canadian life (notably in the savagely amusing novel, *General Ludd,* 1980), the more deeply probing side of his creative consciousness cannot acclimatize so quickly. His most serious and accomplished stories are English in tradition and

> attitude as well as in subject and setting, and for all their delicacy and subtlety (or perhaps because of them) seem off-centre in a Canadian context. The English child is as yet an uncertain father to the Canadian man, though in his more recent stories, especially the novella 'Girl in Gingham' (1978), we can see him adapting his considerable talents to the material around him. (171)

C+ again? If he were in a generous mood (on the eve of his birthday, perhaps), it's just possible that Metcalf might allow a B-. I pride myself that he could probably name a number of Canadian critics likely to offer a less satisfactory account (and at least I spelled his name right), but I'm not happy with my assessment. The emphasis isn't quite right; there is no discussion (shame on me!) of the quality of his writing-style; and in my justified enthusiasm for 'Girl in Gingham', I make no comment (and there are quotation marks coming up here) on his 'Private Parts'.

But my major point remains, I think, valid. There *is* a difference between his English and Canadian material, the retrospective stories of boys and young men feeling their way tentatively and often painfully in a harsh adult world (albeit written with spatial as well as temporal detachment in Canada) and those more immediate stories of married or divorced men set in Ottawa or Montreal or Fredericton. The distinction can be pinpointed by Metcalf's comments in the interview by Barry Cameron: 'The kind of short stories I like most and the kind that I want to write most move always closest to poetry and to imagery ... a short story – at least the kind that I appreciate most – tends to be almost plotless and concerned with a moment of emotional insight' (402, 403-04). A little later, he refers to 'really great short stories, like Joyce's *Dubliners* ... one of the greatest books of short stories' (404, 411). These remarks are perfectly fitted to narratives like 'Keys and Watercress', 'The Estuary', 'The Children Green and Golden'; they do not fit 'Girl in Gingham', 'Polly Ongle', or 'The Nipples of Venus'.

What are the differences between these two sets? Metcalf has given the autobiographical answer to this question in the Cameron interview:

> ... I could never write a story about a child or an adolescent in Canada for the very simple reason that I could never be quite sure that I'd got exactly the right expression that they used in, let us arbitrarily say, 1957.... I can only write, really, about a semi-expatriate, adult Canadian living in a city because that's my experience. (422, 423)

That is clearly an important factor – it makes sense on a number of levels – but it is not, I think, the whole story. In what way do the Canadian stories not fit? First, if these later stories are 'closest to poetry' (and I'm more than a little uneasy about such cross-genre comparisons), it's a decidedly different kind of poetry from the earlier; and, more to the point, while the stories continue to be 'plotless', the phrase 'a moment of emotional insight' fails to catch the peculiar character of these later writings. There is something more than 'emotional' insight here, and it is that 'something' that we should explore.

Take 'The Teeth of My Father'. Superficially, it is another story of retrospection, of trying to come to terms with the past and with people – here, parents – who made up that past. We may notice that the speaker has distanced himself by emigrating to (where else?) Canada, and I think this *is* significant, though it's a minor point in itself. More crucial are the narrative dislocations of what is apparently the main subject – the interpolated short stories (Metcalf's own, though the author in the narrative is not Metcalf himself) and especially the self-contradictions and changes of tactics on the part of the narrator. If you know the story well, you will remember the disorienting parenthetical insertion after the first two innocent-seeming paragraphs:

> (I have decided to tell the truth. My stories in the River Room were not purely nostalgic; they were calculated to be funny and entertain my friend. My friend was more an acquaintance, a man

> I admired and wanted to impress. And 'wilful legs' [a phrase already used] was plagiarized from Dylan Thomas.) (*Teeth* 59)

Last time I read that, something clicked and I found myself saying out loud: 'Alice Munro!' And then I noticed the dedication (a rare thing in Metcalf's short stories) under the title: '*For Alice Munro*'. What Metcalf is doing here for his father is surely what Munro in 'The Ottawa Valley' does for her mother – both explore these relationships by transforming autobiographical memoir into invented story, with continual reminders, to themselves and their readers, that the truth is always relative and always subject to revision.

Can this be a case of Canadian 'influence', the faint beginnings of a Canadian tradition? I suspect so, but the sixty-four-thousand dollar question is: which way was the influence going? *Something I've Been Meaning to Tell You,* containing both 'The Ottawa Valley' and the somewhat similarly constructed 'Winter Wind', both previously unpublished, appeared in the spring of 1974, and 'Home', the other story by Munro that most noticeably employs this technique, was published elsewhere in the same year. 'The Teeth of My Father' first made its bow in what I gather was the characteristically late Winter 1974 issue of the *Journal of Canadian Fiction,* and so must have appeared at almost exactly the same time as the Munro collection. A scholarly dead-end? Not necessarily. We know that Metcalf and Munro had been corresponding for some years. Munro reports that Metcalf first wrote to her in appreciation of her work when she was virtually unknown. After that, she remarks in 'On John Metcalf', 'we wrote about what we were working on' (6). They met some time later, and Metcalf, of course, interviewed her for the *Journal of Canadian Fiction* in 1972. I suggest that some of Munro's experimentation with narrators trying to tell the truth about their relatives (and knowing that they will fail) rubbed off on Metcalf, that Munro was in a position to stimulate him towards further experiments in this direction at a time when he could not have got the same encouragement from the great writers of modernism to whom he pays tribute. All right, he learned from Munro (if I'm right) not because she was Canadian but because she was a writer he respected. Yet the fact remains that she *was* Canadian and (*I* think) influenced him in a way not unconnected with their Canadian situations.

A similar line of influence could be posited for 'Private Parts'. First of all – shades of Alice Munro again – a similar parenthesis. After a skilful re-creation of childhood reminiscence, the narrator renounces his artistry as falsification:

> (This will not do. The paragraphs flow too evenly, the sequence of statements rounds off the subject too neatly....) (*Girl* 17)

I'm prepared to bet dollars to doughnuts that Metcalf could not have produced that effect if he had stayed in England, had not gained the spatial distance provided by Canada, had not come into contact with congenial Canadian writers. I say 'writers' in the plural, because Munro is not the only influence involved here. By this time, Clark Blaise would seem to be a palpable presence behind the writing, and Metcalf has indeed acknowledged this in *Kicking Against the Pricks*:

> Clark's work offered me constructional and rhetorical ideas. These influences haven't worked themselves out in open or obvious ways but stories of mine like 'The Teeth of My Father', 'The Eastmill Reception Centre', and 'Private Parts: A Memoir' probably grew in their own dark from the seeds of Clark's 'Extractions and Contractions'. (79)

A comparative study of Metcalf and Blaise would be fascinating: their autobiographical narrators appearing and reappearing with similar backgrounds yet differing names; not just retrospection but a similar meditative tone of retrospection; a comparable fastidious preoccupation with the right word, rhythm, nuance. The influence is, I am sure, mutual, and I hope I do not have to insist, to this audience, that when I talk of influence I am in no way impugning the originality of the writers concerned. I am thinking of Metcalf's own beautifully precise formulation about Hugh Hood in *Kicking Against the Pricks*: 'Hugh offered me an example of how to relax my own style.... I didn't relax *in Hugh's manner* but that I managed to accept the possibility of relaxation is largely owing to his influence' (79). I am also reminded of the phenomenon that received its classic definition from Gerard Manley Hopkins: 'The effect of studying masterpieces is to make me admire and do otherwise' (294).

PROBE 8 (which might well be subtitled: Probing Metcalf's Private Part): Yes, John, I know, influence is *not* the same as tradition. But when enough writers inter-relate and stimulate and influence each other, a tradition eventually develops. I am merely trying to establish the following point: that alongside the influence of the major writers of one's experience (who are always primary, and should never be confined to one's own country, or even one's own language) there needs to be a secondary influence-cum-tradition from one's own personal experience and place. This may be made up of actual friends and acquaintances, with whom one can discuss, argue, amplify, clarify – not just the distant examples of the indispensable great (who can sometimes be as much a burden as an inspiration). I know what you mean when you maintain in the Cameron interview that national characteristics show up in content only (413), but I think the issue is more important than that because, as I hope to have shown, *the content inevitably affects the art, and vice versa.* I agree wholeheartedly when you insist: 'I don't think that one learns emotional positions from other writers, because if you're learning emotional positions, you're merely parroting somebody else's sensibilities' (414) – a comment remarkably close to Leavis in *The Living Principle* when he wrote (critics rather than writers being in question): 'My critical judgement is mine, in the sense that I can't take over anyone else's (if I did, it would cease to be a judgement)' (46). Or, to quote Hugh Hood from 'The End of

Emma', 'Nobody can take a bath for you' (152). However, John, I would like to add to your statement that your own positions, emotional and otherwise, will be profoundly affected by your experience (including your national experience) as well as, certainly, by your international reading.

I can't therefore go along with you totally in your 'deconstruction' of the idea of a Canadian tradition. I think the need for such a localized tradition is precisely what distinguishes the native Canadian writer of the present time from an immigrant like yourself. One thing which you never experienced (and which Canadian writers are continually referring to) is the frustrating sense, in youth, that literature was something produced somewhere else by dead people. In an Old World culture, this response never arises, and is difficult to imagine. Let me give one instance. In *What Is A Canadian Literature?* you quote Margaret Laurence with approval when she says: 'I think the thing that matters least about a novel is whether it's Canadian or American or English or African' (40). Fair enough, but you don't quote a balancing and equally important remark in which she describes encountering Sinclair Ross's *As For Me and My House* soon after it was published, at a crucial period in her early development:

> When I first read his extraordinary and moving novel, *As For Me and My House,* at about the age of eighteen, it had an enormous impact on me, for it seemed the only completely genuine one I had ever read about my own people, my own place, my own time. (Introduction 7)

Canadian literature – and I still think it exists! – took a long time to develop *because* that essential example (*this* can be done *here*) was too often not forthcoming. You talk about the relative inaccessibility of early writings which Canadian critics claim to be influential. But Laurence *did* come upon *As For Me and My House* on the wartime Prairies, and Raymond Knister *did* read and (rightly or wrongly) was impressed by Duncan Campbell Scott's

In the Village of Viger, however scarce a book it may have been. (This, I should explain, is a test-case Metcalf discusses in considerable detail in *What Is A Canadian Literature?*.)

What I have been trying to do in these probes is to pay you a compliment (left- or back-handed? not really, but in any case heartfelt and genuine) of applying the principle with which I started: the good critic often provokes you into disagreeing. By the same token, such a critic causes one to modify some of one's own assumptions, and you've certainly caused me to re-think some of mine. One obligation remains, so far as I am concerned. I must vindicate my title by demonstrating that the last part of it wasn't just a piece of dubious self-indulgence. 'Criticism in practice': that I have, I think, shown as applicable. Whatever you write critically arises out of the basic situation of writing or reading books, of tracing the possibilities and effects of words as they undergo their curious, often perilous journey from writer to reader. No abstract ivory-tower theorizing for you, and I bless you for it. But 'John Metcalf's Private Part' seems apt because only someone who possessed the necessary strength of character to maintain a private, individual, single-minded course amid the bizarre funhouse or even loony-bin of Canadian criticism could produce the much-needed (but not sufficiently appreciated) challenge you have offered over the years. You will not be widely thanked any more than Leavis was, but many of us believe it to be essential that, following the example of *Kicking Against the Pricks* and *What Is A Canadian Literature?*, you carry on bumping wherever you get a chance, and persist in what Leavis in his later years called 'necessary opportunism'. A private part indeed. As Robert Lecker noted some time ago: 'The private parts of [your] title are sexual, spiritual, emotional, temporal, spatial, and structural all at once' (*On the Line* 90). To which I would merely add that for you to be rigorously literary-critical at this time and place is to play an all-important private part.

There is much more that I would like to add. I wanted to pay tribute to the way in which you *embody* your critical principles within your critical writings – specifically illustrating, for example, how 'punctuation' becomes 'score'. I wanted to praise you for your courage and honesty in naming names in your campaign against literary-critical inadequacy, in asserting that many of the self-appointed emperors of CanCrit have no clothes. But all this yakketing, like Browning's kissing and Aldous Huxley's Time, must have a stop. All that remains, on *my* private part which will immediately become public, is a personal message. So here's to you, you fifty-year-old frowning private man, 'resident alien' (there's Canadian tradition for you), 'resident curmudgeon' (in Sam Solecki's phrase), immigrant gadfly, and, above all, writer extraordinary. Many happy returns – or 'many 'appies', as they used to say in my Cockney past – and long may you prosper.

PART TWO

Fiction

The Art of Frederick Philip Grove: *Settlers of the Marsh* as an Example

Douglas O. Spettigue's sensational discoveries in the early 1970s about Frederick Philip Grove's early life in Germany as Felix Paul Greve sparked new interest in a writer whom many forward-looking commentators would as soon have written off as dull and outmoded. But this interest was primarily biographical. My own interest in Grove involved a pressing literary problem: according to all the principles of literary criticism, Grove *ought* to have been a poor novelist, but I was unable to dismiss him so easily. Despite obvious faults, his work seemed to me to have a solidity, a stature, an importance that could not be gainsaid. Above all, I was convinced that he possessed artistry – an artistry, however, that was not manifest in his indifferent prose style. I therefore explored aspects of Grove's art in a series of articles on individual novels. I have chosen my critique of *Settlers of the Marsh* for inclusion here because it addresses most directly the issues in Grove that seem most pertinent to the other literary-critical matters dealt with in this book. It originally appeared in the *Journal of Canadian Studies* in 1974, and is thus the earliest of my critical writings to be reprinted here. I would qualify a few of my more enthusiastic judgements now, but in the main I am prepared to stand by what I have written.

EVER SINCE ITS FIRST PUBLICATION in 1925, *Settlers of the Marsh* has attracted varied and often contradictory critical responses. It has been hailed as an example of Prairie realism and distinguished from Grove's other Prairie novels; it has been condemned for alleged obscenity and praised for its frankness and integrity; it has been commended for its dour starkness and criticized for its 'happy ending'. Unfortunately, it has rarely been the subject of any rigorous literary criticism. Commentators have recorded their reactions and stated their positions but have generally neglected to demonstrate its artistic qualities. There has been little attempt to probe beneath the surface of the narrative, no exacting scrutiny of the novel's texture. The same might be said, indeed, of all Grove's work. There exists, I suspect, an uneasy feeling that his fiction would not respond satisfactorily to such treatment. But the time has surely come when this kind of experiment needs to be made. Grove's reputation will not, I think, suffer in consequence; on the contrary, it should be strengthened. I have chosen *Settlers of the Marsh* for examination because I believe that here Grove employs his artistic virtuosity, not indeed with complete success, but with a deliberation and a sense of conscious purpose that we do not encounter again in his work until *The Master of the Mill* (1944). However, the uncharacteristic subject matter of the later novel renders it a unique case. It is in the story of Niels Lindstedt that Grove's habitual artistry can be most readily isolated, examined, and discussed.

The inevitable classification of *Settlers of the Marsh* as a Prairie novel has been the cause of some natural, but no less unfortunate, limiting of critical judgements. The realistic presentation of pioneering life in the Canadian midwest is obviously an important ingredient in the total effect, but it would be a mistake to assume that the novel is confined to this level of interest. If we ask ourselves what the novel is about, we soon realize that it is not confined to a single topic. Though a number of other subjects could doubtless be added, the following list may be useful in isolating what seem to me the most significant themes: the relation between an individual and his environment (the creation of 'roots', etc.); the natural versus the artificial; town versus country; the distinction between innocence and *naïveté*; an exploration of the nature of duty; the human response to what Grove describes – not altogether happily – in a chapter title of *Our Daily Bread* as 'the leaven of sex' (38). If this breakdown of themes is accepted, two conclusions surely follow: first, that the novel concerns itself with issues that transcend the boundaries of purely regional fiction; second, that the attempt to combine these themes into a single work – an attempt which I hope to show is impressive but not entirely successful – can only be accomplished by means of a conscious and very controlled artistry.

Again, a literary approach to *Settlers of the Marsh* can easily be inhibited by unjustified assumptions concerning the nature of the chronicle form. The temporal and realistically descriptive aspects of the book are thus emphasized to the neglect of less obvious but ultimately, I believe, more crucial artistic effects. Commentators have tended to concentrate on general discussions of the main characters – at what, I am bound to say, seems to me a superficial level – and to touch on other matters, such as dialogue, style, credibility (e.g., is Clara Vogel a likely character to be found in a pioneering community?), presentation of the natural environment, etc., as if these were isolatable elements and not inter-connecting parts of a complex literary design. I hope in the following pages to explore this design, to emphasize the creative contribution of Grove not merely as observer and describer but as novelist, and to argue that the resultant effect involves a depth and subtlety which may have been sensed by individual readers but has never been critically analysed and demonstrated.

Before proceeding, however, it is necessary to anticipate two possible objections. The first concerns the well-known claim that *Settlers of the Marsh* is no more than a 'garbled extract' from a much more ambitious three-volume chronicle (see Grove's own statement in *In Search of Myself* 352). The numerous ellipses in the novel, which at first reading give it a decidedly fragmented quality, are generally cited to bear out this claim, and it might well be argued that my approach is therefore unfair or inappropriate. In countering this position, I would insist that Grove published his novel as a complete and separate work of art, that this is what we have and what must concern us. In any case, as Thomas Saunders has observed in his introduction to the New Canadian Library edition, these abrupt, ellipsis-ridden paragraphs are often curiously effective in conveying an impression of seasonal change (Grove is essentially a novelist of slow processes and gradual deteriorations), and there is no *necessary* correlation between them and the alleged mutilation of a larger manuscript.

They exist, at worst, as typographical irritants, and need in no way interfere with critical analysis.

The second hypothetical objection is more crucial. Since I have promised a predominantly literary approach to the novel within the tradition of 'practical criticism', a close verbal analysis of specific passages may be expected and my failure to provide this might be challenged. But the fact is (and the admission certainly bears witness to a limitation in his art) that Grove's 'style' is not remarkable for sensitivity or even consistency. Indeed, while reading Grove one is all too easily reminded of the character in Somerset Maugham's novel *Cakes and Ale,* said to be based on Hardy, who always gave the impression of writing with the blunt stub of a pencil. Desmond Pacey has adequately characterized the general qualities of Grove's prose style in his *Frederick Philip Grove* (1945), and I need not repeat the points here (110-11). The strength of Grove's art lies rather in the stolid appropriateness of certain elementary but highly effective technical devices and the mature judgement with which he presents the complex pressures working upon his protagonists. It is upon these aspects of his artistry that I wish to focus.

Settlers of the Marsh opens with two Swedish immigrants, Lars Nelson and Niels Lindstedt, on their way to the bush settlement which, we soon learn, is to provide the all-important setting for the novel. At this point, we do not know which of the two is to become the centre of interest, but the consonantal similarity in their names suggests that some kind of comparison or contrast will ultimately be made between them. In fact, of course, Grove has planned his opening with particular care.[1] His 'hero' (the term will be qualified as the novel proceeds) is the newcomer

---

1 'The First Day of an Immigrant', included in *Tales from the Margin,* is presumably a discarded first chapter of *Settlers of the Marsh.* Though effective as a short story, it is clearly inferior to the present opening, and Grove did well to relegate it to its present status.

Niels, and the function of Lars Nelson, who has 'three years' standing in the country' (15), is to introduce both Niels and the reader to the countryside of the Big Marsh. Through him we become conscious of the tough but invigorating conditions and are made aware of the constant tension between human existence and natural forces – readers of Grove's earlier work will immediately recognize not merely the geographical locale but also the meteorological conditions of *Over Prairie Trails*. We may also note, as a contributing detail, the unformed nature of the landscape into which the two men are moving; this is made evident in the contrast between the specific names they leave behind (Balfour, Minor) and the generalized, not-yet-differentiated names of the physical features through which they pass (the Big Marsh, the Muddy River, Grassy Creek). The first notable incident, their accidental arrival at Sigurdsen's homestead, may at first reading seem merely a piece of 'local colour', but in the overall effect of the novel it will be seen to foreshadow some of the narrative's most significant features. Not only does the old man's misanthropic, hermit-like existence offer a symbolic example of the essential loneliness of the individual – a loneliness that Niels will experience through the greater part of the novel – but the initial image we have of him ('a shotgun in his hands, with one finger on the trigger' (17)) admirably anticipates Niels's act of violence that forms the climax of his story.

The rest of the opening chapter lays foundations upon which the novel is to be built. Niels is identified as the chief protagonist and his position is acutely analysed. While Grove is at pains to stress his basic isolation ('it was his nature to be alone, even in a crowd' (31)); 'He looked on. He was not concerned'(32)), Niels is gradually drawn into the life of the community. He meets the two women who are to dominate his life, Ellen Amundsen and Clara Vogel, and a similar dichotomy is established through his visits to the homesteads of the Amundsens and the Lunds ('Amundsen's house represented a future; this one, the past. Amundsen's, growth; this one, decay' (31)). The two major aims of clearing the land and founding a family unite in

Niels's consciousness. By the end of the chapter, 'it somehow was clear to him that this was his future home' (43). The point is made, simply but subtly, through landscape: 'the pretty junipers of Sweden had been replaced in his affections by the more virile and fertile growth of the Canadian north' (55). The chapter closes with Niels's vision of rootedness (clumsily presented, as I shall show later) which inevitably centres upon his conflicting responses to the two women.

This conflict is, of course, crucial not merely to the plot but to any critical response to the novel. The choice between two radically different types of women is a time-honoured convention in the novel form. Obvious examples include Sue Bridehead and Arabella Donn in Hardy's *Jude the Obscure* and Miriam Leivers and Clara Dawes in Lawrence's *Sons and Lovers.* The point I want to make here is not that we should compare Grove's treatment with these, but that we should recognize his success or failure as dependent less upon his choice of subject than upon his treatment of it. If we are more likely to stress the adverse connotations of the word 'conventional' in Grove's case, this is because he has failed to assimilate the convention fully to his artistic purpose.

For Grove, the choice between Clara and Ellen is not primarily the choice between lust and love (as Niels would probably describe it), nor between ephemeral sensual satisfaction and continuing domestic fulfilment; it is, rather, the choice between town and country. The realism of the presentation is here tempered with symbolic purpose, and the result can often strain our credulity. Clara Vogel is continually associated with the city and, moreover, with the artful and the artificial. On two occasions Niels meets her in circumstances indicated in both cases by the word 'chance' (86, 119), but the locations are by no means accidental so far as the controlling novelist is concerned. The first takes place at a railroad station, the second outside a shopwindow display of 'soaps, face-powders, and similar toilet goods' (120). Both settings are symbolically appropriate to Clara and her way of life. She represents urban restlessness as opposed to rural stability, the artificiality of the man-made city against the naturalness of God's earth.

Throughout the novel, Clara is seen within a context of powder and paint, silk, scents, dyed hair, mirrors, electric lights, and the vagaries of fashion. This raw dichotomy is discernible in almost all Grove's novels, and he may legitimately be criticized for overdoing what is in any case an excessively simple distinction. We may grant that he does his best to develop this imagery, using Clara's 'make-up' to explore the difference between inner and outer, between surface and reality, but the references tend to become a somewhat perfunctory kind of symbolic shorthand that all too often fails to convey the significance that Grove expects us to derive from it. Thus, when Niels brings Clara home to the house he has built with such loving care, and she proceeds to fill it with her city gewgaws, Grove is clearly intending to superimpose on the realistic narrative an allegorical meaning suggestive of the corruption of rural principles by degenerate town values. He may even be asking us to see in Clara's seduction of Niels the urban rape of rural innocence. On consideration, we may indeed be prepared to grant that Grove has a legitimate if simplistic argument, yet the fact remains that he fails to unite the realistic and the symbolic values within his novelistic texture. But the main point for my immediate purpose is that this represents a failure of art rather than an absence of it. Grove is trying to do too much, and as a result his art becomes over-insistent.

The contrasting image to Clara is that of Ellen who, though dressed in the sexless overalls of the farmyard and working close to the soil, at the same time retains (almost in spite of herself) a natural femininity. Niels's frustrated attempt to marry Ellen, to choose the right woman for the central place in his 'vision', leads to two intimate and dramatic scenes which require close attention since they represent important examples of the success or failure of Grove's art.

Why is the first of these scenes, in which Niels and Ellen walk into the storm, so effective? This would seem the obvious question to ask, though I find that at least one commentator, Isabel Skelton, has described it (along with other scenes between the two characters) with the adjectives 'unconvincing' and 'wooden' (35). To me it seems an obvious triumph. It is clearly a crucial test for those interested in Grove's artistic method, yet the secret does not lie in an elegant and euphonious choice of words. Indeed, the style trembles continually on the verge of cliché ('More than ever before she was the only woman in the world for him' (94); 'The moment was coming. It had prepared itself. It was rushing along the lane of time where neither he nor she could escape it' (95)). Grove's effects are technical rather than verbal. The most obvious of these is his use of the storm not merely as background material (though it is magnificently *there*, another example of Grove's vivid meteorological descriptions) but as an external correlative of their internal state. 'I believe a storm is coming', says Ellen (95), and we are aware as she says it of the convergence of outer and inner landscapes. Yet (and this is typical of Grove's unostentatious subtlety) the point is no sooner made than it has to be qualified. As the sultriness of the atmosphere grows more and more oppressive, the tension between the two human beings decreases. The violence of the approaching storm unites them while at the same time reflecting the ominous condition of their relationship. The effect is one of counterpoint rather than comparison.

As the scene develops, Niels and Ellen revert from the tensions of adult self-consciousness to the simple, impersonal, sexless pleasures of childhood. 'Man and woman' become, literally and deliberately, 'boy and girl' (94). This begins as an almost desperate, willed process with suggestions of a vaguely morbid escapism, but their accidental arrival at the deserted schoolhouse releases them into an innocent and uncomplicated past ('they laughed at the sight of benches and blackboards, thoughtlessly, happily, as children laugh' (96)), and it is noteworthy that at this stage the prose itself takes on a simple felicity. 'As if in play' (96), they hide from the pair in the democrat, who represent, on an uninsistent symbolic level, the questioning and suspicious adult world of oppressive responsibility and mistrust. At the same time, a suggestion of Puritan guilt is thrown over the innocent and youthful lovers; they realize, as we realize, that the world of adult decision cannot be evaded. As they try to postpone the inevitable moment by fleeing deeper into the bush, Grove employs a new effect:

> Again the girl stopped, breathless, flushed, but laughing. 'Oh Niels!' she sang out, exuberantly, exultantly.
>
> In an instant he was by her side, reaching out for her hand. 'Ellen!' His voice is hoarse, intensely serious of a sudden.
>
> 'No,' she begs. 'Not now. Let's be happy!' (97)

The switch from past to present tense is one of the most elementary tricks of style, obvious to the point of being hackneyed, yet it succeeds here, like so many of Grove's effects, because its very obviousness is appropriate to the occasion. Ellen and Niels *must* return to the present and face up to the future; how could the point be made more economically? To take a final example, during the storm they seek refuge in the sheltering cave Niels has scooped out of the haystack 'in which all the fragrance of the meadow is concentrated' (99); Grove surely expects us to remember this detail when he comes to describe the languorous and artificial scents with which Clara defiles Niels's home. These are just a selection from a number of varied artistic effects with which Grove augments the literal force of his narrative.

Lest it should be thought that I am exaggerating Grove's artistry, I now pass to the second climactic scene between Niels and Ellen which, though it has been praised by some reputable critics, seems to me an example of artistic failure. This is the scene in which Ellen explains the reasons for her abjuration of marriage. It consists for the most part of dialogue, and its inadequacy becomes evident when we realize – as surely we must – that stylistically it differs little from the rest of the book. Grove can manage the semi-articulate everyday conversation of Prairie farmers, but their more serious and elaborate speeches fail to ring true. Niels states his case with an impressively smooth eloquence that we find difficult to accept in the mouth of an immigrant who, a few years previously, could barely speak a word of English. Ellen's words are often stiff and stilted, and although this is appropriate enough to be generally acceptable, we are sometimes tempted to wonder whether the awkwardness does not lie in her creator. When she insists to Niels that a number of girls in the settlement 'will gladly be your handmaiden' (104), the phrase seems ludicrously inadequate in context. Nor does the scene improve with Ellen's long speech of explanation. Her very introduction ('It's a long story; and I don't know whether I can tell it' (105)) is a danger signal, and there are times when Grove appears to abandon any illusion of realistic speech ('A number of things were said back and forth which I remember with great distinctness but which have nothing to do with my story' (108)). The scene is tremendously bold in design. Grove never flinched from the ambitious, and neither his nor Ellen's sincerity is ever in question. His motives may be praised as admirable, and the full revelation of Amundsen's callous treatment of his wife is a model of authorial clearsightedness and integrity. But it is an integrity independent of artistic value, and as literary critics we cannot afford to recognize intention at the expense of achievement. What effectiveness the scene possesses comes through in spite of, rather than because of, the way it is presented. If we apply the standards by which Grove at his best deserves to be judged, we are forced to record that, in this instance, his artistry has failed him.

These two scenes with Ellen in the third chapter are in many respects the most memorable in the novel. With Niels's marriage to Clara, a decided falling-off in credibility and interest occurs, and one suspects that Grove is attempting to explore realms of experience to which he is a stranger. By means of a series of skilled technical manoeuvres, he endeavours to maintain interest, but it is difficult not to detect – in the texture of the narrative as well as in the quality of the prose – a decline in artistic control which ultimately implies a decline in basic seriousness. For page after page, from Niels's clumsily unconvincing seduction onwards, he undergoes a suffering that has no vent in action, and when he is at last driven to act, the result bears an uncomfortable resemblance to conventional melodrama. This is not to deny the effectiveness of many incidental scenes. The opening pages of Chapter 4 in which Nelson and Hahn drive their steers into Niels's cow-lot obviously carry a symbolic suggestiveness which is all the more impressive for being both unstated and unemphatic. The point is recalled in the succeeding chapter when, in a scene that neatly links the two strands in Niels's life – his work on the land and his marital disaster – he savagely chastises his horse Nellie in a burst of anger caused by the behaviour of his wife. The image-association is ultimately fixed, of course, when Niels follows up the murder of Clara by shooting one of his horses, a gelding, through the head. Commentary and elaboration could only vulgarize and debase what Grove achieves. It would be easy, only too easy, to invoke the assistance of popular psychology, and describe Niels as regaining his virile integrity by a violently masculine act; but Grove has avoided the deadening mechanism of theoretical abstraction. His scenes communicate, as those of an accomplished novelist should, by a process of imaginative insight that is beyond the reach of case-book generality.

In other ways, too, Grove demonstrates his technical proficiency. Up to the scene of the shooting, he has limited the narrative viewpoint to coincide with that of his hero. Niels is 'on stage' throughout the novel, and almost the whole of the action is seen through his eyes. This in itself may not be remarkable, though the way Grove controls the narrative so that the reader, while limited to Niels's viewpoint, is invariably ahead of Niels in understanding is a very impressive achievement for which Grove has received insufficient recognition. However, he carries his technique a step further when Niels's central position as focus of consciousness is withdrawn from him just before the climax. The sudden shift to Bobby Lund's puzzlement and concern increases suspense and prepares us for the catastrophe, while the following section devoted to Niels runs parallel in time and accounts for his absence. A subsequent section in which Niels sleeps and Bobby can only speculate on what has happened adds to both the tension and the pathos of the situation. Once again, Grove has made this effect by means of a few simple, unemphatic technical devices.

UNFORTUNATELY, TECHNIQUE is not enough. It is amazing that Grove could ever have been assumed to lack art. Here one can see him assembling all his considerable resources to carry his scheme through, but his skilled craftsmanship cannot disguise the fact that he has failed to penetrate to the core of his characters. Clara Vogel never comes alive; Grove presents her with intelligence but without ultimate understanding. In her long speech in which she throws Niels's reproaches back upon him (153-57), we can see what is being attempted. The speech is obviously supposed to balance Ellen's disclosure (both are open to the charge of being 'set speeches'), and it demands an acute and mature response. The 'sophisticated' reader will be in danger of falling completely for Clara's eloquent but highly selective and specious argument; the naïve reader will miss even the minimal vitality that can be allowed to her position. All this is to Grove's credit; but he cannot persuade us of Clara's imaginative reality. She is too stereotyped, too much a 'symbol'. She can be said to 'represent' town values while we could never say in the same sense that Niels 'represented' the pioneer life. It ought to be irrelevant to question the likelihood of Clara's presence in the bush settlement, but Grove makes such a query inevitable. The point is, perhaps, that Clara would fail to convince in *any* context, since her creator has formed her out of a stereotype, not moulded her from life.

By contrast, Niels Lindstedt is credible as a character, even when his innocence appears extreme. Grove succeeds in presenting him sympathetically while at the same time offering him as both immature and incomplete. He can convey with remarkable subtlety Niels's inarticulate yearnings on the very threshold of a profound insight that he can never quite attain. Technically, his character develops in distinct and deliberate contrast to that of Lars Nelson, who becomes coarser and more self-centred as he increases in material success. It is only when Grove offers Niels as a particular kind of Puritan that he encounters difficulty, and this is because we become conscious of an insufficient distinction between the novelist and his invention. When Grove writes in *In Search of Myself* of Niels 'fighting the devils in his blood' (262), it is evident that the author shares many of Niels's attitudes. In the text of *Settlers of the Marsh*, when the attractions of Ellen and Clara are referred to as 'both temptations' (57), or sexual intercourse is described as 'the forbidden fruit' (140), it is impossible to decide with certainty whether the phrasing is Grove's own or whether he is merely reporting the sentiments of his protagonist. As the novel proceeds, however, we come to suspect that Grove is unable to view Niels with the detachment seemingly essential for this part of his story. At times, indeed, their attitudes seem virtually identical. When we find ourselves contemplating the possibility that Niels's failure to understand his wife is matched by a similar puzzlement on Grove's part, we have come close to questioning the writer's control over his material. Such questions recur in the fourth and fifth chapters and they point to a serious rift within the texture of the novel.

In the final chapter, however, Grove is able to return to the subject matter that brings out his strengths rather than his weaknesses. Curiously enough, the ending has frequently been criticized, chiefly because it is believed to contradict Grove's published theories about the novel as an art form. Desmond Pacey is the most distinguished and influential critic who has taken this view. 'The logical conclusion of the tragic train of events', he writes, 'is Niels's murder of his faithless wife; our interest flags as we read of the trial and its aftermath' (*Frederick Philip Grove* (1945) 46). I can only record my own diametrically opposed reaction. While I find that the novel sags dangerously in the scenes involving Niels and Clara, it recovers as soon as the melodramatic action of the murder has taken place. The trial and imprisonment are presented with an admirable economy (Niels is convicted, serves six and a half years of his sentence, is released and on his way home within four pages that read briskly without giving the impression of excessive hurry), and the account of Niels's return – a return all the more poignant since it is to a home he has created with his own labour – is surely one of the most moving, consummately achieved scenes in Canadian literature. Grove writes with confidence and a rare sureness of touch; he is never more at ease than when writing about 'the small, trivial things of life' (213), which after his description can no longer be considered trivial. The changes in the landscape are recorded simply and clearly as Niels would notice them. The prose admirably blends a crisp narrative account with personal rhythms and halting observations that suggest Niels's own 'stream of consciousness':

> Niels felt intimidated. This prosperity which had invaded the Marsh was unexpected; the old pioneers had receded to the margin of civilisation; a new generation had taken hold. The change was not entirely welcome: he was of the old generation which had been evicted. On almost every farmstead he saw a garage: cars had always been his pet aversion....
>
> This was no longer the bush land he had loved.... (196; ellipses in original)

Unexceptional as this may seem at first reading, it is in fact a skilled combination of the detached and the personal – both an accurate presentation of a historical process and a sympathetic rendering of a human response. Sentiment there may be, but again a distinction needs to be made between the genuinely sentimental (the honest reproduction of true feeling) and the false variety (the undisciplined wallowing in private emotion). Niels's homecoming is in no facile sense 'happy' (to complain about a 'happy ending' to the novel is to employ an inadequate critical vocabulary). The little detail of Nellie the horse scampering away from the intruder who may either be mistaken as an alien or vaguely remembered as one guilty of ill-treatment (197) brilliantly suggests the tensions that Niels will encounter on the more complex human level. Mrs Lund's embarrassed phrasing ('Mr Schultz was frozen to death the year after ... well, you know' (203)), the honest and touching poverty of Bobby and his family, Niels's reluctance even to mention Ellen's name – all these convey naturally and movingly the painful process of readjustment. The question of Clara's stored furniture is a concrete reminder of the undiscussed past, and Niels's method of dealing with the problem holds out hope for the future:

> Next day he went out into the bush and searched till he found the shanty, well hidden in willows, and piling some brush against the wall, he set fire to it without ever looking inside.... (208)

Who but Grove, one wonders, could have made the point in precisely this way? In acting firmly, Niels is not trying to eradicate the past but is demonstrating that he has learned from it. He must make a new life out of the wreckage of a soiled past, just as previously he had created a home out of the wilderness. Grove allows the human action to speak for itself; Niels is seen accepting his duty as both a pain and a stimulus.

The final reconciliation between Niels and Ellen (final, it should be noted, only in reference to the frame of the novel) is adroitly managed, and may be claimed as a conspicuous success in an area that we might expect to be outside Grove's range. It is a scene that draws together not only the two protagonists but a number of the novel's most important strands of meaning. The deliberate repetition, with significant variants, of elements in the earlier relationship is effective without ever suggesting that too neat a connection is being made. Ellen has been absent from the novel for many pages – and, indeed, for many years – and it is with something of a shock that the reader sees, with Niels, 'a middle-aged woman, knitting, with shell-rimmed glasses on her eyes' (211). Moreover, at their first encounter seventeen years earlier, hers had been 'the face of a woman; not of a girl' (21); now, in a bold transposition, it is 'the face of a girl, not a woman' (211). This scene, then, is to be no mere repetition of the past. Although we may legitimately see the scene as a re-enactment, the common motif is, as it were, repeated in a different key that allows a different resolution. In their walk, they follow the same paths as in their earlier scene of decision, but the season is different ('it is spring, not autumn' (216)) and the storm emblematic of passion has been replaced by a calm that is conducive to mature love. A lesser novelist would have set his finale in an appropriate autumn, but Grove suggests the interchange of season without becoming a slave to its conventions. Nor does the scene attempt to guarantee any sentimentally positive resolution. The concentration is rather on time lost and the uncertainties of the future. 'The years go by,' says Ellen; 'we both are passing through life. There is nothing that will remain when we are gone ...' (217). When Niels faces up to the real problem and asks if they can live down what lies between, she replies: 'I believe we can. And whether we can or not, we must try ...' (217). The effect is muted, and the only excuse for confidence lies in the responsible awareness with which the attempt is made. In recognizing a duty (in this case, to each other), Ellen offers a connection with the other main theme in their lives, their duty towards the land. In closing his story at the end of a phase without committing himself or his readers to the particular fortunes of his protagonists in their life together, Grove has created what we would now call an 'open-ended' novel, but has subtly indicated a tying-up of strands that we associate with more traditional narrative.[2]

---

2 In his *Frederick Philip Grove,* Douglas O. Spettigue considers manuscript evidence demonstrating that Grove considered a sequel to the book in which the marriage seemed unlikely to prove a success (73). Interesting as this is, it represents material outside the completed novel and thus cannot be given undue weight. The tone of the conclusion, I

Settlers of the Marsh is a very remarkable achievement and, in the climactic scenes with Ellen, Grove explores depths of human experience with an insight that he was never to surpass. It is important that this be recognized and his accomplishment in the art of the novel accepted; at the same time, we need to grant that it is a flawed achievement, that Grove has not *quite* succeeded in communicating the full force of what he tried to present. The point can be made most economically by observing that, with the possible exception of *The Yoke of Life*, Grove is never closer to the lapse into cliché than in parts of this novel. Often, as I have already indicated, this occurs at the verbal level. When describing Niels's response to Clara Vogel's advances, Grove can do no better than tell us that 'a wave of hot blood ran through him' (116). This is the language of the popular magazines of the period, and recurs oddly in a novel that is in other respects remarkable for the maturity of its attitudes. Sometimes, too, we detect what can only be called the falsely sentimental. Here, for example, is the first description of Niels's recurrent 'vision':

> Suddenly, as they were entering the bush, where the moonlight filtered down through the meshes of leafless boughs overhead, a vision took hold of Niels: of himself and a woman sitting of a mid-winter night by the light of a lamp and in front of a fire, with the pitter-patter of children's feet sounding down from above: the eternal vision that has moved the world and that was to direct his fate. (36)

There can be little doubt, surely, that this passage strikes a false note, and that the falsity lies primarily in the slackness of the diction. Most of the images – the filtering moonlight, the leafless boughs, the lamp, the pitter-patter of feet – are merely counters soliciting a response that, because it is not upheld by any delicacy of wording that could suggest a similar delicacy in the situation,

maintain, suggests neither an unqualified 'happy ending' nor intimations of failure.

the discriminating reader has a right to reject.

This last instance is a crucial one, however, since it raises the possibility that the element of cliché resides not merely in the words but in the conception. There is a sense in which Niels's polarizing of his attraction to Ellen and Clara is itself an oversimplification for which Grove is as much to blame as Niels. At one point, for example, Grove writes, following Niels's thoughts: 'One of these women had seemed to demand; the other to give. Yet one was competent; the other, helpless. One was a mate; the other, a toy' (57). Here the fault is not in the words but in the simplistic dichotomies they represent – dichotomies which I hope to have shown are integral to the structure of the novel. There is no reason why distinguished fiction cannot be created out of this basically simple pattern, but this is only possible when the novelist is capable of enriching the material and not merely reporting it. In neglecting to 'place' either Niels's vision of domesticity or his classification of womanhood, Grove fails to reveal the more profound implications of his theme. A rawness of presentation is discernible in long stretches of the book, and the puzzling contrast with juxtaposed scenes of achieved excellence interferes with the reader's attempt to appreciate the novel as an artistic unity.

Few, I suppose, would be moved to challenge the impression that the least successful parts of the book are those that deal with love-relationships. When Grove concerns himself with the relationship between man and the land, the novel flows smoothly and convincingly; but, whatever else it may be, *Settlers of the Marsh* is clearly not 'a profound artistic treatment of sexual love', which was how one of the original reviewers. V.B. Rhodenizer, described it (116). Since Grove claimed to 'abominate the common love-story' and maintained that 'in life, both young men and young maids are peculiarly uninteresting when they see each other as they are not' (*It Needs* 124), it is curious that he made the subject play so important a part in the action of this book. It is, in fact, the only Grove novel in which a love-situation may be said to occupy the forefront of the narrative. Even in *The Yoke of Life*, the emphasis is rather on Len Sterner's temperament than on his human relations. His love for Lydia is a part of his story, and important because it inhibits the achievement of his other aims, but he does not possess Niels's vision of domesticity. Despite his general scorn for contemporary taste, one cannot help wondering if in this early work (and whatever the ultimate result of investigations into Grove's chronology, it is difficult to believe that *Settlers of the Marsh,* at least in conception, is anything but early work) Grove did not create a story of love-relationships because he believed that the novel form demanded it. He may also have felt that the comprehensive nature of his aims in fiction necessitated treatment of the subject. At all events, it is not easy to escape the conclusion that the overall effect of the novel is dissipated because of the imperfect fusion between the pioneer-theme and the love-theme.

The chief criticism that can be brought against the novel would seem to be its lack of unity. I began by listing six major themes explored in the book, and this in itself would suggest that the difficulty of keeping all these themes in control might be considerable. Again, in drawing attention to Grove's wealth of artistic effect, I have been conscious of Grove's tendency to display one aspect of his craft and then, in the enthusiastic awareness of undemonstrated powers, to follow up with another. While each of the effects I have described is successful in itself, the overall result can be disjointed. Had Grove been less lavish in both his ideas and his methods of revealing them, he might have produced a more balanced, though perhaps less compelling, novel. It would be improper, however, to end on a negative note. *Settlers of the Marsh* is memorable as the first manifestation of Grove's challenging powers as a novelist in English; here the qualities that were to dominate the rest of his fiction – his remarkable structural imagination, his critical intelligence, and his admirable steadiness of purpose – are all present. There are few writers in any country's literature of whom it can be said that their art demands the fullest critical attention on the part of their readers at all times. Grove, I believe, is one of this select few.

Overview: Ethel Wilson, Providence, and the Vocabulary of Vision

This paper was delivered at the University of Ottawa Ethel Wilson Symposium in 1981 and published in the proceedings, edited by Lorraine McMullen, the following year. It gave me an opportunity to extend the remarks I had already made about Wilson in 'The Thematic Approach to Canadian Fiction' and present a literary-critical case for a writer whose achievement has still to be fully acknowledged.

'OVERVIEW'. This is one of several ambivalences in my title. I hope in the next few minutes to present, among other things, a general survey – a bird's-eye view, perhaps – of Ethel Wilson's major work; but I also want to lay emphasis on her own customary viewpoint – a particular kind of authorial omniscience that has been described by W.H. New (in a phrase I hadn't encountered when I chose my title) as 'Mrs Wilson's overviewing eye' ('"Genius"' 42) and earlier by Desmond Pacey as 'the vision of the innocent eye' ('Innocent' 43). 'Vision' is also in my title, and is meant to refer not only to the plain act of seeing, but to that more exalted sense of irradiated understanding. And I have included the word 'Providence' because I see Ethel Wilson's authorial stance as presupposing and in some respects even embodying the sense of a divine purpose. I shall attempt, then, to move to and fro between a specifically literary-critical approach and one more concerned with philosophical and religious attitudes. Perhaps I shall fall between the two stools; but it is important, I think, to try to show the significant relation between Ethel Wilson's artistic techniques and what might be called, inadequately, her 'philosophy of life'.

This relation has not, in my opinion, been sufficiently stressed, and the reason for this may well be that Wilson's first novel, *Hetty Dorval,* apparently goes against my thesis by employing a first-person narrator. I consider that Wilson is extraordinarily successful at handling this essentially Jamesian technique (the communication of Hetty's 'experience' through Frankie Burnaby's naïve 'innocence' is surely comparable with James's method in *What Maisie Knew*), yet at the same time I cannot help feeling that this is *not* Wilson's natural mode. I also suspect that she came to realize this and so never repeated the experiment in a full-length novel. She needs the freedom to expand and generalize that only omniscient narration can provide. Some commentators have criticized the descriptions in this novel (though excellent in themselves) as extraneous and unintegrated, and the reason for this is surely that they represent the characteristic awareness of Wilson herself (as we learn from her later work) rather than the interests of her young narrator. Others have complained that Frankie's narration betrays, in the words of R.D. MacDonald, 'a "wisdom" which is not won or not genuine even as she speaks retrospectively' (42). Given the high quality of the achievement – there have surely been few better 'first novels' – such criticisms may seem over-harsh, but once again they suggest that Wilson herself has not yet found the most suitable viewpoint from which to tell her story.

Nonetheless, even if *Hetty Dorval* is the one Ethel Wilson novel that doesn't (at least at first glance) fit my thesis very well, it provides an important clue to her artistic method. Perhaps the most memorable scene in the book is that in which Frankie and Hetty watch the wild geese on migration. I will quote the crucial sentences:

> I reined Maxie [her horse] in at once, and, quite forgetting the importance of Mrs Dorval, pointed up and said, *'Look!'*
>
> Mrs Dorval reined in too, and said, 'What? Where?' She shaded her *eyes* with her hand and *looked up* as I did. She could not *see* as quickly as I could that out of the north came a thin long arrow, high in the sky. Then her *eyes* picked up the movement of the fluid arrow rapidly approaching overhead, and the musical clamour of the wild geese came more clearly and loudly to us.... As we *gazed,* the moving arrow of great birds passed out of *sight*

> on its known way to the south, leaving only the memory of *sight* and sound in the still air. We drew a long breath.
>
> '*God*', said Mrs Dorval. Then, 'What a *sight*!'
>
> ... We remained standing there and *gazing* at the empty sky. (14-15; except for '*God*', all emphases mine)

'Look', 'eyes', 'see', 'gazed', 'sight'. The passage is full of the vocabulary of vision – and so, indeed, is the whole novel. I recommend the experiment of going through the book marking such words; for myself, I was amazed at the frequency of instances. Here, however, it will be sufficient to recall actual scenes in which seeing is all-important. At the opening Frankie and her friend Ernestine watch the arrival of the train and (significantly in view of later developments) draw wrong conclusions from what they see. After contact is established between Frankie and Hetty, frequent references are made to Hetty's bungalow and to people looking either out of or in through the windows. The most important of these is when Frankie and Ernestine peer through the darkness into the lighted room at 'Mr Dorval'. As the novel progresses, the imagery of sight develops from a mainly literal to a mainly metaphorical usage. In the climactic scene in which Mrs Broom reveals herself as Hetty's mother, Frankie and Hetty first gaze at her, surprised at her emotion, and then, when the truth is out, 'Hetty went quite white and *stared* at Mrs Broom as though she had never *seen* her before, and perhaps she never had' (82; my emphases). But Frankie sees. Indeed, the whole of the novel is concerned with Frankie coming to 'see' Hetty in her true light – seeing her, and then seeing through her.

Bearing in mind Ethel Wilson's preoccupation with the vocabulary of vision, let me turn now to *The Innocent Traveller,* a novel in which her particular overview becomes clearly manifest. The splendid opening scene in which the young Topaz slides down beneath the dinner-table and observes the assembled company, including Matthew Arnold, at boot-level, is often quoted and praised. In memory, it may seem a classic example of limited viewpoint – but we should take another look. My extract is radically foreshortened but it is not unfaithful, I think, to the movement and intention of the whole:

> She put her head on one side and looked at Blakey's clod-hoppers.... Topaz regarded Blakey and his boots coldly. He, the sharp-nosed boy, was already the farmer, the jockey. He was to sail cheerfully across an ocean and a half to Australia....
>
> Here were the good shoes of Mary. Out she went to India, poor Mary, to marry a missionary. Glory surrounded the absent Mary, who soon bore two little spinsters in the heat and died....
>
> Oh, the beautiful slippers of Annie.... She was to marry James Hastings, Father's brilliant young man at the Works. She was to be the gentle and obeyed mother of nine. She was, in her charming matriarchal old age, to go far away across sea and land to join distant sons yet unborn. (5-6)

The effect here is remarkable. At the very moment when literal perspective is at its most circumscribed – a toddler's view of what she calls 'a world of shoes' (4) – Wilson expands her own perspective so that we see the Edgeworth family *sub specie aeternitatis.* We may be intended to move from the viewpoint of Topaz as child to that of Topaz in old age, but the impression is one of omniscience. This is a paradigm, I suggest, of Wilson's mature artistic method.

We can see a related effect in the long chapter, 'The Journey', in which Annie (now the Grandmother) and Rachel and Topaz cross Canada by train. Their view of Canada is limited by the train windows (we recall the windows of Hetty's bungalow, and I shall have more to say about Wilson's use of windows in general towards the end of my paper). The three immigrants can achieve only 'the travellers' vision' (105): '"Oh, look!" and "Oh, look!" they said' (106). But as the train progresses, Wilson's lovingly detailed descriptive passages increase, and again we notice a corresponding expansion of viewpoint:

> All day the illimitable prairie spread before them and slipped

> behind them. Far to the north (and to the south) the prairie spread, defeating imagination, like eternity. They did not know that further north still were great irregular lakes, and rivers, and a great river flowing to the Arctic Ocean, where only a few of the hardiest white men had been. (118)

And a little later:

> The birches with their white maidenly stems and honey-yellow leaves shone against the dark conifers. Far to the north of them, but still east of the Rockies, east of Jasper House, the Athabasca River flowed widely through a land that was all gold.... Few travellers along the brave steel way had ever heard of this golden world. (119)

The movement is from what the travellers see to what they do not see, what they cannot see. While they move west across Canada, Wilson follows the spreading prairie north beyond their horizons. The sense of two complementary viewpoints – the human one, bound by time and place, and another, authorial though verging towards the divine – becomes increasingly evident in Wilson's later work.

One of Ethel Wilson's supreme artistic qualities is that she never repeats herself. The novels have a family resemblance but each differs significantly from what has gone before or will come after. The same is true of her narrative viewpoint. In 'Tuesday and Wednesday', the first story in *The Equations of Love,* she comes closer to the divine perspective by the presentation of Mort and Myrt's 'angels'. This is a curious device, and I am bound to say that I do not find it wholly successful, but one can see readily enough the writer's intention. The angels not only represent the better selves of her characters – their consciences, their senses of decency and moral duty – they also represent ways of looking at the characters from the outside and yet at the same time intimately – from just over the shoulder, as it were. So Mort's angel, we are told in the opening chapter, 'stepped for a moment outside its domicile, also stretched, and then returned to its simple yet interesting spiritual or shall we say psychic quarters' (3-4). The prose is, I think, a little stiff and pert by comparison with Wilson's best standard, but we can see the way in which the angel acts as an intermediary between Mort's own inner viewpoint and the narrator's external perspective. There is a constant movement between these two ways of looking, and we are only mildly jolted when, after showing Myrtle coming to her own conclusions about a woman in a street-car wearing alligator shoes, Wilson claims the extreme authorial privilege and tells us omnisciently what the woman is really like.

We come to understand the significance of this procedure on Wednesday if not on Tuesday. After Mort's death by drowning on the second day, the main questions posed by the story are: what sort of man was he? and what sort of death did he die? When the two policemen break the news to Myrtle, giving her the supposedly uninterpreted facts that he had been drinking (not actually true – he had had nothing stronger than, of all things, Postum) and then drowned in the company of 'that souse Hansen' (9), Myrtle *sees* him (I use the word deliberately) as 'the idle lying drunken loafer who had so deceived her time and time again' (119). It is the romanticizing, movie-going, innocent Victoria May Tritt who maintains that 'Morty died the death of a hero' (122), and even persuades Myrtle that it is the truth. Of course, it isn't. Only Ethel Wilson (along with Mort's angel, now departed) knows that 'the truth' – if there is such a thing – lies somewhere between the two extremes. An adjudication between imperfect perspectives, only communicable with any clarity through omniscience, is therefore one of the central concerns of 'Tuesday and Wednesday'.

'Lilly's Story', the second story in *The Equations of Love,* follows the fortunes of Lilly Walker alias Maudie Watkins alias May Bates, and her later transformations into Mrs Walter Hughes and eventually into Mrs Lillian Sprockett. The important point to be made about Lilly is that she is never quite what she seems. One of her employers, for instance, thinks of her, albeit affectionately, as 'this common common girl' (201), but as readers we know (thanks to Wilson's omniscient instruction) that she is anything but common. At the same time, Lilly herself has not been blessed with – perhaps has been spared – a capacity for vision. We are told that 'Lilly had never in her young animal life looked below the surface of things as they occurred, nor had she looked within herself' (160). Lilly is admirable – Wilson admires her, loves her, and so do we – but hers, like Mort's, is the life of surface and the challenge of the immediate moment. Her 'angel', we might say, is undeveloped, not even needed. She knows something of time (the past haunts her, and after one bad early experience she has periodic nightmares about the police), but she knows nothing of the greater reality that her creator knows and celebrates. Here is an important passage:

> It was very strange that Lilly to whom the world of the invisible senses was closed should have given birth to this daughter who, when her day should come, would experience love and friendship and beauty, joy, sorrow and the poetry of experience. On such a day as this and in such a place Eleanor would – some day and days – be aware of the incorporeal presence in air, and light, and dark, and earth, and sea, and sky, and in herself, of something unexpressed and inexpressible, that transcends and heightens ordinary life, and is its complement. Without it, life is uninformed, and life in Lilly was uninformed, without poetry or ecstasy or anguish. (194)

It is supremely characteristic of Ethel Wilson that these intimations of immortality (her effects often recall Wordsworthian phrases) should be articulated in a story whose leading character is blind to them. Here, in its extreme form, we see the writer's need to maintain an overview beyond the imagination of her protagonist. 'Lilly's Story' told exclusively from Lilly's viewpoint is imaginable – indeed, many a modern author could be imagined writing it – but it would be limited. That awareness of an incorporeal presence unknown to Lilly would be absent; only Ethel Wilson's providential vision can give us that.

Swamp Angel begins with Mrs Vardoe watching, through a window in Vancouver, free-flying birds returning on migration. It ends with Maggie Lloyd (who was Mrs Vardoe) throwing the Swamp Angel revolver high into the air above Three Loon Lake and watching it fall, pierce the surface of the water, and vanish into the depths where the fishes scatter in fright and then resume their way. The birds remind us of the geese in *Hetty Dorval* or of the sea-gulls that, by the end of *The Innocent Traveller,* are all that the aged Topaz can see of the living world of nature. And the world of fishes in Three Loon Lake may remind us also of Wilson's preoccupation with surfaces, as in her account of the 'water-gliders' in *The Innocent Traveller,* those insects that, like Topaz, move upon the surface of life, 'unaware of the dreadful deeps below them' (103). And Lilly, we have just noted, 'had never ... looked below the surface of things'. I mention these connections at this point because, in their inter-relatedness, they suggest the recurring sense in Wilson's work of an overall pattern, of regulated if still mysterious laws within the visible universe, of a larger world beyond our own that can be seen and experienced in part but never apprehended as a whole. 'Vision' and 'visionary' now begin to merge. We are moving here, of course, into a religious dimension – a concern for the *un*seen, for something that cannot be perceived visually but whose larger dimension can occasionally be sensed in glimpses – the world of eternity, if you like, only fitfully discernible in the world of time.

In *Swamp Angel* Wilson is particularly concerned with this larger world. Maggie Lloyd, revitalizing herself in isolation in the cabin by the Similkameen River, feels herself 'on a margin of life, ... that margin of a world which was powerful and close' (39-40). Much later, Mr Cunningham, saved by Maggie when he becomes exhausted while in a fishing-boat on the lake, thinks of 'the margin between what might have been and the validity and comfort of the warmth and of this woman who offered him life in a chipped bowl' (137). *Swamp Angel* explores these intimations of a wider life, a larger existence. Nell Severance, in her old age, confined to her room and her memories, talks about what she believes, about Providence and God (102-03), and then speaks to Maggie, during their one meeting in the novel, of 'the miraculous interweaving of creation ... the everlasting web' (150). She describes herself as 'an unusually religious woman' (128), and her daughter says of her: 'Mother, you are so used to playing God' (65).

The novel, too, is a 'miraculous interweaving of creation', and although the number of threads can sometimes seem bewildering, I hope that a sense of pattern is gradually becoming clear. There is much of Ethel Wilson herself in Nell Severance, and a novelist inevitably, I suppose, gets 'used to playing God'. While we see the world from the viewpoints of Maggie Lloyd and Nell Severance, we need also the novelist's overview, her fictive control that in turn suggests an overall meaning and purpose in the universe. The effect is analogous to that already noted in *The Innocent Traveller* where Topaz's viewpoint from under the table is juxtaposed with an omniscience that knows and tells the fates of the whole Edgeworth family. Here in *Swamp Angel* Wilson makes the point through what I call omniscient parenthesis. Thus Maggie, just escaped from her husband, is portrayed as 'free of care or remembrance as if she had just been born' – and then, from the viewpoint of a generalizing, philosophizing omniscience, the parenthesis: '(as perhaps she had, after much anguish)' (34). Or, more chillingly, as she swims in Three Loon Lake much later in the book: 'She could never sink, she thinks' – and the all-knowing narrator adds: '(but she could)' (100).

The 'world' of *Swamp Angel* – and, indeed, of all Wilson's fiction, though it is more readily demonstrable here – is a world that makes sense. It is by no means perfect, and some of its manifestations are cruel or unpleasant, but it is a world in which meaningful lives can be led, and joy and fulfilment can be achieved. R.E. Watters, I think, made the point well: 'This world and its known inhabitants are a continuing delight to Ethel

Wilson – a delight unshaken by the predatory "tooth and claw" rampant in Nature or by human vices and follies' (22). When she comes to write *Love and Salt Water,* however, the 'human vices and follies' are decidedly more pronounced. True, one is aware of many of the old preoccupations, and I suspect that the vocabulary of vision is quantitatively more frequent in this novel than in any since *Hetty Dorval.* At the beginning, Ellen Cuppy is taken by her mother to a park where 'they would watch from the shore, looking westward, a gliding freighter which had just shown its bow around the distant southern point of land' (5). Not many pages later, after the mother's death, Ellen is herself on a freighter with her father, and now they are the ones to be watched: 'watchers on the shore or at windows feel afresh the kindling interest in the long in-coming or out-going deep-sea freighter, and something in the mind says I will go some day, somewhere, anywhere' (31). Much later, from the windows of her sister's apartment, Ellen watches the sea (the 'unplumb'd, salt, estranging sea', perhaps, of Arnold's poem 'To Marguerite: Continued'), and it is in that sea that disaster almost strikes when Ellen is disfigured in an accident and the nephew for whom she is responsible almost drowns.

The same cluster of images is present (windows, watching, 'seeing' in both senses) but the view of the world is much more sombre. The young Ellen suddenly comes upon her mother dead. Her sister loses her first child, her second is mongoloid, and the third doomed to deafness. Her first fiancé, Huw Peake, is an ill-tempered, embittered ex-prisoner of war; one of the minor characters has lost a hand in the war. Ellen herself has experienced war at close quarters: 'Walking again in St. James's Park with Alan Brown who was soon to be shot down, and seeing and hearing – aghast – the buzz-bomb ride, land and demolish the Guards' Chapel, and the Guards within the Chapel' (121). This is not, I submit, a passage that, were we confronted with it on its own, we would identify as 'typical' Ethel Wilson. Though the move from the individual viewpoint to omniscience – 'who was soon to be shot down' – is characteristic, there is a brutal directness about this passage that we do not normally associate with her. *Love and Salt Water* is surely the darkest of her novels.

'Dark', indeed, becomes an important image in this novel, and I must quote a crucial passage at some length:

> Lying flat on her back at two o'clock in the morning, Ellen reflected upon the nature of reality, which she found to be one (or almost one) with the nature of light – light implying, of course, also the absence of light: that is, darkness.
>
> This was because the ceiling of her bedroom at which she looked, while being in its own nature a white ceiling, was dark, since the night was dark. But a light in the street below made the ceiling partially pale, luminous, and ... the light and the darkness between them made stationary patterns upon the ceiling, so that curiously irregular wedge-shaped quadrilaterals of light and dark lay there in a design of great beauty. (67-68)

This is described a little later as 'a pattern of still light and dark, and of light moving across the pattern' (68). Both light and darkness are part of the pattern, part of the 'design of great beauty'. Even here, then, in her darkest work, Wilson insists upon a world that makes sense, that has form and meaning. She does not ignore pain or violence or injustice (consider, for example, the number of sudden deaths even in a novel as affirmingly positive as *The Innocent Traveller*), but her 'overview' includes both light and darkness, and allows her readers to see the complete pattern even if her characters do not. Hers, then, is invariably a providential vision, and Wilson's authorial intrusions, so culpable to the advocates of modernism, are justified because they reflect and interpret a world-view that presupposes a larger meaning.

I could go on for a long time citing passages and details from these and other works, but that would become tedious. I must, however, examine in some detail one of Wilson's short stories (first published in 1958 after the last of her novels) in which all the elements I have been discussing are contained in conveniently small compass. It has not, so far as I know, attracted much attention, but it seems to me one of her finest achievements. Perhaps significantly, it was placed last in her collection *Mrs Golightly and Other Stories.* Its title, appropriately enough, is 'The Window'.

The window in question forms 'the entire transparent north-west (but chiefly north) wall of Mr Willy's living-room' (194). Mr Willy is an English businessman now retired who has left his wife (in some respects presenting the reverse-pattern to Maggie Lloyd at the opening of *Swamp Angel*) and come to live in Vancouver. We soon realize, however, that he has retired not only from business but from the world. He looks out at the world, his magnificent view over sea and mountains (here we may be reminded of Adolphus in the short story 'A Drink with Adolphus'), but the world is separated from him by the supposedly protecting glass. Appearances, however, are unreliable. Thus the mountains look beautiful, but Wilson's omniscient narrator tells us that they are 'deceptive in their innocency, full of crags and crevasses and arêtes and danger' (195). Mr Willy (like so many of her main characters) watches the birds flying freely – cormorants, wild duck, but also smaller birds that are injured or killed when they collide with the glass window (the same image is the central preoccupation of the short story entitled 'The Birds'). For a time Mr Willy feels himself 'at peace' (195), 'contented' (197), but his retreat into this palace of art is ultimately dissatisfying. He becomes aware 'that he had left humanity behind, that a man needs humanity and that if he ceases to be in touch with man and is not in touch with God, he does not matter' (197). In other words, to use that favourite phrase from John Donne which is never far from the front of Wilson's consciousness, 'No man is an Iland, intire of it selfe.'

And at this point the perspective, the narrative viewpoint, changes dramatically, albeit only for a moment. From Mr Willy, looking out of his window at the world from which he has withdrawn, we move to an unidentified man, an intruder, a criminal, looking in through the window at Mr Willy and his material goods. But, we are told, 'this time, as evening drew on, the man outside went away because he had other business' (199). 'This time' is ominous; and the seemingly casual word 'business' links the man, ironically, with Mr Willy himself. Both men, the respectable and the disreputable, are 'involved in Mankinde'.

Mr Willy is gradually lured back into the world, but at first only into that dismal society of black-tie dinner-parties and bridge that he had previously found so tedious. But his depression deepens and he finds that the visible world (the view from his window) is insufficient. He begins to look – and again we notice Wilson's inconspicuous but significant use of the vocabulary of vision – within or beyond, below that surface with which so many of Wilson's earlier characters had never been concerned:

> He found himself looking this way and that out of his aridity for some explanation or belief beyond the non-explanation and non-belief that had always been sufficient and had always been his, but in doing this he came up against a high and solid almost visible wall of concrete or granite, set up between him and a religious belief. This wall had, he thought, been built by him through the period of his long life. (202-03)

As we read, we cannot but connect this metaphorical 'wall of concrete or granite' with the actual window of glass that he has built into his home. And at this moment we return once more to the man outside the window – still watching, and planning violence.

Mr Willy now feels that he must reciprocate hospitality and holds his own party; that is to say, for the first time he asks that outside society from which he has withdrawn into his house. He invites them one Sunday: is it reading too closely to point out that the climax of the story occurs on God's day? The guests arrive and duly admire the view, but some – businessmen of the kind he had once been – want to see the extent of his property. On returning with them he fails to lock the glass door that protects him from the deceptive world. Later, when the guests have gone and Mr Willy is alone once more, the man outside sees his opportunity.

And now what one can only, I think, call Providence intervenes. As the intruder raises his arm to strike from behind, he sees his own action reflected in the glass of the now dark window. Mr Willy hears a slight movement and sees the danger – also reflected in the window. And at the same moment the telephone rings (one of the sillier guests has left her handbag behind). The intruder panics, flees through the glass door, and bangs it behind him. Mr Willy's immediate response is 'Damn you! ... you might have broken it!' (208), but later, with the door safely locked once more, he realizes that he 'must in some way and very soon break the great wall that shut him off from whatever light there might be' (209).

Because 'The Window' is not as familiar as much of Wilson's work, I have felt bound to offer a digest of the plot, but in such a way, I hope, that her major preoccupations have become clear. The cluster of images and ideas which I have been trying to trace elsewhere all converge within this story (almost, one feels, within its title) to form a concise and central statement.

So far, I have derived my argument wholly from Wilson's fiction. In conclusion, I want to test my findings against biographical evidence and the more direct statements she has made, in non-fiction articles, about her attitudes and intentions. I begin with an extract from a memoir by George Woodcock: 'She and her husband Wallace ... would entertain one in their succession of apartments, which were always chosen so that they faced on to English Bay and Stanley Park, with a view of the North Shore mountains and of the Gulf of Georgia out beyond Point Grey' (*World* 121). The shock of recognition we encounter here measures the extent to which Wilson draws upon personal emotion and experience. We find a similar instance in the article she herself contributed to the first issue of *The Tamarack Review*. Entitled 'On a Portuguese Balcony', it involves Ethel Wilson travelling, meditating, but always watching and seeing, and the elevation of the balcony allows her the characteristic 'overview'.

An article she contributed to Woodcock's *Canadian Literature* also provides eloquent support for what I have been saying. It is entitled 'The Bridge or the Stokehold?: Views of the Novelist's Art'. Both perspectives, up on the bridge or down in the stokehold, represent possible angles of narration, and the ships that she has watched so often from her apartment windows present her with an image for her 'views' on the art of fiction. 'A novelist', she goes on to say, 'is, no doubt, a born watcher. He may not be as planned and deliberate as a bird watcher, yet he cannot help watching' (44). So once more birds enter the pattern, their free flight representing for her that living movement of life, the observation of which is the novelist's prime concern. (When, at the beginning of this paper, I said I would offer a 'bird's-eye view' of Wilson's major work, I chose my image with care.) At the close of her article, moreover, completing her design and fulfilling her title, she relates an anecdote about looking out (and down) at a trawler 'just below our study windows' (46).

I must now draw my argument to a close. In doing so, however, I cannot forgo quoting three brief scattered extracts from her non-fiction work that bear witness to the imagistic and intellectual design that I have been discussing. I have said that Wilson's authorial stance embodies the sense of a divine purpose. We know that her parents both came from Dissenting backgrounds, but what was her own religious position? She states this most explicitly in a passage where she recounts meeting the critic and Catholic convert John Sutherland for the first time. He immediately asked her if she was a Christian, and she replied: 'I am indeed a Christian and very grateful and not a good enough one, and not entirely conventionally a Christian – in formal belief and observance, I meant' ('Series' 6). We might have derived this position from her work, but it is reassuring to hear it directly from her own statement.

Again, in 'Reflections in a Pool', where once more she meditates upon her art, she speaks of 'turning the binoculars of the living on to the far remembered dead' (29). The reference to binoculars reasserts her preoccupation with seeing, but the whole phrase reminds me that I have said little about that important concern in all her fiction: the relation between time and memory. I have concentrated for the most part on Wilson as watcher of external events, but we must never forget the 'eye of the mind' which has its own vision.

Finally, there is an essay called 'A Cat among the Falcons', and the title recalls another aspect that I have neglected: those recurring scenes in which human beings watch significant incidents in the world of nature. I quoted the description of Hetty and Frankie watching the geese, but have said nothing about the scene where Lilly and her daughter watch an eagle mobbed by gull and crow ('Lilly's Story', ch. 6) or the similar one in which an eagle robs an osprey of its fish in *Swamp Angel* (ch. 18) or the scene later in the same novel in which Maggie sees her kitten stalking the fawn at first light outside her cabin (ch. 20). These are scenes of watching and learning that recall Wordsworth and the influence of natural objects. In 'A Cat among the Falcons' itself (with these outdoor scenes in mind) the closing sentence proves central to my purpose: 'It will be better now, I think, to take my convictions safely indoors and sit looking out of the window at what I can see, and at the sky which is so beautiful' (19). Looking at what she can see, inside or out. Here, surely, we come close to the essence not only of Ethel Wilson's vision but of her affirmative but sober wisdom that has heard 'the still, sad music of humanity' and sees 'into the life of things'. Like Wordsworth's, hers is 'an eye/That hath kept watch o'er man's mortality'.

Novelist or Essayist?: Hugh MacLennan and *The Watch That Ends the Night*

This paper was written for the 'Hugh MacLennan: 1982' conference at University College, University of Toronto, and subsequently included in the proceedings published by the Canadian Studies Programme of the college, under the editorship of Elspeth Cameron. It explores the blurred no-man's-land between fiction and non-fiction which I find a recurrently important feature of modern Canadian fiction, and one that is considered again in later articles in this section, notably those on Robertson Davies, Hugh Hood, and Jack Hodgins.

THIS PAPER IS INTENDED to be exploratory. I hope to pursue a number of literary-critical hares in the next few minutes, but I don't guarantee to catch any of them. My aim is to open up rather than to survey fully (let alone exhaust) my subject.

The Watch That Ends the Night is commonly (though by no means unanimously) regarded as Hugh MacLennan's finest novel. I myself believe it to be easily his best. Alongside this evaluation, however, let us set another, very different one. George Woodcock recently articulated the commonly held belief 'that MacLennan is really an essayist whom circumstances have forced into the role of a fiction-writer', and he went on to remark: 'Certainly he is a writer whose unfictional prose arouses less doubt in the critical reader than his novels do' ('When the Past' 94). I would not be prepared to go quite that far, yet I suspect that, if pushed to the wall and required to name the book by MacLennan that I most admire after *The Watch,* I would probably plump for a non-fiction work, *Seven Rivers of Canada.* Yet these two positions – that *The Watch* is his best novel and that he is at heart an essayist – are not, of course, contradictory. I juxtapose them because they may offer a clue to the curious effectiveness of *The Watch That Ends the Night*.

And at this point, let me make what appears at first sight to be a drastic change of tack. In Part Seven of the novel, Catherine is dangerously ill, about to undergo an operation, and not expected to live. MacLennan begins the fourth chapter of this part by making George Stewart write:

> I can continue with this story and make sense of what follows only if I succeed in explaining something very difficult. (340)

The remainder of the chapter (just over four pages) reads like a personal confession, a deeply felt statement by one who has loved and suffered greatly. It is, of course, precisely that, and I cannot imagine any sensitive reader who would not be profoundly moved by it. But, artistically, it raises problems. If, for example, one were to undertake an experiment by reading it to intelligent people who did not know its origin, and then asking them to identify the kind of work from which it came, I suspect that few would argue that it formed part of a novel. Save for a casual reference to 'this story' (341), there are no indications within the text that it belongs to a fictional narrative. Is this ultra-realism or a breakdown of art? The chapter ends, it is worth noting, with a series of paradoxes concerning the nature of reality that stand in a recognizable tradition of mystical writing, and closely resemble passages from sources as various as the medieval *Deonise Hid Divinite* and T.S. Eliot's *Four Quartets*:

> This, which is darkness, also is light. This, which is no, also is yes. This, which is hatred, also is love. This, which is fear, also is courage. This, which is defeat, also is victory. (344)

I quote this not merely as a sample of the 'un-novel-like' quality of the prose but also because that last word, 'victory', is the title of a non-fiction essay by MacLennan written just before *The Watch.* As many of you will know, it is a tribute to his late wife Dorothy Duncan, an essay that represents in many respects an alternative version of the material transfigured (and I use the word deliberately) at the end of *The Watch,* an essay containing the following sentence that might just as well have appeared in the novel:

> Through this experience became manifest some of those mysterious things spoken of in the last chapters of St. John's Gospel, and I knew that they were true. ('Victory' 183)

This chapter-length piece of discursive prose embedded in *The Watch* is exceptional for its length as well as for its power, but numerous other passages could be cited from MacLennan's novels that have the 'feel' of non-fiction. As early as the first section of *Barometer Rising* we find Neil Macrae climbing Citadel Hill and looking down over Halifax. There follows a meditation on the geology, geography, history, and character of Halifax that, though perfectly fitting to a novel in which, as MacLennan has stated himself, 'the background is the most essential part of the book' (*Thirty* 53), might well have found an equally appropriate context in a familiar essay. And, moreover, it bears an interesting resemblance to 'Portrait of a City' (*Cross-Country*), an article on Halifax that MacLennan wrote almost a decade later.

Such passages are particularly common, though, in *The Watch*; they include generalizations about politics, descriptions of Montreal during the thirties, philosophical meditations. Indeed, if we have been away from the novel for any length of time, we remember it, I believe, as much for its non-fictional elements – its evocation of Montreal, its analysis of the politics of the Depression, its impassioned portrayal of a non-sectarian religious experience – as for the story of George Stewart, Catherine, and Jerome Martell. And if the blending of these different elements is achieved more smoothly and more successfully here than in any of the novel's predecessors (or, I think, successors), the reason is not far to seek.

On the opening page George Stewart, the central figure, introduces himself as 'a political commentator over the radio and a writer of free lance articles on political topics for our magazines' (3). Like his creator, he is both lecturer (he teaches history at McGill at the time when MacLennan was beginning a new career there as part-time lecturer in English) and commentator (Stewart primarily on radio, MacLennan primarily in magazines). Stewart is, then, a figure for whom the communication of fact and opinion is both habitual and natural. Moreover, in this novel MacLennan experiments for the first time in his published fiction with first-person narration. By making George Stewart not only a socio-political commentator but the voice through whom the story is told, MacLennan employs a technique by which he is able to integrate his own didactic interests into the form and texture of his fiction. While some argue that, in creating Stewart as a mouthpiece, MacLennan has failed to distance himself sufficiently from his chief character, I would maintain that he has deliberately – and successfully – evolved a protagonist who can communicate the author's own sentiments and experience with a minimum of strain. Alec Lucas is right to assert that MacLennan is 'neither journalist, nor historian, nor sociologist *manqué* writing fiction', that his novels 'are not fictionalized essays' (12, 44), but it is an argument that should be made positively rather than negatively.

At this point, it is well to be reminded that, despite its predominantly positive critical reception and its continuing commercial popularity, the book has received its share of criticism. And most of this has, indeed, centred upon the character of George Stewart. Such criticism complains of his ordinariness, even his 'squareness', and (curiously, in view of the praise generally accorded MacLennan's non-fiction writing) the flatness of his prose. Perhaps the most extreme condemnation came from Warren Tallman, who complained in the first issue of *Canadian Literature* of Stewart's 'mania for handing out crashing complacencies on almost every imaginable major consideration in life: marriage, religion, modern love, art, war, sex, neurosis, politics, philosophy, peace, the seasons' ('After-Glance' 81). One can understand this charge without in any way agreeing with it (whatever words may be employed to characterize Stewart's attitudes, 'complacencies' is certainly not one of them). Personally, I would begin a rebuttal of Tallman by insisting that, in context, Stewart's statements are not *ex cathedra* pomposities; rather, Stewart is seen throughout the book as struggling desperately to come to terms with all these matters. We are concerned not only with the justice of his comments – their profundity or, if you will, their banality – but with the intensely realized situation that provokes them. (Romeo Pronovost, the taxi-driver, is surely introduced into the novel to show what true banality – however it may coexist with goodness and decency – actually sounds like.) The fact that our modern world forces individuals, not just the political leaders but ordinary responsible people, to respond to these topics, even if they have no hope of influencing the course of events, is the unusual preoccupation of this novel.

Yet this leads, in turn, to a related point. There is a sense in which *The Watch That Ends the Night* is a revolutionary – or perhaps I should say counter-revolutionary – book in that it challenges so much that was taken for granted in the society and literary-cum-intellectual context in which it was written. Stewart is at the centre of the controversy for a number of reasons. For the literary élite, the king-makers of the book-trade, he was insufficiently interesting; he lacked glamour. MacLennan's American publishers at that time rejected the book because, we are told, 'the characters (except Martell) are too trifling as people to be equal to their destiny, especially George Stewart' (E. Cameron 289). In other words, novel readers want heroes, and as a hero Stewart is a queer fish. And for the literary Marxists, of course, MacLennan had not only presented a world in which the thirties communists were as gullible and as wrong as anyone else, but had compounded his errors by offering an archetypal bourgeois as his central figure.

In fact, both sides disliked the book because they recognized that MacLennan was saying something that challenged their basic assumptions. He touched too many exposed nerves; he had been bold enough to suggest that the George Stewarts of this world are at least as worthy as the Jerome Martells, that both the right and the left political extremes are objectionable because of their common belief that the cause is more important than the individual. As Elspeth Cameron has noted, MacLennan told the Royal Society of Canada in 1955, while *The Watch* was being written, that fiction 'must return to people again and a belief in the value of the individual' (262). Stewart is offered, sympathetically, as bourgeois and unashamed. He comments at one point: 'Adam Blore was right when he called me a bourgeois at heart. What else is a bourgeois but a man who wants a home, some respect from his fellows and a feeling that he has a future and belongs to a human group?' (157). Such characters are not fashionable in the current literary ethos, but, as Hugo McPherson wrote in a review, 'Hugh MacLennan has dared to sound old-fashioned' (qtd. in E. Cameron 296).

As bourgeois, Stewart (whose name – deliberately, I assume, given MacLennan's Scots ancestry – combines the surname of the aristocratic 'good old cause' with the Christian name of the first of the bourgeois Hanoverians) believes in middle-class values, which include an acceptance of middle-class realism. And this brings me back to the combination of essayist and novelist. MacLennan believes wholeheartedly in the necessary relation between art and life – in the responsibility of literature to comment on 'the way we live now', to hold an artistic, mimetic mirror up to the contemporary human situation. 'There it is', says Stewart in this novel, 'just as it happened' (14). That Stewart, a fictional character, should speak with the same sentiments and in the same accents as Hugh MacLennan, regular essayist in *Maclean's* and *The Montrealer*, is not a sad proof of inadequate artistic detachment but a bold refusal to separate imaginative literature from everyday experience.

This line of thought leads outward in two possible directions, which I will explore so far as time permits. First of all, this mingling of essay and fiction, of discursive commentary with imaginative narrative, has – in some cases, perhaps, as a result of MacLennan's influence – become a feature of modern Canadian writing. The tendency dates back, of course, as far as Frances Brooke and *The History of Emily Montague*, but, along with the current interest in 'documentary poetry', we find a remarkable number of our contemporary novelists exploring the interconnections between fiction and essay, between novel and memoir, between narrative and description. I think of Hugh Hood creating the curiously Hugh-Hood-like Matthew Goderich as central figure for his *New Age* cycle that attempts to present in fictional-cum-documentary terms the whole panorama of twentieth-century Canada as Hugh Hood is in the process of comprehending it; or of Margaret Laurence, an aging novelist in a cottage overlooking the Otonabee River, beginning *The Diviners* with a fictional aging novelist in a cottage looking out over the Otonabee River; or of Mordecai Richler, writing those detachable, hyperrealistic, descriptive vignettes of Montreal life that embellish and all but interrupt the action of novels like *The Apprenticeship of Duddy Kravitz*; and especially of Robertson Davies, who reviewed *The Watch That Ends the Night* shrewdly and justly on its first publication, and who, in *Fifth Business,* wrote another novel in which, in his own words, 'the story-teller and the self-explorer are one' (*Well-Tempered Critic* 214), and who created another (albeit very different) article-writing, schoolmastering bourgeois who discovers that a world of horrors can also be a world of wonders. And note that all these writers, though most prominent as novelists, are known also for their non-fiction. MacLennan is often portrayed as a writer with an almost uncanny knack of catching the nation's pulse at a particular moment in time – with *Barometer Rising* at the beginning of the Second World War, with *Two Solitudes* at the end of it, with *Return of the Sphinx* during the quiet revolution in Québec that was about to become not-so-quiet, and with the apocalyptic warnings of the barometer falling in *Voices in Time* as recently as 1980. This gift presupposes an essential connection between what we read in our fiction and what is going on in the world of *Realpolitik* that impinges upon us at every moment, between the two functions of novelist and essay-commentator.

Finally, where does Hugh MacLennan stand not in the immediate and comparatively small world of Canadian literature, but in international terms? Along with Richler, Davies, Atwood, and Laurence, he is one of our best-known novelists abroad, but like them (with the possible exception of Atwood) he hardly commands a reputation with the literary intellectuals. My colleague D.J. Dooley recently observed that 'he has always seemed the pre-eminent example of the major Canadian literary figure – who else was there to rank above him? – who was never good enough to command international attention' (79). Perhaps 'never *fashionable* enough' would be more accurate. I have already noted how, in its own time, *The Watch* seemed too middle-class in its philosophy to satisfy the cultural élite. Now critical fashions have changed once again, and it may well be MacLennan's 'old-fashioned' mixture of essayist and novelist (who's afraid of Truman Capote?) that is a barrier to critical acceptance. His kind of fiction runs against all the basic principles of contemporary critical theory, of structuralism and especially post-structuralism. If one believes that the signifier can never in fact indicate or represent the signified, that (in the words of Paul de Man) 'sign and meaning can never coincide', or that, in the paraphrase of an opponent of such theories, 'meaning does not mean' (qtd. in Graff 173, 168n), one is hardly likely to display much enthusiasm for MacLennan's work. His move from an omniscient storytelling tradition to that of a fallible, blundering first-person narrator would be seen as a step forward, but his assumptions, his values, his very attempt to find meaning in a world that is assumed *a priori* to be meaningless, would provoke nothing but amused dismissal. 'There it is just as it happened'; 'I knew that they were true' – what impossible statements!

George Woodcock once described MacLennan as 'a writer emphatically, but not necessarily fatally, out of period and fashion' (*MacLennan* 27). I can't help feeling that, in this instance, it may not be so much a matter of the writer being out of fashion as of the critical theorists being out of touch. It is difficult to believe that a novel as unequivocally human as *The Watch* will not have something to say to sensitive and thoughtful people at all times. Moreover, one of the healthy qualities of Canadian literature over the past quarter of a century has been the insistence of its writers on fulfilling the terms of their own talent rather than on tailoring their work to preconceived models of what a good or acceptable novel should be. I'm thinking of books like Sheila Watson's *The Double Hook,* Rudy Wiebe's *The Blue Mountains of China,* Hugh Hood's *A New Athens,* Jack Hodgins's *The Invention of the World,* and (most recently) Robertson Davies's *The Rebel Angels.* These works do not follow fashion, and because they are inimitable they cannot create it. *The Watch* is less formally original than these, but in its underlying values it is strikingly independent. There are advantages to writing in a country that makes no pretensions towards setting the international pace. Hugh MacLennan may have failed, at least for the present, to create universal interest in Canadian writing, but this admission can lead in turn to a more radical thought: that Canadian practice and achievement – and *The Watch That Ends the Night* is surely a magnificent achievement – may indeed reveal serious weaknesses in present-day literary-critical assumptions.

The Roots of Fantasy: Document and Invention in Robertson Davies's Fiction

I have long been of the opinion that Davies's popularity and humour have led Canadian critics to underestimate not only his special importance as a writer but also his curious contemporaneity. Here, in an article that appeared in the *Journal of Canadian Studies* in 1985, I tried to make the case for Davies's claim to one of the many mansions within the 'post-modernist' present. My comments on his interest in fakes and his fascination with documents have, I am pleased to note, been borne out by his subsequent novels *What's Bred in the Bone* (in which faking is a central topic) and *The Lyre of Orpheus* (which concerns itself with, among other things, the literary-archaeological aspect of restoration and the problems involved in pastiche).

THAT ROBERTSON DAVIES'S NOVELS combine a circumstantial realism with frequent forays into the realms of wonder and fantasy is well known. What concerns me here is the curious, and surely important, interconnection between the two – the way in which Davies on the one hand persuades us that the amazing and the wonderful are a part of reality, and on the other invests the ordinary with a glow of romance. But he is also adept at blurring the distinctions for a particular artistic purpose. *Fifth Business* provides a convenient initial instance. When discussing the novel with undergraduate students, I have often mentioned the apparent contrast between factual historical details (exact dates, carefully identified places, references to actual historical events, etc.) and the emphasis on magic and mystery that is so often a prominent ingredient in his work. In doing so, I am accustomed to ask where they would place the stories about Wilgefortis-Kummernis, the saintly and bearded virgin of Portugal. Almost invariably, they set this part of the narrative firmly on the side of fantasy, and are somewhat surprised when I point out that Davies is not giving rein to his imagination here but is referring to authentic legends recorded in Catholic tradition. 'Authentic legends' is, indeed, a happy phrase that itself catches the complex blend of documentary fact and elaborate invention that Davies so delights in.

An attempt to explore the whole subject of the factual versus the fabricated in Davies's work would be a large-scale, ambitious undertaking. As it happens, however, a number of commentators have already thrown light on particular corners of the subject. Thus Robert G. Lawrence has shown how Davies uses Sir John Martin-Harvey's theatrical tours of Canada as a basis for the fictional Tresize tour in *World of Wonders,* and Patricia Monk has demonstrated how the cave scene at the conclusion of *The Manticore* – which most readers, I imagine, accept as fictional invention – is in fact grounded firmly in archaeological discoveries in the vicinity of St. Gall (see Lawrence and Macey). I shall limit myself in the present paper to a small but, I think, crucial section of this extensive subject. Taking my cue from Dunstan Ramsay's emphasis on 'documents' in *World of Wonders,* I want to examine the way Davies incorporates, alludes to, invents, or in any way depends upon books and documents to give substance and credibility to his fictions.

ALTHOUGH THEY MAY BE SAID to maintain diplomatic relations with the conventions of realism, the novels that make up the early Salterton trilogy are all based upon age-old romance conventions. In all of them the sense of make-believe is strong, though each book is twisted in the direction of irony, parody, or sheer good fun. Thus for all its absurdity, Hector Mackilwraith's hopeless love for Griselda Webster in *Tempest-Tost* (1951) is recognizable as a variant on the standard romance-situation, and at the conclusion he duly ends up in Griselda's bed, though hardly in the way he hopes. In *Leaven of Malice* (1954), a mischievous hoax leads ironically to a comic resolution in which what was advertised as false becomes true. *A Mixture of Frailties* (1958) is clearly a Cinderella-type story, though Monica Gall, the Cinderella in question, has to shed her conventional 'goodness' in order to qualify as heroine, and Sir Benedict Domdaniel ('Brum Benny') in no way resembles the orthodox fairy-tale prince. These highly contrived structures, with all the strands appropriately tied at the end, display an artifice that was acceptable enough at the time of Jane Austen or even Charles Dickens; but until the recent appearance of 'magic realism' it has been unfashionable in fiction purporting to comment on 'real life'. Davies is obviously attracted to the tradition-sanctioned older mode, but wishes at the same time to display his talent for contemporary social satire, to comment in witty but nonetheless cogent and acceptable fashion on existing Ontario mores. How does he create the necessary bridge between romance and reality?

In *Tempest-Tost* he fuses the two at the outset by telling the story of an imaginary production of an authentic play. Shakespeare's *The Tempest* is a play that all his readers may be expected to know, or at least know about. It provides references and even quotations that can be verified outside Davies's text. But (and this is a typical Davies touch) the real play is far more fantastic than his invented plot. It represents a world of 'romance' against which we respond to the more mundane romances (love affairs) involving the amateur and sometimes amorous cast. The narrative focus upon putting on the play, the creation of an artistic illusion, also contributes to Davies's effect, though he does not make so much of this as readers who are familiar with the complexities of his more mature novels might expect. Nonetheless, anyone who has had experience of amateur theatricals will be in a position to appreciate the justice of Davies's portrayal, and most readers will derive pleasure from his skilful if not, ultimately, very searching presentation of the interconnections between the imaginative and the mundane.

Leaven of Malice is rather more complex in this respect. We are immediately confronted by a solid-looking 'document' in the form of an engagement notice from a provincial newspaper, and may or may not query the anomalous date (November 31) as we read. It is, of course, a fake, and the plot develops from all the embarrassment experienced by the pair who have been erroneously mentioned and by the editor of the newspaper that failed to detect the hoax. Yet, if we pause to consider the matter more deeply, we may note an oddity. Though we are prepared to accept the Salterton *Evening Bellman* and its editor Gloster Ridley as 'real', they are in fact no more and no less figments of Davies's rich imagination than the fake notice itself.

Perhaps because the novel is centred upon a newspaperman, it is strewn with references to books and writing. Some, like the quotation from *All's Well That Ends Well* that fascinates Ridley, are genuine; others exist only within the world of the novel. There are, indeed, three full-length imaginary pieces of writing that appear in *Leaven of Malice* – Solly Bridgetower's mercifully unwritten academic thesis on Charles Heavysege (himself an authentic literary-historical figure); the publisher Clerebold Warboys's memoirs, *Politics: The Great Game*; and reporter Henry Rumball's unpromising Prairie novel, *The Plain that Broke the Plough.* There is also the parody best-seller *Plonk,* which Rumball is asked to review, and fictive specimens of newspaper prose from the prewritten obituary on Professor Vambrace to Shillito's sub-Lamb-like familiar essay, 'A Vanishing Amenity'. Even Ridley, the editor, is in the process of preparing an academic lecture. Moreover, we also see him tinkering with stories and anecdotes from other newspapers to use as possible fillers. These are also, in a small way, fakes: 'One always attributed any foolish remark upon which one intended to pun either to an eminent scientist, a prominent physician, or a political commentator; it gave authenticity' (18). It is precisely 'authenticity' that Davies is aiming at, though he makes no explicit capital out of the relation between Ridley's fake filler and the fake engagement notice that causes him so much trouble. *Leaven of Malice* is a lighthearted, extremely amusing novel, but at its centre lie ideas about the power of words and also about the slippery slope from creation through invention to fabrication that are adumbrated but never fully developed.

With *A Mixture of Frailties* we move from the world of books and writing to that of scores and music. Once again the plot springs from a document (albeit a fantastic one), Mrs Bridgetower's idiosyncratic will, but we move quickly into a world of singing, opera, and recital. Here Davies displays the breadth of his learning, and can easily dazzle the uninitiated by his easy reference to musical personalities of the past. As readers we may not be able to vouch for the accuracy of the information but it sounds genuine enough. (It is worth noting at this point that Davies wrote music criticism for *The Peterborough Examiner* in the 1940s.) But here again he deliberately breaks down the barrier between what is clearly fact and what is clearly fiction. Monica Gall (an invented character) is made to sing authentic musical pieces ranging from Tosti's *Goodbye!* to a part in the *St. Matthew Passion,* but she also sings imaginary pieces by the invented composer Giles Revelstoke.[1] Moreover, Revelstoke himself uses for his invented music authentic texts in Reginald Scot, Coleridge, and Apuleius. To make matters all the more complicated, when Monica gives her Bridgetower Trust recital, she mixes music from the real world and music that only exists in the world of the novel on the same programme. Once again, the possibilities are not developed very far. The 'real' references provide a grounding, I suspect, for the not very likely Cinderella story already mentioned. But the process has wider possibilities, and Davies goes on to exploit them in the Deptford trilogy.

Fifth Business (1970), as we might expect, is rich in these inventive complexities. We do not have to go further than the novel's

1 Revelstoke, though an invented character, appears to be based on Peter Warlock (Philip Arnold Heseltine, 1894-1930). Warlock seemingly committed suicide, though the jury was unable to reach a clear verdict. A few years later, Davies was to lodge in the very street where Warlock had lived. For this information, which adds to the complexities I discuss here, I am indebted to Professor Michael Peterman of Trent University.

epigraph, which claims to explain its arresting title. The Salterton novels, we should note, all contained epigraphs, identifying their titles and drawing from *Macbeth,* the Prayer Book, and Earl Halifax respectively. The epigraph here is from Thomas Overskou's *Den Danske Skueplads,* and it attracted much comment when the novel became popular. Some have cast doubt on its authenticity, but both author and book undoubtedly exist (as both British Museum and Library of Congress catalogues testify). Personally, I have never seen a copy, and I do not know where the English translation comes from, but these are matters which dutiful scholars will doubtless track down in the near future, if they have not already done so. More important to my purpose is the fact that, for English-speaking readers, this is a decidedly unfamiliar text and, although the quotation itself is apparently genuine, the phrase 'Fifth Business' which it purports to explain is by no means a familiar theatrical term (despite the unwary assumptions of some commentators). Moreover, the phrase is later glossed in the text of the novel itself by an imaginary character whose extraordinary name, Vitzlipützli, is an erudite allusion to a minor character in an early German *Faust* play, as Davies eventually tells us in *World of Wonders,* and the title of a poem by Heine, as F.L. Radford has since demonstrated.[2] (Her first name, Liselotte, presumably involves a relevant pun.) Davies has created a tangled web of allusion and reference here that enables him to begin his story with the distinctions between the real and the imaginary expertly and appropriately muddied.

The first book mentioned and quoted in the novel, then, proves somewhat elusive and ambiguous. In the body of the text itself, references to books and documents are at least as numerous as in *Leaven of Malice.* I shall consider the documents first. The novel takes its ostensible origin, it will be remembered, from an article, 'Farewell to the Cork', that is supposed to have appeared in the Colborne College *Chronicle.* This document (an

---

[2] For other erudite allusions here, see Gertrud Jaron Lewis.

invented article by an imaginary author about an imaginary individual published in the invented magazine of an invented school) is quoted in full and challenged by Dunstan Ramsay (the imaginary individual in question) as false. But in what sense false? Ramsay himself is writing the novel, comprising events that Davies has made up, in the form of a fictional report to an imaginary headmaster. How do we separate the 'true' from the 'false' in so complicated a mass of invention?

Another 'document' in *Fifth Business* is reproduced by Ramsay much later in the novel. This is the letter he is supposed to have received from Hippolyte Delehaye, S.J., formally accepting his article on Wilgefortis-Kummernis (the bearded female saint) for the *Analecta Bollandiana.* Here we have an invented letter to an imaginary addressee about an imaginary article. But the article is on an authentic subject, the writer of the letter is historical, and he was indeed the editor of the journal in question at the time in which this section of the novel is set. Yet this is not all. Dr Judith Skelton Grant has informed me that articles on this particular saint appeared in the *Analecta* shortly before and after this period but not in the particular year in which Ramsay's imaginary article is supposed to have been published. No document of fantasy could be more firmly rooted in a historical reality.

There are, of course, numerous books mentioned in *Fifth Business*: among the 'real' ones are Robert-Houdin's *The Secrets of Stage Conjuring* (which Davies draws upon heavily in *World of Wonders*). Others are imaginary, including *A Hundred Saints for Travellers*, *Forgotten Saints of the Tyrol,* and *Celtic Saints of Britain and Europe* – and, we must not forget, the 'autobiography' of Magnus Eisengrim (entitled *Phantasmata,* as we learn later from *World of Wonders*). The distinction between an imaginary false book and imaginary books of genuine scholarship is subtle indeed. Moreover, in *Fifth Business* as a whole, which is itself an invention, we find side by side in an imagined world an invented false book, invented 'true' books, and books that we can consult in real libraries – libraries, be it noted, that can be expected to contain at least one copy of *Fifth Business.* It is, when we come to think of it, a strange combination of imaginative experiences, though Davies's artistry is such that we rarely pause to examine the extraordinary texture of his art.

The Manticore (1972) is decidedly less complex than its predecessor so far as documents are concerned. However, the narrative itself contains two long imaginary documents, David Staunton's 'Zurich Notebook' (Part 2), in which he writes down his memories and dreams for Dr van Haller, and his 'Sorgenfrei Diary' (Part 3).[3] Other documents are fairly minor ones, like Pledger Brown's imaginary advertisement in the authentic *Times Literary Supplement,* and his equally imaginary visiting card which is given the illusion of genuine status by being reproduced in the text. There are, in addition, several learned references to legal precedents and definitions that sound genuine (more opportunities for specialist research here) and so lend an air of authenticity to this aspect of the novel.

World of Wonders (1975) is concerned with theatre and film rather than books, though Robert-Houdin's *Confidences d'un prestidigitateur* is a notable presence behind the imaginary film, and, indeed, behind Eisengrim's narrative which makes up the bulk of the book.[4] Some interesting changes are, however, rung on the differences between the imaginary Eisengrim's 'real' autobiography, as told by himself within the novel, and the false autobiography, imagined to have been written by Ramsay, that I have already mentioned. Eisengrim's actual (albeit invented) story replaces the mythical version, though, if Davies's statements about the composition of this series of linked novels are to be trusted, he hadn't thought up the actual version when he invented the false one in *Fifth Business.* But *World of Wonders* is of special interest to my subject because reference is made within

---

3 I ought to have pointed out at this stage in my argument that one of these documents is linked to a real place (Zurich), the other to an imaginary one (Sorgenfrei). [1989]

4 See Keith, 'Text and Subtext'.

the text to 'the extraordinary importance of documents' (18), and Ramsay is eager throughout the book to compile his own document that will eventually take on historical validity (though it can only do so, we realize, within an essentially fictional world).

There are, moreover, some interesting blendings of fact and fiction in this novel. As I have already noted in passing, Sir John Tresize is invested with many of the attributes of the real-life Sir John Martin-Harvey; his cross-Canada tour is based on a number of actual tours by Martin-Harvey's company, including some real plays from their repertory but inserting some existing though, in terms of theatrical history, fictional alternatives. Moreover, within the narrative Eisengrim acts as 'double' to Tresize, deputizing for him in certain athletic and acrobatic sequences. There is therefore a true and a false Sir John Tresize as there must have been a true and a false Sir John Martin-Harvey. Once again, then, we find true and false within an invented world, based partly on historical evidence. There are other nice touches in *World of Wonders,* notably several references to the distinguished British theatre critic James Agate, including extracts from what must be a fabricated (or, at the very least, adapted) review from his pen about one of Tresize's revivals.

WE COME FINALLY to *The Rebel Angels* (1981), Davies's most recent novel at the time of writing and apparently the first part of another trilogy. Since it is set in a university, the novel has a decidedly bookish and archival atmosphere – even more so than *Leaven of Malice* and *Fifth Business.* References are made to numerous books, from ancient volumes like Aretino's *Sonnetti Lussoriosi* and Gesner's *Historia Animalium* to first editions of Edgar Wallace and a classification of anatomical types by W.H. Sheldon. But two individual books play prominent parts within the plot. One is the 'Gryphius manuscript', the text of a hitherto lost book by Rabelais entitled *Stratagems* that has turned up among the effects of a rich Toronto collector. We are then told within the novel that Rabelais's book 'was supposed to have been published' but that 'no copy exists' (90). This is a sufficiently accurate account of the bibliographical facts, though the Toronto manuscript is, of course, Davies's invention, as are the three holograph letters from Rabelais to Paracelsus tucked into the folio. Davies offers us an unlikely though not impossible fictional situation (after all, a Traherne manuscript surfaced in Toronto quite recently) based on some actual facts within the real world. This, then, is a half-imaginary book by an authentic author, but balancing it is the manuscript of Parlabane's notorious novel, an invented text by an imaginary character. These two books dominate *The Rebel Angels* and appear together at a crucial point in the plot.

In *The Rebel Angels,* as in *World of Wonders,* there is much discussion of faking. When the Gryphius manuscript is first mentioned, reference is made to letters of Pontius Pilate and Christ himself which are said to have been sold to a gullible purchaser in the nineteenth century; later, Mamusia and Yerko produce violins that are 'not precisely what they seemed' (composite instruments made up of authentically ancient and recently constructed parts) and so shock the heroine, who has apprenticed herself 'to the hard trade of scholarship, which shrieks at the thought of a fake' (207). Faking has always fascinated Davies. On at least two occasions, he is said to have himself produced fake documents in the real world (a new variation on my theme), once when he offered – very much 'tongue-in-cheek', to be sure – what he called 'The McFiggin Fragment' to a body of Stephen Leacock experts at an academic conference.[5] One wonders, indeed, whether faking may not become an important subject in the volumes to follow *The Rebel Angels.*

There are numerous other references in the novel to books and documents. One of the narrators is writing a doctoral dissertation on Rabelais; another (who, perhaps significantly, is an authority on the Apocrypha) is collecting material for a memoir imitative of John Aubrey's *Brief Lives.* There is, moreover, a

5 See Rehak and Slopen 12.

particular 'document' reproduced within the text that is of special interest: the place-setting for the Ploughwright College dinner (173). Similar charts are not uncommon in detective fiction but relatively rare elsewhere. Here, however, Davies has inserted an interesting 'in-joke' for those who know the original of Ploughwright College: the imaginary document is in Davies's own handwriting.

What are we to make, ultimately, of all this intellectual play between the real and the imaginary, the complex series of allusions to texts within texts? The practice is continually to be found in Davies's work. Even in his recent amusing but not very important collection of Massey College ghost stories, *High Spirits* (1982), books and documents are again prominent, and the fantastic stories are all placed within an identifiable context which includes the real names of Massey Fellows. How does all this fit into the developing tradition of fiction?

The artful mixing of the factual and the invented is not in itself, of course, unusual in literature. Imaginary toads are continually appearing in real gardens. There are, first of all, the fictional realms superimposed on an authentic geography, like Hardy's Wessex, Faulkner's Yoknapatawpha County, or Laurence's Manawaka. Then there are those fictions where the movements of fictional characters can be followed on real maps. This is true of a good deal of Joseph Conrad, Malcolm Lowry, and a particularly good example (which Davies has praised in print (*Enthusiasms* 209-11)), John Cowper Powys's *A Glastonbury Romance.* Canadian instances can be found in the work of Mordecai Richler and Margaret Atwood. Similarly, the traditional historical novel has always created situations in which fictional heroes and heroines rub shoulders with authentic historical figures (Davies creates a deft version of this in *Fifth Business* when Dunstan Ramsay looks into the eyes of King George V while receiving his V.C.). One thinks of Joyce's compulsive insistence on accuracy and verisimilitude in *Ulysses,* where his invented characters (and some that are not invented) move through a minutely reproduced historical Dublin – even though it is only eager research scholars armed with the appropriate Dublin street-guides who can appreciate the extent of his meticulousness. One especially intriguing instance of this kind of authenticity has recently been explored by Louis Dudek. In an article entitled 'Interface: Reality and Literature' he demonstrates how, in *Pale Fire,* Vladimir Nabokov has an imaginary character from a non-existent country reading *The New York Times* on 21 July 1959 and noting details from certain advertisements that did in fact appear in the 'real' *New York Times* of that day. This example seems decidedly closer to the procedures we have observed in Davies, and it is interesting to note that he is an admirer of Nabokov (Davies's bibliography contains several reviews of Nabokov's fiction, including two of *Lolita*).

Canadian examples of this kind of effect do not appear to be common, at least on a complex level – though one may remember with pleasure Robert Kroetsch giving his own address in Binghamton as that of the demented Professor Madham in *Gone Indian.* Perhaps the most interesting instance outside Davies may be found in Hugh Hood's novel series, *The New Age/Le nouveau siècle.* All the volumes hitherto published are full of subtle telescopings of fact and fiction, and I will limit myself to a single illustration. In *The Swing in the Garden* (1975), a text that is positively studded with (usually genuine) book titles, the infant Matt Goderich is inspected in his bedroom by his father and a visitor. His father, Andrew Goderich, is an author (within the fiction) of invented philosophical works entitled *The Place of Conceptual Thought in Ethical Judgments* and *Property and Value*; the visitor is the factual Jacques Maritain, the distinguished French Catholic philosopher and theologian who was living in Toronto during the period in which the novel takes place. Later, in *Reservoir Ravine* (1979), set earlier in time than *The Swing in the Garden*, we learn that the first of Andrew Goderich's books already mentioned (an invention, I must repeat) is to be published by an authentic publishing house in an authentic philosophical series. Hood's aim, however, is what he calls 'super-realism'; 'I turned out', he writes, 'to be a moral realist, not ... a magic realist' (*Governor's Bridge* 127). Yet, while there are resemblances between their two attitudes, Davies's art is ultimately more playful and free-wheeling than Hood's, without the support but also without the possible constrictions of commitment to a fixed religious and philosophical position. Davies tends to create (to borrow a phrase used by André Maurois of Jorge Luis Borges) 'a game for the mind' (Borges xii).

While it would be absurd to try to pin the label of 'magic realist' on Davies, the term is more fruitful in relation to him than we might at first expect. Borges is, of course, the writer who has made most artistic capital out of inextricably confusing the real and the invented. Once again, I can only cite a brief selection of available examples. His well-known 'Tlön, Uqbar, Orbis Tertius' takes its whole imaginative flight from an invented entry in an invented '*Anglo-American Cyclopaedia* (New York, 1917)' – though I note with interest that an actual *Anglo-American Encyclopaedia,* dated 1917, is listed in the Library of Congress catalogue; and a little later in the story, references to an imaginary book about an imaginary country are rooted in the historical reality of 'the catalogues of Bernard Quaritch's book shop' (3, 5). Elsewhere, Borges is fond of writing real reviews of imaginary books ('The Approach to Al'Mu-tasim', for example), and invests his most fantastic flights of fancy with a battery of impressive-sounding scholarly documentation in which the authors are generally authentic but the view attributed to them impossible to track down in their work. 'Three Versions of Judas' is another fascinating instance, in which Borges purports to discuss a series of invented theories backed up by references to actual and invented authorities. As one of his translators has noted, in words that could be applied to Davies, 'we are transported into a realm where fact and fiction, the real and the unreal, the whole and the part, the highest and the lowest, are complementary aspects of the same continuous being' (Borges xix).

Here I can't resist pointing out another (doubtless coincidental) resemblance. Just as Robertson Davies created the imaginary Samuel Marchbanks in the 1940s as a convenient mask and *alter ego* who could be used for various comic and satiric effects, so Borges, along with Adolfo Bioy-Caseres, later invented the character of Honorio Bustos Domecq, whose *Chronicles* enable his creators to lampoon a variety of pretentious artistic and intellectual movements. Typically, however, Borges has succeeded in carrying his joke one step further. The copy of the English translation in the University of Toronto Library is catalogued under 'Bustos Domecq, Honorio' with no mention of the actual authors; and this, I find, is because it is classified as such (albeit with the insertion 'pseud.') in the Library of Congress Cataloguing in Publication Data. Within the library system, then, only the shelf number gives any clue to the actual authorship, despite the fact that the authors' names appear clearly on both spine and title page. Davies cannot quite equal this success, though Samuel Marchbanks's article entitled 'The Double Life of Robertson Davies' (first published in *Liberty,* April 1954), in which the creation gives a biographical sketch of his creator, is an extravaganza in the same vein.

My remarks on this subject are, it will be recognized, both tentative and incomplete. My aim has been to open up an aspect of Davies's achievement that has not been sufficiently explored hitherto. It is, I hope, needless to say that in the foregoing paragraphs I was not arguing that Davies is in any way influenced by Borges – that seems to me unlikely. I merely wish to emphasize that his effectiveness, like that of Borges, derives in large part from the abundant citing of documents that creates a convincing sense of authenticity. As Dunstan Ramsay notes in *World of Wonders*: 'Historians come and go, but the document remains, and it has the importance of a thing that cannot be changed or gainsaid.... It might be honest and it might be complete; on the other hand it could be thoroughly crooked or omit something of importance. But there it was, and it was all succeeding ages possessed' (19). In many respects this passage embodies all that I have been trying to say. As a statement it is important, but we have to remember that it is uttered by a historian who is himself an invention, who exists only in an imagined document. Moreover, he is hoping to create a document (*World of Wonders* itself, I suppose) that will provide a permanent record of the 'truth' of the imaginary Magnus Eisengrim whose false story – within an illusory world within a fiction – he has already fabricated! That, I submit, is a complexity as rich as anything in Borges.

I would argue, then, that Davies's technique and artistry are such that he deserves to be considered at a highly sophisticated critical level. This is not yet generally recognized – partly, I think, because there is a superficial straightforwardness about his control of narrative pace that too often disguises the complexity of what is going on beneath the surface. Adequate explorations of his range of reference and allusion will take time, and will require the cumulative efforts of many scholars with different areas of expertise. Such investigations will doubtless risk the charge of pedantry. If general readers are unable to pick up the subtleties, if they often have no idea what is fact and what is fabrication within Davies's artful mix, then why, it may be asked, should we concern ourselves with such erudite clue-following? I would insist, however, that clue-following is in fact an important part of the pleasure that we derive from such writing. Borges's created world is one through which we wander in congenial puzzlement, exploring the beckoning side-roads whenever our own special knowledge coincides with the writer's. This, surely, is part of the artistic intention and effect. Much the same is true, I think, of Davies. Whether our knowledge extends to the theatre, or music, or hagiography, or Jungian psychology, or magic, or the strange intellectual and physical passions of university academics, there will be something to absorb in addition to the engaging plot. Whenever Davies's erudition overlaps with what we know of our own 'real' world, then his world of wonder will take on a corresponding immediacy and credibility. Because of its intimate rooting in what we recognize as the here and now, his fantasy is often more compelling, and more convincing, than the standard realism of less inventive and less exuberant writers. Davies's fictional world, in the words that Borges uses of Tlön, 'is surely a labyrinth, but it is a labyrinth devised by men, a labyrinth destined to be deciphered by men' (17-18). In that resides much of its fascination.

The Not-So-Divine Comedy of Robertson Davies

In 1981 Davies published both a novel, *The Rebel Angels,* and a collection of critical commentary, *The Well-Tempered Critic: One Man's View of the Theatre and Letters in Canada.* I was invited to review them both for the *Journal of Canadian Studies* in 1982, and welcomed the opportunity to explore his range. My approach to *The Rebel Angels* by way of Davies's non-fiction enabled me, I believe, to get close to the heart of this unusual, possibly unfashionable, but certainly intriguing novel of ideas.

SAMUEL MARCHBANKS ONCE OBSERVED that 'Canada will only respect the theatre when plays are called "works"' (*Well-Tempered Critic* 27). *The Rebel Angels,* by Samuel Marchbanks's *alter ego,* is an absorbing novel, but it is many other things as well; perhaps one needs now to talk of the 'works' of Robertson Davies. Certainly, the pleasant accident that caused the publication in the same year of his latest novel and a selective gathering of his earlier writings on Canadian theatre and literature encourages a critical approach that looks to the work, if not to the works – an approach that ignores the formal generic distinctions of novel and criticism, fiction and non-fiction, and considers the unifying interests and attitudes that characterize Davies's writings as a whole.

The wide range of Davies's concerns is no news in 1982; nor is the fact that, as a prolific and versatile writer, he makes the maximum use of his specialized 'enthusiasms'. For example, he knows the drama inside and out as actor, playwright, obsessive theatre-goer, dramatic critic, and theatrical historian, and in *World of Wonders* he produced a novel that used the theatre as both subject and metaphor. In *The Rebel Angels* he turns his attention to another world of wonders, the world of the university that he came to know intimately in his eighteen years as Master of Massey College. But this involves not just a matter of collegiate architectural detail and a presentation of the fanaticisms and perversions of people who happen to be university professors; it comprises the house of intellect itself, and Davies can draw upon the full range of his intellectual resources to encompass the novel's form, content, plot, themes – its whole *ambiance*, in fact.

The Well-Tempered Critic reprints a selection of Davies's commentaries on drama and literature between 1940 and 1979. Much of it was produced under less than ideal journalistic conditions, and its wit, intelligence, and grace are astonishing. Along with *A Voice from the Attic* (1960) and *The Enthusiasms of Robertson Davies* (which Judith Skelton Grant edited from his non-Canadian literary criticism in 1979), it embodies the experience of an intelligent lover of books and drama over a lifetime of voracious but by no means indiscriminate reading and theatre-going, one who fosters an independent Canadian cultural tradition without exaggerating the extent of the national achievement. His articles and reviews collected here represent his own personal attempt to qualify the general truth that 'informed criticism is an uncommon thing in the periodicals of our country' (58). (But why, I wonder, did he decide to appropriate Northrop Frye's title for his book? To distinguish himself at all costs from that generally ill-tempered critic Marchbanks? Perhaps, but it will surely cause confusion.)

As a reviewer, Davies displays a remarkable capacity to keep in balance his responsibility to both author and reader. He can be sympathetic and informative where one might well have expected the opposite; thus I did not, I confess, anticipate that much of value would be forthcoming from his review of Irving Layton's *A Red Carpet for the Sun*, since the personalities of reviewer and author seemed wholly distinct. But Davies used the occasion to broaden his readers' conception of what poetry is and can be, and moreover (in 1959, when Layton was so obviously a raging bull in the genteel china-shop of Canadian literature) to emphasize what needed to be emphasized – Layton's 'high-coloured, abounding delight in the physical world' (218) and his achievement as 'a man who pierces through triviality to something that is enduring' (219). Yet Davies does not, when the occasion requires it, shirk the critic's awkward responsibility to be cruel in order to be kind. His insistence, when Marie-Claire Blais was being lionized as a literary prodigy, that her early fiction bore too uncomfortable a resemblance to the world of *Cold Comfort Farm* (221, 245) was courageous – a minority viewpoint that needed to be expressed.

Doubtless his editor has omitted some reviews and articles that would read oddly – perhaps unfortunately – today, but for the most part Davies's judgements have stood the test of time remarkably well. In April 1941, for example, he told his readers in *The Peterborough Examiner* that 'three first-rate books' had been published within the year. These were identified as the translation of Ringuet's *Trente Arpents,* E.J. Pratt's *Brébeuf and His Brethren,* and Sinclair Ross's *As For Me and My House* (142). What critic writing forty years later could match that for an evaluative bull's eye? If anyone wonders about Hugh MacLennan's *Barometer Rising,* it was not published until six months after the article in question and was duly praised by Davies within ten days of its appearance (148-49).

But the theatrical section of the book shows Davies in yet another light: as one who might be called – though these days it sounds more like an insult than a compliment – a cultural politician. When the whole story of the development of a native Canadian theatre is told, the name of Robertson Davies will loom large, not merely as playwright but as propagandist and moulder of public taste. 'Why Not a Canadian Drama?' he asked as early as 1944: 'In the opinion of the present writer something could be done which might eventually give us a Canadian theatre and which would soon give us a body of Canadian drama' (24). By 1951, he was again arguing the same point – 'I am quite sure that a robust Canadian theatre would bring forth a large body of Canadian plays, some of them good enough for export' (60) – in a contribution to the Royal Commission on National

Development in the Arts, Letters and Sciences. (It is typical of Davies, incidentally, that he should grace so bureaucratic an occasion with a lively dialogue presented as a dramatic script – a demonstration of the imaginative qualities waiting to be released.) And he was in on the Stratford Festival from the beginning, not only as adviser – he served on the Board of Governors for the first seventeen years of the Festival's existence – but as a shrewd critic who nurtured both the interest and the taste of a new, keen, but inexperienced theatre-going public. The accounts of early productions are valuable as historical documents though they can't be tested like book reviews: who can summon the spectre of a past performance? But it is fascinating to watch Davies educating his readers, telling them both what they should look for and what they should not expect. He is generous to a company that needed support and encouragement, but never at the expense of the high standards without which such a Festival has no *raison d'être. The Well-Tempered Critic* can teach us much (particularly if we are academics) about the humane and readable expression of firm and judicious criticism.

But what has all this to do with a novel like *The Rebel Angels*? Much more than one might initially expect. We find in both books interest in a wide range of human experience in all sorts of manifestations, and an emphasis on wit, polish, and civilized discussion. And there is one remarkable entry in *The Well-Tempered Critic* concerning 'Light-Hearted Scholarship' (190-91) that, though written as early as 1953, offers an ideal introduction to the novel of 1981. Can Judith Grant have brought it back to Davies's attention when she was beginning her compilation, and so set off a creative chain-reaction? At all events, we have references to 'scholars in the tradition of Rabelais' and to 'the snail-like progress towards the PH.D.' (one of the chief characters in *The Rebel Angels* is writing her doctoral dissertation on Rabelais), and there is even mention of '*the* man in the Borrow field' suggesting an interest in Romany lore and language (the same character is part gypsy). It is as if these chance-gathered associations combined like the *atomes crochus* in John Livingstone Lowes's

The Road to Xanadu and reappeared over a quarter of a century later in novel form (and I solemnly swear that I mentally composed this sentence before noticing that there is actually a reference to Lowes's book in the same article).

Perhaps the best way of communicating a concise sense of the paradoxical richness of *The Rebel Angels* is to suggest that in it the subject matter of Rabelais is filtered through the fictional method of Thomas Love Peacock. But that won't quite do, since the first thing that needs to be said about the novel is that it is compulsively readable. The temptation is to read too quickly, for the simple reason that one wants to know what will happen – not so much because it is a novel of suspense but because (to use an appropriate image for Davies) one wants to see what the author-magician will pull out of his hat, or mortar-board, to tie up the main strands of his peculiar plot. Indeed, I recommend two initial readings of the book, one fast to get the full feel of the whole, one slow in order to savour the wit and wisdom that Davies so generously supplies.

The novel flows smoothly, but has a deceptively intricate form. The role of story-teller is shared between two people (one male, one female; one a professor, one a student) whose alternating accounts interweave without undue overlap to provide the continuing narrative. But beneath this layer lies the organizing form of a symposium – not in the modern academic sense of a conference (though that, too, is appropriate for the university setting) but in the ancient Greek sense, which my dictionary defines as 'a convivial meeting, usually following dinner, for drinking, conversation, and intellectual entertainment'. Indeed, a central scene, where the Peacockian method is most evident, involves a Guest Night at a University of Toronto graduate college, complete with closed court and fountain, called Ploughwright (no prizes for identification). Can this be the first serious novel in which a table-plan is reproduced within the text? At any rate Davies escorts us in and out of various academic and not-so-academic conversations, and at a first reading (for plot) the scene may appear as a long-winded excrescence. A second reading reveals its centrality (it is literally in the middle of the book), and the subjects discussed – the idea of a university, cultural fossils, the Fall of Man, the Devil, murder, the nature of evil, Rabelais, 'Indecency and even filth' (175) – are the major themes of the book.

'Indecency and even filth'. This is doubtless the aspect of the novel that will get most initial attention – legitimately enough, as it happens, but it will probably be for the wrong reasons. One might say that Davies has rung all possible changes on Yeats's observation, in 'Crazy Jane Talks with the Bishop', that 'love has pitched his mansion in/The place of excrement'. There is Professor Oazy Froats, whose research project involves the scientific examination and analysis of human *faeces*; the *bomari,* a gypsy process for restoring ancient violins that requires generous supplies of high-quality horse-dung; Professor Clement Hollier, whose 'rooting about in the kitchen-middens and trash-heaps of the Middle Ages' (28) includes an interest in filth-therapy; Father Simon Darcourt, whose love of food – 'How many visions of Eternity have been born of low blood-sugar? (This as I prepare a third piece of toast thickly spread with honey.)' (57) – is a mirror-image of the same concern; and Professor Urquhart McVarish, whose end is appropriate, unpleasant, messy, and too important to the resolution of the plot to be revealed here.

But this is not just an original, *risqué* subject about which Davies can be daringly witty while keeping more or less within the bounds of the old-fashioned conventions and proprieties. It opens up to provide a dominant and unifying image for the whole book – not merely an opportunity for verbal play like the description of a history of the university as 'three heavy volumes of unilluminated crap' (13) but (like Dickens's dust-heaps in *Our Mutual Friend*) a way of classifying scenes and welding the individual parts of the novel together. Other examples of this interconnecting imagery include the 'great heaps of stuff' (14) that constitute Francis Cornish's accumulation of art treasures (the collector as dung-beetle?) and even the presentation of the university itself as a wonderfully complex mass/mess in which the sublime blossoms out of the dirt. It is in fact a novel of transformation, metamorphosis, and endless mutability. Professor Froats searched 'in the dung-heap for a jewel he suspects may be there' (157); a minor character argues that civilization depends upon two things: 'the discovery that fermentation produces alcohol, and voluntary ability to inhibit defecation' (177). When Froats's research is described as 'discovering the value that lies in what is despised and rejected' (250), the subject is raised into cosmic, even quasi-religious terms. The novel presents the university as a microcosm of our whole world of wonders in what might be called a vision of fundamental recycling.

But why have I called this review 'The Not-So-Divine Comedy of Robertson Davies'? Because I wish to emphasize his splendid capacity for artifice, for 'making' in the sense of imaginative creation. The book ends with marriage-bells (I won't reveal for whom the bells ring), and this is so unusual in a modern novel that the age-old convention comes almost as an original surprise. All Davies's novels are technically comedies, and the so-called Salterton trilogy offered the comic pattern in the most direct form possible. The so-called Deptford trilogy was well-made in a different sense, since the whole action is determined by and contained within the perfect circle of a weighted snowball. *The Rebel Angels* finds its sense of an ending unfashionably by means of a wedding (albeit an idiosyncratic one), and this piece of whimsical but satisfying artifice serves to draw attention to the decidedly unorthodox variations on comic form that are played out in the rest of the book. In my title I allude to the Florentine trilogy-writer to demonstrate that Davies, by contrast, is concerned here with an unashamedly earthly (and earthy) comedy. This novel is, as Davies has stated on more than one occasion within my hearing, a celebration of the university as a human (and therefore fallible) institution, but it is also a celebration of the world, of the jewel within the lotus that is also the jewel within the shit. Contemporary writing has a rather tiresome habit of exaggerating the shit and neglecting the jewel;

Davies has returned to the supposedly outmoded convention of 'the happy ending' to jolt us into the realization that what is as old as the (earthy) hills can seem challengingly and refreshingly new.

G. Wilson Knight (once a teacher at Trinity College and worthy of a professorship at Spook) taught us to read Shakespearean plays spatially as well as temporally, for the patterns of image and idea as well as for the linear progression of plot. Northrop Frye (at home in Ploughwright if not in Spook) invites us to examine a literary work as we might look at a painting: peer closely to admire the minutiae of the brushwork but also stand back to appreciate the shape of the total design. *The Rebel Angels* responds well to both methods. Almost at the end of the book is another of those comic funerals (cf. Boy Staunton's in *The Manticore*) that Davies stage-manages (I use the word deliberately) so well, and at least metaphorically the funeral baked meats furnish forth the marriage-tables with comedic blatancy and zest. Weddings and funerals; meals (there are many in the novel, and this is another of Davies's specialities – cf. Father Blazon in the restaurant in *Fifth Business*) and defecation; or, in the metaphor introduced into the text by the impossible but irrepressible Parlabane, root and crown; these are not just rich bonuses cluttering the texture of a great buggerly Rabelaisian novel but controlled patterns of word and imagery that revolve like satellites around its central theme. Davies mixes a strong brew, and (like the love-potion prepared within the novel) it is composed of some very strange ingredients indeed; but one can be sure that nothing is irrelevant to the whole in *The Rebel Angels*.

Here is another reason, of course, why the novel demands to be read more than once. To extend Frye's analogy, we can approach this book as if it were not merely painting but sculpture – a three-dimensional construct that we can walk around and even move into. Having followed the linear progression, we need to go back to explore the intellectual and artistic connections. *The Rebel Angels* is, in the *patois* of our age, a great read, but its traditional qualities in no way lull us into the soul-deadening producer-consumer syndrome that belongs more to the world as supermarket than to the world as university. Davies's intellectual curiosity is infectious; he invites us into a bracing fictional world in which the permutations and interconnections seem unending. It is a place where we can exercise our minds and experience the joy of re-creation if not of creation. Above all, it is a pleasure-ground where we grow even as we are entertained and prodded to entertain ourselves. The myth of the rebel angels, Davies suggests, explains the existence of the true university professor, and as novelist Davies proves to be a rebel angel himself. The adventure of following him can sometimes be perilous (one thinks of *The Manticore* again) but it is never dull; in this novel it is by turns amusing, disturbing, chastening, and for some it will doubtless be shocking, but it is characterized throughout by what Davies – through, of all people, Parlabane – calls at one point (118) 'the big salutary humour that saves'.

Margaret Laurence's *The Diviners*: The Problems of Close Reading

Margaret Laurence was clearly one of the finest of our contemporary novelists. Because she was also the best-loved, however, critics have been reluctant to make discriminating judgements about her work. I had been unhappy about certain aspects of *The Diviners* ever since it was originally published, and at last expressed my view in the following article which appeared in the *Journal of Canadian Studies* in 1988. It pays Laurence the compliment of bringing high critical standards to bear on her work. While it finds weaknesses in this particular novel, it helps ultimately, I believe, to throw into relief her most enduring qualities as a writer of fiction.

MARGARET LAURENCE'S FELLOW NOVELIST Marian Engel was one of the first to comment in print on the critical unease surrounding *The Diviners* (1974), the last novel in the Manawaka series. Engel reports that she was continually invited to review the book in circumstances which suggested that she was not the first choice: 'I knew enough about the rules of the game to understand that the first-choice people hadn't liked the book and didn't want to say so.' She then records the private response of an unidentified male critic: 'I didn't like it. I thought *A Bird in the House* was marvellous, an almost perfect book. Beside it, *The Diviners* looked big and sloppy.' Engel goes on to remark: 'the Toronto critics ... are terrified of the monumental, particularly in the works of women' (72).[1] There are, however, at least three

1 Engel, who reviewed the book for *Chatelaine* in May 1974, also wrote about *The Diviners* in 'It's the Grit: Laurence Is Unforgettable Because She Is Us', *The Globe and Mail* [Toronto] 19 Apr. 1975, reprinted in W.H. New, ed., *Margaret Laurence,* Critical Views of Canadian Writers (Toronto: McGraw-Hill Ryerson, 1977) 219-21.

elementary (and revealing) lapses of logic in that last judgement: a) the critics in question were by no means confined to Toronto; b) 'monumental' is not the same as 'big and sloppy'; and c) the implication of sexist prejudice is both unsubstantiated and unlikely (would these conveniently unnamed commentators have passed a similar judgement on, say, *Middlemarch* or *The Golden Notebook*?).[2]

In the same issue of the *Journal of Canadian Studies* in which Engel's article appeared, guest editor Michael Peterman gave different – and far more cogent – reasons for his own unease: he found the novel's 'explicit political qualities ... more clearly defined and more urgently felt' than in Laurence's earlier work, and argued that a more 'delicate balance between personal vision, artistic skill, and public purpose' had been achieved in the previous books in the series. In addition, he pointed out that 'it is possible to argue that what troubles many readers of *The Diviners* is not so much the fact that Morag is a liberated heroine who, as Engel puts it, achieves her "apocalypse" without "the agency of men"; rather, it is that the three men in Morag's life fail to take hold as flesh and blood characters' (103, 104).

Later commentary (whether by men or women) has tended to move on to the positive side. The novel won the Governor General's award despite Engel's claim of dissatisfaction in influential

---

2 It is worth noting that the reviews of *The Diviners* listed in the section devoted to Laurence in Robert Lecker and Jack David, eds., *The Annotated Bibliography of Canada's Major Authors: Volume One* (Downsview, ON: ECW, 1979) 96-98, do not support Engel's insinuations. Out of sixteen reviews, only four can be said to include critical reservations. Two of these appeared in American journals, and one in the Vancouver-based *Canadian Literature.* And only two of the four were written by men. Moreover, both the women who registered criticisms were novelists, the American Marge Piercy and (much less emphatically) the Canadian Audrey Thomas. For a fuller bibliographical listing of reviews of *The Diviners,* see C. Thomas, *Manawaka* 209-12.

places. Moreover, it is now well established as a text frequently taught in schools and universities. Scholarly discussion has even tended to focus on its 'monumental' qualities and the way in which it rounds off the Manawaka series thematically. Nonetheless, the unease remains, and I have to confess that I share it. *The Diviners* seems to me an admirably ambitious, often deeply moving, but at the same time decidedly flawed work, for reasons that are compatible with Peterman's but go beyond his inevitably brief and assertive account. On the one hand, I believe, the book demands to be read closely; on the other, a close reading reveals some fundamental weaknesses as well as expected strengths. The problems centre crucially upon the verbal and structural elements of the novel, and I intend in the following pages to examine each of these in turn.

IN THE OPENING PARAGRAPHS of the book, Morag Gunn is immediately preoccupied with 'style of writing' (4); over three hundred pages later, the final one-sentence paragraph reads: 'Morag returned to the house, to write the remaining private and fictional words, and to set down her title' (370). We realize, of course, as several critics have pointed out, that the title in question will be 'The Diviners'. The earlier books in the series conformed – despite bold uses of flashbacks, interior monologues and fantasies, and occasional typographical effects to indicate newspaper headlines and media announcements – to a fairly conventional tradition of fictive realism. So does much of *The Diviners,* but in addition it is obviously feeling towards a post-modernist or self-reflexive mode. Each chapter begins with Morag as novelist wrestling with the problems of novel-writing as well as with daily domestic chores. We are continually reminded that her memories of the past are not pure recollections but subtly crafted creations of an imaginative novelist who knows that she has embroidered on the prosaic facts ('*I am remembering myself composing this interpretation*'; '*I don't recall when I invented that one. I can remember it, though, very clearly*'; '*And that is the end of the totally invented memories*' (7, 8, 9)). Even a

'Memorybank Movie', we realize on reflection, presupposes a movie-maker. Above all, Morag is continually drawing attention to language by challenging her own words, questioning meanings, and generally alerting us to tricks of emphasis and rhetoric. This should encourage us, as readers, to be especially attentive to the use of language within the novel.

A flexible narrative style is evident from the first page. The opening ('The river flowed both ways', etc.) is at once formal and beautiful, and apparently derives from a detached and seemingly omniscient narrator. But the writing soon reflects Morag's interior monologue, which consists of abrupt, staccato, and often colloquial phrases. These two styles are soon found in juxtaposition within a single paragraph. Thus one paragraph begins with detached third-person narration – 'Morag read Pique's letter again, made coffee and sat looking out at the river' – but ends in Morag's idiom: 'No wonder the kids felt themselves to be children of the apocalypse' (4). We find ourselves constantly moving between an external and an internal perspective. We also discover that Laurence inserts indications of Morag's verbal facility at each stage of her growth from small child to mature novelist, and that these examples of developing idiom are not only present when dialogue is reproduced but also blended into the narrative commentary. For example, when Morag's parents are dying, we are told that 'Mrs Pearl's face looked scary when she put Morag to bed'; and when, next morning, the neighbour tells Morag that her parents have 'passed on ... to a happier land', she does not believe that 'they have gone to a real good place' (13). Clearly, 'scary' and 'real good' are the words of the child, not of Morag the adult novelist – although it is Laurence the adult novelist who has intermingled the language-levels for her own deliberate effect.

This process continues throughout the book. As readers, we listen to Morag growing up verbally as well as physically and intellectually – from 'It smells like pee or something' (24), through the recurring constructions 'is why' and 'what means...?' and her flaunting of bad language picked up from Christie and school ('Why doesn't Prin go and get her own goddamn blistering bloody shitty jelly doughnuts?' (36)), to an awareness of proper and improper speech ('... which makes Morag feel bad, that is, feel *badly*' (89)), and her (temporary) renunciation of the same bad language ('If you swear at fourteen it only makes you look cheap' (89)). We are also constantly reminded of Morag's fascination with the sounds of words (such as '*spittoon*' and '*mooner*' (11, 42)) and with their associations and meanings ('*Scavenger*' and '*Nuisance Grounds*', '*bluebottles*' (30, 33)), just as we are made aware of her precocious sense of the differences between levels of speech. In the second chapter, for example, when still at the age of seven, Morag begins to recognize the deficiencies in Prin's way of talking:

> Prin's family was English. She has told Morag about it. Prin's father was a remittance man. That meant his family in The Old Country didn't like him so good, and were pretty mean and all, even though he was a gentleman, a real one, and so they made him come to this country where he didn't want to come to, and for awhile, there, they sent him money, and then they didn't. He wasn't much of a farmer but he meant well, Prin said. She was the only child and wasn't none too bright (you were supposed to say wasn't *any* too bright but Prin didn't know that) ... (28-29)

Here Laurence moves from the distanced narrator to Morag and then to Morag's reproduction and criticism of Prin's speech. A full appreciation of this effect requires considerable linguistic sensitivity on the part of readers.

Unless we are alert to the incongruities of language, we shall miss many of Laurence's subtleties. When Morag encounters Millie Christopherson at Simlow's Ladies' Wear, for instance, Morag's belief that 'Millie has very Good Taste' is immediately undermined by Millie's speech: 'Good Taste is learnt, ... and I am going to learn a tiny bit of it to *you*.' And a few lines later: 'You catch on quick, dear. It's a pleasure to tell you things' (91). But the same close reading that responds to the use and misuse of language in such instances can also reveal difficulties within Morag's – and Laurence's – own style. For example: '*Hill Street was below the town; it was inhabited by those who had never and never would make good*' (24). '... had never ... make ...'? The sentence occurs in the novel's present when Morag the novelist is thinking back over her early days. Is the grammatical lapse Morag's or Laurence's? A little later, we encounter the following: '*everyone is constantly changing their own past*' (49). Authorial slip or deliberate effect? Later still, the experienced novelist makes the common error of using 'presently' instead of 'currently' (173) – a minor lapse, to be sure, but odd in one who, we are told, aims at 'exact use of words' (43). Other examples occur in passages where the error *may* be attributable to the younger Morag, but with these instances in mind we can never be certain. An especially problematic example occurs at the time when Morag has just left school and is working on the local newspaper. Her editor tells her that she can 'clean up the punctuation, grammar and spelling' of their correspondents; but, since we have just been told that she 'calls him Lachlan, like everybody else in town does' (125), we may well be sceptical about her qualifications. This example is complex because it inevitably raises the question: what precisely is Laurence's intention here? Is she expecting us to note the irony and draw our own conclusions, as is obviously the case with Millie Christopherson? The assumption seems not unreasonable, given the stylistic range I have already noted, yet an uneasy doubt remains that Laurence may have stimulated a level of close reading that her prose cannot invariably sustain.

Such thoughts lead naturally to a consideration of our impressions of the adult novel-writing Morag as they are conveyed to us through her own words. We can certainly see the adult Morag emerging convincingly from the child, but the credibility of Morag as established novelist is another matter. Thus her ambivalent attitude towards slang is puzzling. When Maudie uses the phrase 'Right on', Morag thinks to herself: 'Right on. Dear little Lord Jesus, what did that mean? Like saying Great, Stupendous. No meaning at all' (44). Yet she accepts, and apparently understands, Pique's slang, and her own speech and thoughts are filled with colloquialisms. She even uses 'great' in this slang sense two pages later (46). Earlier in the book she has referred to '*totally individuated persons (as the pretentious phrase has it, when describing okay fiction*)' (10). The judgement on pompous jargon is characteristic and understandable, but '*okay fiction*' jars. Would a novelist of Morag's stature express herself, even informally, in this way? And should she? Maudie's husband, Alf Smith, is nicknamed 'A-Okay' for his verbal (or sub-verbal) trademark. Are we to connect Morag's usage with that fact? The Smiths' style seems infectious: 'They had rented the farms, with an option to buy, always supposing A-Okay could whomp up the necessary money ...' (82). 'Whomp up'? One is tempted to quote Morag's phrase back at her: 'No meaning at all'. If this is supposed to be Smith talk – even a parody of Smith talk – it remains disturbing.

Individually, these may seem small details. They accumulate, however, and eventually we come to doubt whether Morag possesses the respect for language that might be assumed in a serious novelist. She is sensitive to other people's clichés – Jules's, for example (133) – but not to her own. Moreover, she habitually thinks in slang. One day she is irritated by an early-morning telephone call requesting literary advice and assuming that her writing is automatically accepted for publication. Laurence reproduces Morag's inner response: '*Oh, sure. Just bash out any old crap and rake in the millions. I get my plots from the telephone directory*' (20). This is doubtless intended as a human touch, and I may well be laying myself open to the charge of romantic idealism in wondering if a novelist ought to think in a more dignified manner. Of course even novelists employ slang – we all say 'okay' continually – but there is something about Morag's *flaunting* of her slang that rings false, especially when we remember that concern for 'exact use of words' (43).

Surprisingly little attention has yet been paid to the verbal texture of *The Diviners*. However, Marge Piercy concentrates on this aspect of the book in her review that originally appeared in

The New York Times Book Review (23 June 1974). She praises the 'strength and zest' of the Memorybank Movies, and responds to the 'chewy idiom' of the Manawaka sections of the novel. But she has reservations about the scenes set in the present, which she characterizes as 'staider, flabby with words like *albeit* and conventional nature descriptions, two adjectives (often with a *somewhat* or an *almost*) where one or a proper verb would do, weak Latinate verbs like *discern* and *attain*' (212). This is perceptive – an example to Canadian critics who rarely seem to be aware of such matters. I would merely add that the problem of Morag's style, as I see it, may be identified as an uneasy combination of this rather flat, conventional prose with the use of a slangy vernacular in contexts where slang, virtually by definition, cannot provide the necessary precision for subtle distinctions or profound insights.

Another brief discussion may be found in W.H. New's excellent article, 'Every Now and Then: Voice and Language in Laurence's *The Stone Angel*'. Despite his emphasis on an earlier novel, New begins with a consideration of *The Diviners*. Morag, he notes, 'retrieves from memory not just the events of her life and the emotions she at least once attached to them, but also the language of different stages in her development.' The result is the creation of a world that 'sometimes rises to eloquence' and sometimes 'descends to the banal'. Because it 'records the different reaches of the Canadian English tongue', New is prepared to defend this: 'That there should be this unevenness of diction does not seem to me a flaw in the work, but instead a deliberate effect: the novelist-author forcing the novelist-character to explore the limits of her verbal understanding, so that in turn the reader might learn the connection between mode of speech and pattern of thought' (171). This is, I believe, an accurate assessment of Laurence's intention; where I differ from New is in questioning whether this intention is fully achieved in practice. Has Morag eradicated the undesirable (because insufficiently precise) language of earlier stages in her development? Are we convinced, from what we see of Morag's own 'mode of speech and pattern of thought', that she is the accomplished novelist that Laurence evidently believes her to be? To take the inquiry one stage further, is Laurence too emotionally involved in Morag's situation to view her with the necessary detachment that, at least in traditional theories of fiction, the novel requires? These are questions that are rarely asked but I believe they need to be asked. New's useful reference to 'novelist-author' and 'novelist-character' should help us to focus more clearly on the all-important distinction between Laurence as novelist and Morag as novelist. It is in this relation that we may find the complex origins of the unease that troubles many readers. To follow this line of thinking, it will be necessary to make brief forays into matters as diverse as biographical connections and concepts of realism, but all these converge ultimately on a consideration of the structure and formal cohesion of the novel.

A NOVELIST WRITING A NOVEL about a novelist writing a novel may well be exploiting a post-modernist preoccupation, but complicated questions about the relation between artist and protagonist are inevitably involved. This is especially true in the present case when, as is well known, Margaret Laurence in the early 1970s was an established novelist known to have escaped from a confining Prairie town and to be living in a riverside cottage near Peterborough, Ontario. The intimate connections between novelist and subject are manifest. While Laurence is doubtless perfectly justified in insisting that *The Diviners* 'is not autobiographical', she has also acknowledged that certain details – Morag's poem about the Wise Men (64), *The 60th Canadian Field Artillery Battery Book* (72), the Louis Riel poem (199), the character of Royland the diviner, an admiration for Catharine Parr Traill, even the plaid pin that connects the novel with *The Stone Angel* (351), and the river that seemed to flow both ways – are drawn from her own experience.[3]

3 See Fabre 208 and Laurence, *Heart* 146, 162, 163, 219. In addition,

These resemblances are not, however, confined to certain biographical patterns, memories, or details; they extend to specific references and tricks of style. Thus a short story that Morag writes at university and shows to Brooke Skelton (155-56) is identical in plot to a story Laurence herself contributed to *Vox*, the United College literary magazine.[4] Again, Morag makes several allusions to the 'Black Celt' in her temperament (186, 264, 337). This is precisely the term Laurence uses of herself in an interview with Donald Cameron that took place while she was writing *The Diviners*: 'I've got this terrible tendency toward what I call the Black Celt in myself' (D. Cameron 100). And here is Laurence discussing *The Diviners* with Margaret Atwood: 'I know it's bloody difficult, it's one of the most difficult things to do, writing about a writer. But I had to. At first, I had her as a painter, but what the hell do I know about painting?' (Atwood, 'Face' 25). The tone, rhythms, and language are indistinguishable from Morag talking about her own novel-writing problems within the narrative.

Laurence even told Cameron that, while at work on the novel that became *The Diviners*, she wrote a letter to a friend and found that it was written in the style of her protagonist (102). This is indeed plausible, since many stylistic resemblances are shared by author and main character. For example, Morag has a tendency towards exaggeration that recurs again and again. Here is the younger Morag: 'The Nuisance Grounds contain a billion trillion heaps of old muck' (68). And here is the older: '[Bridie] has

Morag's friendship with Ella Gerson and her family is based in part on Laurence's introduction to the 'Winnipeg Old Left' through Adele Wiseman (see Morley 20), while her residence in Vancouver and Hampstead clearly derives from Laurence's own experience. Furthermore, Morag is a name remarkably close to Margaret, and Morag and Laurence are the same age.

4 This story, 'Tal des Walde', has since been reprinted in the Margaret Laurence special issue of the *Journal of Canadian Fiction* 27 (1980): 15-22.

an old-fashioned washing machine, into which she dumps approximately three tons of clothing' (311). In view of this tendency it is odd that Morag describes Julie Kazlik as 'slapdash' when she says that 'thousands' of Manawaka people may be living in Vancouver (248). But it is even more instructive to compare Morag's exaggerations with the following from Laurence's non-fiction essay 'Down East': 'You listen to the radio in the morning and hear the city's air-pollution index and wonder if you should venture as far as Yonge and Bloor without a gasmask.' Or, from 'The Shack': 'I sometimes feel sorry for the people in speedboats who spend their weekends zinging up and down the river at about a million miles an hour' (*Heart* 160, 188. 'Down East', incidentally, was one of Laurence's non-fiction contributions to a Vancouver newspaper – another biographical link with Morag). We come to realize that at least some of Morag's weaknesses as a writer are those of Laurence herself. In turn, this may lead to two related questions: is Laurence closer to Morag – in style, attitude, and basic responses – than she knows? and is this as much a liability as an asset?

'I never had the feeling [in childhood] that as a woman I couldn't choose the profession that I wanted to choose. Two of my aunts were nurses, my step-mother had been a high-school teacher of English and my mother had been a pianist' (Twigg 265). Laurence indicates here how far her own early life differed from Morag's. At the same time she obviously wanted to present in *The Diviners* a portrait of the artist as woman novelist that would inevitably be based, at however much a remove, upon her own creative experience. When she embarked upon the writing of her last Manawaka novel, however, Laurence was faced with a number of serious literary problems. First, she had already portrayed the lives of four women who had grown up in Manawaka; all were Scots in origin and had come from middle-class backgrounds, so there was clearly a danger of repeating herself or working a vein that was already exhausted. Second, Morag was destined to become a novelist, but Laurence had already presented a potential writer in Vanessa MacLeod. Furthermore, in *A Bird in the House* she had already drawn extensively on her early experience both as individual and as future novelist from a Prairie town; indeed, she described this volume of linked short stories (before she embarked on *The Diviners*) as 'the only semi-autobiographical fiction I have ever written' (*Heart* 16). Third, she needed to extract her protagonist from Manawaka, the setting with which she was most familiar, and give her a life that was as distinct as possible from her own.

I suggest that Laurence solved some of these problems but in so doing created others. Morag Gunn is yet another descendant of Scots immigrants, but, by what at first seems a brilliant stroke, she is made to grow up on 'the wrong side of the tracks' so that we get a new and refreshingly different perspective on Manawaka society. Laurence had to ignore the fact that two writers out of five Manawaka heroines constituted an unusually high percentage, but there was obviously nothing that could be done about that. Getting a child from an underprivileged background to university would be tricky, but this was the only – or, perhaps, the least unlikely – way of providing an escape into a more literary atmosphere. Finally, Morag would need inevitably, in the interests of her career, to move to an urban publishing centre. Toronto was the obvious choice, despite the fact that the university milieu of Toronto in the late 1940s and early 1950s was outside Laurence's range of personal experience. As she has admitted, 'natural imagery comes to me easily whereas urban imagery does not' (Fabre 207). Here the structuring of the novel demanded a change of direction that conflicted with Laurence's commitment to meticulous literary realism.

Despite its metafictional accretions, *The Diviners* is still set well within the realistic mode.[5] The Manawaka portrayed here is the same Manawaka so accurately presented in the earlier books,

5 A discussion of *The Diviners* and realism is obviously complicated by the element of fabrication implicit in the 'Memorybank Movies'. It seems clear, however, that Laurence does not intend the metafictional

although seen from a different angle. We need to believe in Morag as a realistic character against a realistic background just as we have believed in Hagar and Rachel and Stacey and Vanessa. This being so, it is surely not unreasonable to query Morag's successful and apparently smooth progress towards enrolment in an arts programme at university. The financial details are (barely and vaguely) covered by the convenient fund set up by Henry Pearl at the time Morag was orphaned (15). But the intellectual and cultural aspects are more puzzling. Morag is brought up in a home virtually without culture. Christie's stories are imaginatively compelling, but she is given little intellectual encouragement. The one lesson in literary criticism that she receives at home is Christie's downgrading of a great Wordsworth poem ('this crap') for a pretentious piece from Macpherson's *Ossian* (51-52).[6] Few books – only a Bible in Gaelic and

qualities of the novel to detract from the realistic presentation of Manawaka and other settings. Once again, close reading can raise difficulties. For instance, we are presumably intended to accept Pique's description of her experiences in Manitoba (86-87) at face value; however, given Morag's earlier undermining of her own reliability as a narrator, it would be difficult to counter an interpretation claiming that Pique's account, which has a suspiciously representative neatness, has already been embroidered (by Pique) into fiction. But I shall ignore these troubling complexities in the discussion to follow.

6 I cannot accept Clara Thomas's description of 'I Wandered Lonely as a Cloud' as 'a poem which has become a cliché for British educational imperialism, especially as practised on children of the tropics who never saw a daffodil' ('Chariot' 56). Morley makes a similar reference to 'cultural imperialism' (128). But Christie does not criticize the poem for political reasons but because 'clouds don't wander lonely, for the good christ's sake' (63). There is no hint of imperialism in Wordsworth's poem, though it can of course be distorted and abused by bad teachers, whether Christie or certain advocates of Wordsworth in the tropics. Besides, would it be culturally imperialistic to teach *The Diviners* outside Canada to students who had never seen a prairie?

The Clans and Tartans of Scotland beyond those already mentioned – are in evidence. We are occasionally told that Morag works hard, but we rarely see her working. The glimpses we receive of her progress at school, with the exception of Miss Melrose's explanation of 'what was good and bad in writing' (99), are hardly inspiring – and even this sounds superficial (avoid Pathetic Fallacy and prefer Browning to Wordsworth).[7] Morag is proud that 'the teachers hate her', and the school scenes are generally framed by such sentiments as 'Who gives a christly damn anyway? ... Who cares?' (50, 54, 55). All this may be credible and human in itself, but it is, to say the least, an unpromising start for a future novelist.

In fact, Morag is a strange bundle of contradictions, an unlikely blend of innocence and experience. At the age of almost twenty, she doesn't understand 'stretch-marks' (176) – despite her unprotected upbringing in wrong-side-of-the-tracks Manawaka and its nature-in-the-raw High School. For all her experience of social prejudice, she has to have the phrase 'lumpen proletariat' explained to her at university and at the same time 'first truly realizes that English is not the only literature' (143, 151). A little earlier, within a year or so of entering university, she not only fails to recognize a reproduction of Botticelli's *Venus Rising from the Waves* – which would be excusable – but seriously believes it to be the work of a modern painter from Winnipeg (127). The more Laurence emphasizes the contrast between Morag's upbringing and, say, Vanessa MacLeod's, the more difficult it becomes to believe in her transformation into a gifted university student and a creative artist.

The presentation of Morag's development as a writer is itself decidedly spotty. As a child, in a burst of religious enthusiasm,

---

7 Are we supposed to remember this incident when, over a hundred pages later, Morag indulges in some particularly blatant 'Pathetic Fallacy' while watching 'the swallow children' (242)? Another critical problem in close reading.

she writes an unremarkable poem about the Wise Men and composes her own versions of stories that are based on Christie's (64, 42, 70). She refuses to allow a story to be printed in the school magazine, but later submits one successfully to the university newspaper. This is perfunctory enough, but we also hear curiously little about her novels, and what we learn does not sound especially promising. *Spear of Innocence* (what a title!), with its heroine who goes to work in a 'seedy nightclub', involves subject matter about which Morag would have known little. As we are told blandly, 'she has never in her life known anyone remotely like Lilac' (184). The problem of credibility arises again when we are asked to believe that a novel could have been published in Canada in the early 1950s in which the heroine aborts herself. *Prospero's Child* is a moral fantasy (270); *Jonah,* about a British Columbia fisherman, also seems outside Morag's range of experience (299); *Shadow of Eden* is historical – Piper Gunn and all that (341). There is also a collection of short stories of which we are told nothing beyond its title, *Presences* (295). B.W. Powe has legitimately asked: 'Who are [Morag's] influences? Why does she write? Who is she writing for?' (139). There is some discussion of point of view and general fictional problems at one point (184), but it is strangely superficial – and we are given no specimen extracts from her work. Oddly, we are offered instead two extended series of extracts from reviews (214, 272) that smack of rather cheap parody. The amount of Morag's work is intriguingly similar to Laurence's own, but we get no sense, as we do with Laurence herself, of an organic *corpus.* What is ultimately disappointing about Morag the writer – and this may be explained but not excused by Laurence's concern to avoid autobiographical references at this point – is that Morag is so obviously inferior as a novelist to her creator.

Most of this artistic development – if that is the right term – takes place outside Manawaka, and there may well be a correlative between the lack of conviction we feel in this material and the more general weakness of the novel after the second section.

As soon as Morag's – and Laurence's – experience expands beyond her native place, we become aware of a lack of cohesiveness, an uncertainty in the writing, the lack of a sustaining environment. Here the problem of Laurence's male characters becomes crucial. Christie, a product of Manawaka, is surely a triumph, one of the most original and memorable characters in Canadian literature, a larger-than-life creation but wholly credible at the same time. With Jules Tonnerre, however, Laurence encounters difficulties. It is hard to reconcile the bullying, foul-mouthed brat of the earlier part of the story with the figure who later attracts Morag physically. Had one of the white Manawaka boys from the respectable side of the tracks behaved like Jules, one imagines that Morag would have despised him. Sexual attraction can never, of course, be fully explained either in life or in literature, but it is difficult to avoid the conclusion that Laurence is forcing a political point here. To put the matter bluntly, she needs Morag to have a sexual relationship with the socially-deprived Jules in the interests of social concern and plot symmetry. This, I presume, is close to Peterman's point, already quoted, about the necessary 'delicate balance between personal vision, artistic skill, and public purpose'. Jules Tonnerre is a little too insistent as a socio-political symbol to be wholly credible as a major figure within Morag's life.

With Brooke Skelton, this weakness is magnified into something close to a disaster. Top-heavy as a symbol, he fails to be even minimally credible as a character. He is given a conveniently extreme and traumatic upbringing in India and England, which at one and the same time provides ammunition for some too-easy attacks on English authoritarianism and leads to facile psychological explanations for his later emotional inadequacy. Like Morag, he is characterized by a supposed sensitivity to language, but in Brooke's case the references rarely ring true. As an English immigrant myself, I cannot understand why he should have drawn attention to Morag's unexceptional 'Up Galloping Mountain way' as one of her 'idiomatic expressions' (156). Far more unconventional, for an Englishman of his time, are some of his own expressions – 'exotic as all hell', 'so goddam beautiful', and particularly 'like my father was' (157, 161, 178).

But it is with Brooke as teacher that close reading of the text raises especially puzzling difficulties. While he is consistently presented as a conscientious and excellent teacher, the corroborative details we are offered prove unsatisfactory. While Morag is a student in his class, for example, they get involved in an argument about John Donne's 'The Canonization' ('For God's sake hold your tongue, and let me love'). She remarks: 'Supposing the lady had been able to write poetry – I mean, I wonder what she might have said of *him*.' To this Brooke replies: 'You would not take it kindly, Miss Gunn, to be asked to hold your tongue?' (155). The whole exchange is based on the assumption that the male speaker of the poem is addressing his lady. In fact, he is addressing a third party, presumably a male friend. It is credible that Morag should misinterpret, but why doesn't Brooke correct her? This is evidently another of Laurence's slips – surely a damaging one. Another difficulty comes when, not long after their marriage, Brooke makes the implausible claim that he has marked 'twenty blasted essays' in a single evening (175). At this point, any close-reading academic reader will recognize Brooke as a phoney, but such, I assume, is not Laurence's intention. Finally, Brooke's comments on Morag's writing are not only incredibly condescending and chauvinistic (especially in one who is supposed to be a sensitive reader and teacher of literature) but also inept. When called upon to make a literary-critical comment, all he can offer is: 'The novel is a complex structure' (184)!

Perhaps more serious than the blurred characterization here is the unfortunate reflection that our response to Brooke casts upon Morag. Even Clara Thomas, generally an enthusiastic commentator, admits: 'Perhaps their basic incompatibility is from the start made too obvious to the reader' (*Manawaka* 151). Since Laurence presents Brooke as so transparently inadequate, only a hopelessly naïve young woman with a damaging ignorance of human nature would ever have married him. That Morag does so is not in itself incredible. What should give us pause, however, is that the Morag who marries Brooke should, within a few years, begin writing novels that presumably demonstrate a mature insight. The impression we gain of her at this time is hardly reassuring, and once again this is caused by Laurence's uncertain command of realistic detail outside Manawaka. After living in Toronto for four years, Morag is 'able to go downtown without getting hopelessly lost. She has long since learned the various colleges of the university, which city book shops are the best ...' (180). This information backfires, presumably unintentionally, when one recalls that downtown Toronto is based on a fairly simple grid-plan, that (excluding a few theological colleges) there were only four college names to remember at that time, and that there were even fewer good book shops. Brooke's appointment as Head of Department will also amuse anyone acquainted with the University of Toronto in the early fifties; a relatively young professor who filled an apartment with second-hand furniture 'painted in startling colours' (175) would hardly have been a serious contender. The texture of the novel at this point, especially by contrast with the convincingness of Manawaka, is thin indeed.

Significantly, the novel regains subtlety and credibility – as well as verbal distinctiveness – on the two occasions when Morag returns to Manawaka. The first occasion is Prin's last illness. As soon as Morag arrives she finds herself 'thinking in the old phraseology', and at the funeral she responds to the dignity and simplicity of the service and the hymns: 'Service for the Burial of the Dead. The old words' (203, 206). On the occasion of Christie's death and burial, which Thomas rightly describes as 'one of the greatest of scenes in Margaret Laurence's work' (*Manawaka* 163), verbal concerns are also prominent. Morag learns from Hector Jonas that the Manawaka Nuisance Grounds are now known as 'the Municipal Disposal Area' (326); this strengthens her resolve to insist upon the bone-bare parts of the service, 'the old words' in the church (328). She also confines the graveyard ceremony to Scotty Grant the piper playing '"The Flowers of the Forest", the long-ago pibroch, the lament for the dead', and is thus, simply and sublimely, 'released into her mourning' (329).

Close reading cannot, I think, escape the conclusion that the post-Manawaka scenes are decidedly inferior to the account of Morag's growth within her own environment. After she separates from Brooke, Morag's life in Vancouver and Hampstead lacks both shape and direction; indeed, this section becomes correspondingly rambling in structure. The phrase employed by Engel's unnamed critic – 'big and sloppy' – is surely apposite here; it seems worth noting that this 'Rites of Passage' section not only constitutes a third of the novel (out of all proportion to its importance or its impact) but is also approximately three-quarters of the length of *A Jest of God.* Prolixity is not the same as monumentality, and the function of this section, its formal relation to the rest of the novel, is far from clear. Fan Brady is an amusing character in herself, and she is perhaps introduced as a chastening example of dangers that could lie in wait for the aging Morag (she may also be 'an Eve', as Thomas asserts (*Manawaka* 159), though I don't see why), but she passes in and out of Morag's story in an oddly perfunctory fashion. And Dan McGraith, presumably introduced as an artist in another medium, is a pallid figure who never attains the stature that one presumes he is intended to possess. B.W. Powe has gone so far as to use Henry James's phrase 'baggy monster' in connection with the novel (138), and the 'Rites of Passage' section particularly invites the charge.

The contemporary scenes, which introduce each chapter in the book, raise similar questions. The characters are for the most part two-dimensional, and, although this matters little in the case of the Smiths, it becomes a serious blemish with Pique. Morag's daughter is, in fact, a walking cliché, a composite of all the naïveties and fatuities of the 'lost generation' of the late 1960s. The clichés in her speech are only slightly less blatant than the notorious example of parody constructed by Frederick Philip Grove in *Fruits of the Earth* (182-83). 'Who cares about the right word?' she asks at one point (193), and once again the close reader is at a loss to know how to interpret the scene. This is a statement from the daughter of an established novelist. Is it legitimate to draw critical conclusions about Morag's failure to educate her daughter in the importance of precise speech? How can the supposedly sensitive Morag endure Pique's verbal sloppiness? Pique's creative act at the end of the book is the composition of a ballad in the style of her father that contains the line 'Leadin' me back to that home I never knowed' (360). The scene is offered as something close to a tear-jerker, and Morag eventually asks: 'Could I have a copy of the words, Pique?' The close reader's reaction is surely very different.

Royland, with his conspicuously symbolic name, is more effectively presented, though the revelation of his earlier life as tub-thumping preacher and wife neglecter (196-97) verges on the contrived and banal. Nonetheless, his function as 'Old Man of the River' (197) transcends its romantic origins. He is important to the total effect since he is the diviner who provides the literal example of the dominating image in the novel. Ultimately, however, it is fair to ask: what is the significance of the title? All we hear within the text is that water-divining is a mysterious process that cannot be explained but nonetheless 'works' (22). '"I don't reckon I really need to understand it," Royland said. "I just gotta do it"'(22). At the end of the novel he loses the gift as inexplicably as he received it: '"I had it for a long while, and now I don't have it. It's as simple as that"'(368). There are other 'diviners' in the novel – notably Christie who divines comically but profoundly from his garbage, and others like Jules and Dan McGraith. But the application to novel-writing, in the last analysis, reveals little. It is merely another version of 'Inspiration' – the creative wind that bloweth where it listeth. Royland is, to some extent, a sentimental figure, and the transfer of the divining image to the art of writing also risks sentimentality. It is a 'theory' – if that is not too exalted a term – that may be appropriate to Morag Gunn but is hardly worthy of Margaret Laurence.

I REALIZE THAT the preceding discussion may irritate – even enrage – many. Although I have concentrated on the imperfections of the novel, it is only proper to insist at this point that *The Diviners* contains much that is moving and effective. One can say with confidence that only a major novelist could have produced it. If I did not believe that Margaret Laurence was a major novelist, I would never have written this article. She is, I am convinced, a novelist who deserves to be read and judged by the highest standards. In other words, her books demand close reading. But in this case close reading reveals complications that lead as often as not to uncertainty rather than to insight. This is not an experience I have had when reading the early books in the Manawaka series. The process reveals minor blemishes, to be sure (the problem begins to manifest itself, along with other difficulties, in *The Fire-Dwellers*), but in no other case does close reading create such acute problems of interpretation. Current literary commentary, alas, has not addressed itself to this topic. Perhaps this is a long-term example of Engel's suspicion that many who had reservations about the novel on its first publication preferred to remain silent. I hope to have demonstrated, however, that the reasons lie far deeper than Engel supposed. The literary-critical challenge posed by this book is not one that can be adequately explained by personal prejudices or sexist fears. *The Diviners* aspires to something close to epic stature, and seems to have strained Laurence's powers to the utmost. In addition to telling the story of another Manawaka heroine, the book dutifully draws the series to a close (as has been abundantly demonstrated elsewhere) and attempts to explain the complex subject of a writer's relation to her work. It is a gallant enterprise, but it does not succeed completely in all that it undertakes. Ultimately, we are doing a disservice to Margaret Laurence if we fail to acknowledge the weaknesses that accompany the strengths of her most ambitious work.

'Layer on Layer': A Reading of Hugh Hood's *A New Athens*

The following article was written for John Moss's collection of essays entitled *Present Tense* (1985), the fourth volume in his series on the Canadian novel. This essay represents an exercise in the kind of literary-critical flexibility I have been advocating in this book. *A New Athens* is not the kind of novel that reveals its qualities in response to standard approaches to fiction. I have tried therefore to follow the clues within Hood's text and to evolve a suitable reading for a remarkably original narrative experiment.

MOST READERS WOULD AGREE, I suspect, that Hugh Hood's *A New Athens* is written in an attractively flowing style that combines freshness of outlook with spontaneity of expression. Yet most of the literary-critical comments that have hitherto appeared suggest an imposed, potentially rigid formal structure. Hood himself, speaking with J.R. (Tim) Struthers about Coleridge and Wordsworth's conversation poems, acknowledges a structural debt to Wordsworth's *Excursion*: 'The largest of them, *The Excursion,* I've imitated explicitly, almost from point to point, in the opening chapter of *A New Athens* which is a big excursion, a modern representative of a great genre' (Struthers 'Interview' 62).

Although the Wordsworthian hint is valuable, it is possible that particular connections with *The Excursion* loom larger and prove more interesting to the writer than to the reader. Margaret's ruined cottage in Book 1 may well have provided Hood with an inspiration for his forays into what the narrator of *A New Athens* describes as 'a kind of instant archaeology' (6), and Hood himself has shown how Mrs Codrington's vision of the New Jerusalem in his final chapter derives from a passage at the end of Book 2 of Wordsworth's poem (Struthers 'Interview' 74). Nonetheless, the more overtly didactic aspects of the later books of *The Excursion* seem to me – and I write as a fervent admirer of Wordsworth – more ponderous and monotonous than Hood's poised and subtly varied prose narrative.

Doubtless in response to Hood's insistence on the numerological significance of the chapter-divisions in all his fiction, other commentators have offered ingenious but somewhat heavy formal interpretations. Thus John Mills, in 'Hugh Hood and the Anagogical Method', observes that the novel 'is divided into four sections which are suggestive, though not strongly, of the four elements – earth, water, fire (of the Pentecostal sort), and air (into which the figures of Mrs Codrington's last painting triumphantly recede)' (104). And Lawrence Mathews, developing Hood's remarks in the Struthers interview about literature as 'a secular analogy of scripture' (32), favours a more specifically allegorical account in 'The Secular and the Sacral: Notes on *A New Athens* and Three Stories by Hugh Hood': '*A New Athens* is ordered by means of a clear biblical structure. Chapter 1 corresponds to Genesis, Chapter 2 to the prophetic books, Chapter 3 to the Gospels, Chapter 4 to the Book of Revelation' (223). There is merit in both suggestions. I cannot help feeling, however, that they have the unfortunate effect of restricting the novel's free movement within a formal strait-jacket. They imply that the structure conforms to a pre-existing model and so neglect the extent to which it arises out of its own organic coherence.

While I am happy to acknowledge a debt to both these writers (Mills, in particular, goes on to make a number of brief but cogent observations), I would prefer an approach that begins, as it were, on the novel's own terms. And I find a clue not in any discussion of *A New Athens* but in Robert Lecker's examination of the first novel in the *New Age* cycle, 'A Spirit of Communion: *The Swing in the Garden*'. Lecker writes:

> Although *The Swing in the Garden* is full of documentary importance, it does not satisfy on the documentary level alone. Hood himself denies that the work is strictly documentary, and hints at

> a method of approaching the text when he notes that the work should be conceived of as a 'documentary fantasy' which tries 'to give an exact account, in the most precise and credible detail available, of something that is purely imaginary. "Imaginary" in the sense of "envisioned" or "made into art".' (189)[1]

Much the same could be said about the subsequent books in the series, and *A New Athens* seems particularly well suited to an approach that combines a consideration of different physical, literary, temporal, and psychological 'levels' with an emphasis on 'vision' and 'art'. What I propose to attempt in the following pages may at first sight seem elementary, but I hope that it will lead to a better understanding of the novel's tonal and formal unity: at the risk of appearing to proceed by means of somewhat simple-minded plot-narration, I shall try to indicate how Hood controls and vindicates the shifts in Matt Goderich's mind and memory.

A New Athens begins with Matt Goderich setting out on a walking tour in the country north of Stoverville (Hood's imaginative transformation of Brockville), and the first major image we encounter is the familiar one, especially to southern Ontario residents, of straightened and modernized roads replacing earlier surfaces. 'Sometimes', he remarks, 'you can see an earlier roadbed cutting a sharp curve around a knoll a hundred feet off, while new paving lies above it on the wider, more direct course' (6). This image recurs later in the chapter when, on following Mrs McCrady to the site of the disused Forthton station, Matt notices 'traces of paving under the gravel' (46). This is precisely the effect that gives rise to the phrase 'instant archaeology'.

But the main event in Matt's walk is his discovery of 'broken old creases in the shoulder of the highway and certain strange upheavals in the tarred surface' (6). The buried past here insists

---

1 Lecker is quoting here from Hood's remarks in Robert Fulford, 'An Interview with Hugh Hood', *The Tamarack Review* 66 (1975): 77.

on obtruding into the present. The road in question is Highway 29, once known as the Victoria Macadamized Road. Hood, as we might expect, makes artistic and symbolic capital out of this (historical) roadmaking son of Adam, and the idea of one name being replaced by another yet still existing – if only in the minds of historians – suggests levels of another sort: both circumstances point up the wider implications of what are at first literal images. After discovering 'at least four different layers of resurfacing' (7) on the highway, Matt then notices a 'strange earthwork' (8). The experience reminds him of days spent tracing thousand-year-old footpaths in England, and we follow the movements of his mind as he thinks back via the Wessex novels of Thomas Hardy to ancient legend and folklore:

> ... we haven't the culture-memory of the people who live in Angla-land, layer on layer on less discernible layer on faint mark on mere suspected prehistoric spume of cross-hatched human purposes, or have we, or have we? Who tarred over those scratches on the roadway? How much past is past? (11)

The unifying imagery of layer and surface is now fully established, applied not only to the humanly adapted and controlled landscape in which he finds himself but to the configurations of Matt's own mental consciousness.

What he soon comes to refer to as 'the barrow' (12) is eventually recognized as the disused roadbed of the Stoverville, Westport, and Lake Superior Railroad. By old-world standards this represents 'instant archaeology': the remains date back no further than three generations and were not abandoned until some fourteen years before the date of Matt's walking tour. Moreover, Matt had himself observed the last ceremonial run of the railway in question; enrolled in the University of Toronto Art and Archaeology course, generally shortened (shades of Noah?) to 'Art 'n Ark' (38), he was 'up the highway looking for the ruins of an old farmhouse [shades of Wordsworth's Margaret?], said to have been built before the beginning of the nineteenth century' (36).

What he stumbled upon at that time is not the ruins from the past but a historic moment in the present – and at the same time he gains a first glimpse of his future wife.

These two events, the walking tours of 1952 and 1966, combine to create a Wordsworthian 'spot of time'; or, in Matt's words, 'this place intersected with that time' (18). This invoking of Wordsworth's name is by no means arbitrary on my part. A specific reference to the poet has occurred on the previous page as if to prepare us for the dramatic moment of recollection and re-creation. Wordsworth has always been a powerful force for Hood. In 1961 he wrote no fewer than three short stories with Wordsworthian titles: 'A Season of Calm Weather' (published in *Queen's Quarterly* in 1963), 'Fallings from Us, Vanishings' (the opening story in *Flying a Red Kite*), and the until recently unpublished 'From the Fields of Sleep' (now collected in *A Short Walk in the Rain*).[2]

All these quotations are drawn, significantly, from Wordsworth's 'Immortality Ode', which also provides the opening phrase in the title of an important essay, 'Sober Colouring: The Ontology of Super-Realism', collected in *The Governor's Bridge is Closed.* It is also worth noting that references to Wordsworth occur in all the *New Age* novels to date. Hood follows the conspicuous practice of George Eliot in constantly alluding to Wordsworth as a way of indicating the particular intellectual and imaginative tradition to which his fiction belongs.

A more deliberate invoking of Wordsworth appears later in the chapter at the site of Forthton station. In another flashback, Matt remembers going with his wife to visit Tintern Abbey, mainly on account of Wordsworth's famous poem that includes the ruin in its title if not in its text. The Goderiches make their way up a trackway to obtain a distant view of the abbey ruins in the belief that they are following the actual footsteps of the poet

---

2 For Hood's discussions of Wordsworth, see Struthers, 'Interview' 28-29, 62, 74-75.

They discover, however, when they examine the path more closely, that 'the damn thing was an abandoned rail-line' (49). In this English instance, which contrasts with the Canadian experience while at the same time complementing it, the disused railway is later in time than either the abbey ruins or the Wordsworth who wrote the poem. And, predictably, Matt goes on to consider the older Wordsworth's complaints about the coming of railways and to discount the poet's fears: '*Pace* Wordsworth, the railways were never invasive, alien; they were new in their beginnings. We turned them into antiquities as fast as we reasonably could' (51).

But this Wordsworthian flashback is introduced by a passage that is not only central to the whole subject of our perception of the Canadian past but extends our understanding of Hood's artistic procedure. Matt is disturbed that he had never previously recognized the Forthton station for what it was: 'What bothered me about this terrible recognition was the way in which the evidence of past things lies before us, trailing clouds of meaning ... and we miss it' (46). 'Trailing clouds of meaning'. The allusion is, of course, to the 'trailing clouds of glory' line in (yet again) Wordsworth's 'Immortality Ode'. The Wordsworthian statement lies, as it were, below the surface of Hood's multi-layered text in much the same way that the SWLSRR roadbed lies beneath the tarred surface of Highway 29. We begin to see how this imagery of layers and surfaces provides a key to the whole form and structure of the book. We might say that the Tintern 'digression' (for want of a better word) is indicative of the layers of Matt's mood; and, by extension, the way in which the fiction is made up of an elaborate series of inter-related actions and reflections is indicative of the layers of Hood's art.

It is at this point that Matt meditates on 'the almost infinite possibilities of recession' (43) and considers 'the strange double-treble optics of the superimposition of the present on many, many pasts' (45). This has already been demonstrated in my discussion of the 'spot of time' during which Matt in 1966 is carried back to the past of 1952 when he had witnessed the last run of a railway that opened in 1888. Yet, when the 1952 event was itself the present, Matt was searching for the ruins of a *pre*-nineteenth-century farmhouse. The remark about infinite possibilities of recession is made (within what is itself a flashback) when Matt is interviewing the current owner of a historic house and discovers that the owner's great-grandfather, who built the house, was born in 1798, the same year that Wordsworth and Coleridge published *Lyrical Ballads.* And here I may perhaps be forgiven for extrapolating somewhat from Hood's text and noting that 'Tintern Abbey' (which first appeared in *Lyrical Ballads*) itself depends upon a temporal recession between the present of 1798 and Wordsworth's previous visit to the banks of the Wye five years earlier.

Within the same section of *A New Athens* Matt recalls being told a local story by an old inhabitant 'about the day it rained on the church picnic and the congregation just about had to swim home – which happened 75 years before I heard about it, *the tale resurfacing in my informant's imagination* as though it had happened the week before' (39-40; my emphasis). Matt's own imagination links the anecdote with traditional flood-narratives ('Art 'n Ark' in another manifestation). Much earlier he had remarked how the folk-mind can link legendary tales with orally transmitted memories of historical events 'on the same *level* of reality' (11; my emphasis). I suggest that Hood subtly introduces these metaphorical phrases to show how our habitual processes of language themselves contribute to the subject he is exploring. Metaphor bears witness to layers in language that suggest resemblances to those other layers of earth and mind studied respectively by archaeologists and psychologists.

I cannot, of course, continue to discuss the later chapters with the same degree of detail that I have used in examining the novel's opening section, but this imagery of layers and surfaces looks forward conveniently to the second chapter where the ghost ship replaces the ghost train as a powerful symbol of the inter-relations of past and present. We learn later that the ship in question was built 'in 1824-25, and scuttled as redundant thirteen or fourteen years later' (195); the inconspicuous link with the fourteen-year span between Matt's walking tours in the first chapter is almost certainly deliberate. Matt and Edie catch a glimpse of the ship under the ice in the dying moments of 1952 after a skating-scene that recalls a well-known Wordsworthian account in the first book of *The Prelude* and is heralded by another quotation from Wordsworth four pages earlier (104). The ship is lying beneath the surface of the St. Lawrence River, and is only visible at certain privileged moments when suitable light effects converge. For Matt and Edie the miracle happens; it is the occasion on which they become engaged, thus connecting by way of their personal romance with the episode of the ghost train when Matt saw Edie 'for the first time' (63).

'The phantom. Really there' (114). These are the words in which Matt describes what might be called the natural supernaturalism of the ghost ship. A little earlier, an important conversation that looks forward to some of the major preoccupations of the latter half of the book alludes to the building of the St. Lawrence Seaway, which is described as 'a pressing example of the interpenetration of reality by vision' (102). The phrase could be applied with equal appropriateness both to the ghost-ship incident and to Mrs Codrington's paintings, which combine the visionary and the local in a way that has since become popular (and distorted) under the term 'magic realism'.

For Matt, her paintings are examples of the way 'vision obliterates fact' (108); realistic perspective is ignored, but an effect of 'coherent unity' is nonetheless achieved. The connection is made quite specifically when one painting, *The Stoverville Annual Regatta,* is described as communicating 'a living atmosphere, and at the same time a distinctly submarine, aqueous impression, as if the viewer were seeing the town through light reflected off water, maybe even from under water' (109). In other words, Stoverville is seen as if from the viewpoint of the phantom but real ghost ship.

Images of layer and surface are less prominent in the third chapter. Nonetheless, various issues that have coalesced around this imagery, matters concerning art and history, continue to develop. Centred upon Matt and Edie's wedding, the chapter shows Matt coming to know Edie's family, and a reference to 'primordial Codringtons' (154) suggests the layered generations evident in familial as well as local, social, and national histories.

The third chapter also contains an account of Matt's frustrating relation with 'the South Nation Village project' (161). As chief historical consultant, he protests at the inclusion of a 'kind of Upper Canadian hotel, in fact almost a motel' (164) designed to accommodate tourists and their cars. He finds that he cannot prevent the absurd anachronism since the franchise chain 'insists on an on-site site' and the chain in question is 'American-owned' (165). So modern political realities can distort and vulgarize a historical vision. But at least Matt learns something from the experience: 'We can't actually live in our own past. All we can do is remember it, love it, and try to understand it' (166).

Matt is roused from his irritation by Mrs Codrington's bringing another picture for his critical response. In the ensuing artistic discussion she complains that most modern Canadian art is 'cut off from the world of vision' (171). She herself is concerned with 'sacred art', with 'the art of revelation' (170). In her paintings real people (the Mayor of Stoverville, the local M.P.) are represented in fanciful guise, and one feels that this blending of the visionary and the real is close to the essence of Hood's own art. This point is, I believe, underlined in the fourth and final chapter when her paintings are gathered and arranged after her death to comprise the 'permanent display at the Codrington Colony for the Encouragement of Visionary Art' (216). 'Twelve in all', Matt adds, and we remember the number of projected novels in Hood's *New Age* cycle.

In the final chapter the emphasis falls upon the archaeological recovery of the ghost ship and its restoration as an emblem of the past, and on the timeless relevance of Mrs Codrington's art, where action 'occurs in space, and outside it, simultaneously' and where she succeeds in communicating a 'vision of the heavenly and eternal rising from the things of this world' (211). In this technical discussion of art, levels and surfaces are replaced by interconnecting planes, but the basic principles of argument remain the same. On the general significance of this section, I am in substantial agreement with the findings of Mills and Mathews; the former asserts that Mrs Codrington's paintings 'seem to act as the visual equivalent of Hood's own technique and viewpoint' (110), while the latter argues that, 'in Matt's analysis of Mrs Codrington's painting, Hood is also explaining how he wants his own work to be read' (227).

I would add only two footnotes. First, as an amplification of Mathews's point, we may detect another Wordsworthian analogue, since the discussion between narrator and Wanderer in Book 1 of *The Excursion* on the subject of Margaret and her cottage may be seen as Wordsworth's explanation of how his poetry ought to be read.[3] Second, Hood has signalled the connection between Mrs Codrington's art and his own in a detail that Mills and Mathews do not appear to have noticed. He makes her insert a little touch of Matt Goderich into her masterpiece: 'The seventh figure is that of a man with face obscured, not old, about my height and weight' (216). One is free to speculate on the relation between this figure and the amount of Hugh Hood that is transformed into Matt Goderich for the purposes of the fiction.

I am further convinced that Hood intends us to make connections between Mrs Codrington's art and his own by the fact that the just-quoted remark about her work presenting a 'vision of the heavenly and eternal rising from the things of this world' paraphrases his reasons for admiring Wordsworth. He praises 'We Are Seven', for example, because 'there, in that poem, is an ordinary and quotidian experience related by poetic meditation to a great religious truth' (Struthers 'Interview' 79). A thorough reading of *A New Athens* shows how 'sacred art' (whether Words-

3 I have argued this point, so far as Wordsworth is concerned, in *The Poetry of Nature: Rural Perspectives on Poetry from Wordsworth to the Present* (Toronto: University of Toronto Press, 1980) 32-35.

worth's, Mrs Codrington's, the poet Maura Boston's, or Hugh Hood's) reveals the visionary below the surface of the real, and sometimes vice versa. It is a quality that unites the prehistoric painters of Lascaux (34, 60) with the best of the present day, and it also links ancient and modern societies. Even the novel's title, in terms of literary layers provided by Alexander Pope and Frances Brooke, connects classical Greece with nineteenth-century Ontario (23). Matt Goderich is at pains to explain that the (historical) alteration of the community's name from Farmersville to Athens is neither presumptuous nor ridiculous:

> What they had done wasn't to insinuate that their village was as great, as central to culture as the city of Athens, but only that their schools were in the tradition of the Academy, that human culture is continuous, that a Canadian school two generations removed from the wilderness is the same kind of school as the Academy, that human nature persists, remains self-identical through many generations of superficial changes. (59)

In conclusion, I should acknowledge that my reading of the novel has been, to some extent, selective. Like any interpretation, mine has emphasized one aspect and has doubtless underestimated others. Thus my approach has laid stress on literature rather than the fine arts, though the novel itself is concerned with painting and references to visionary-cum-realistic painters, from Dürer to Stanley Spencer, are significantly more frequent here than elsewhere. Besides, Wordsworth is by no means the only writer to be an important inspiration for Hood. Proust is a strong presence in other fictions, and it is surprising that, although *A New Athens* is clearly a book about the discovery of lost time, and although Proust is named on several occasions in *The Swing in the Garden*, *Reservoir Ravine*, and *Black and White Keys*, he is never specifically named here. One suspects, however, that his influence can be felt 'below the surface'. Dante, mentioned twice in the text (168, 170), seems prominent, named or unnamed, in all Hood's later work, Joyce pares his fingernails inscrutably in the shadows, and even Stephen Leacock (complete with his own ghost train) takes a bow here as a token Canadian (25; cf. *Swing* 139-40, and Struthers 'Interview' 25-27).

But I would argue that Wordsworth is absolutely central: the Wordsworth for whom common things were 'apparelled in celestial light', for whom the poorest leech-gatherer can be seen as 'a man from some far region sent' by 'peculiar grace', for whom the meanest flower that blows – and Matt picks a large posy of them in the first chapter – 'can give/Thoughts that do often lie too deep for tears'. Moreover, following through the developing imagery of the 'Immortality Ode', *A New Athens,* though a sun- and light-filled book, is also a deeply probing one that, as in the serene scene that presents the death of Mrs Codrington, keeps 'watch o'er man's mortality'. Yet for Hood, Wordsworth provides not only an attitude and an imagery but also a form, and I agree with Dennis Duffy in 'Space/Time and the Matter of Form' when he finds *The Prelude* a more promising clue to Hood's choice of form than *The Excursion* (140). But I would not, as Duffy does, speak of 'looseness of form' (142) – except as a necessary balance to the rigidities of elemental or scriptural reference. What this Wordsworthian form allows, rather, is a freedom of intellectual movement between times and places that allows for a remarkable variety of tone and is unified by the continuing development of an individual mind.

No less Wordsworthian is the strong sense of local place.[4] In Hood's case, however, this manifests itself in an exhilarating emphasis on a specifically Canadian experience which is firmly presented without any trace of shrill nationalism. The layers that are uncovered are those of Ontario history. Matt's thesis, we remember, was called *Stone Dwellings of Loyalist Country*; with his

4 Between the writing of this article and its original publication, Anthony John Harding published an excellent article on the relation between Wordsworth and Hood, 'Field of Vision: Hugh Hood and the Tradition of Wordsworth'. [1989]

wife he is preparing 'an illustrated guide to eastern Ontario architecture' (36); and in later life they see themselves as 'recapitulating ... the constitutive, essential story of life in the colony' (185) when they turn away from the riverfront to build a summer cottage near Athens. The action thus takes on much larger dimensions. Matt lays claim to the title of 'first prophet of the Canadian style', remarking: 'There must be something in my guts that is finally Canadian' (120). We might say, indeed, that in the last analysis, both above and below the surface, *A New Athens* is as quintessentially Canadian as Wordsworth's poetry is quintessentially English.

The Case for Hugh Hood

This review of Hood's collection of short stories *None Genuine Without This Signature,* commissioned by *Canadian Forum* in 1980, seemed a good opportunity to draw attention to Hood's importance for a broader readership than that provided by the average academic journal. It therefore uses this particular volume to generalize about Hood's work as a whole. One slight oddity should be explained. The review was written from an advance copy of a 'text edition' containing an introductory essay by Keith Garebian. This introduction was not included in the 'trade edition' of the book.

IS HUGH HOOD IMPORTANT? If so, why?

The first question is (for me) readily answered: yes, definitely – though I have to admit that many whose opinions I respect would not share my certainty. But to offer reasons proves anything but easy. It requires as a preliminary a personal confession for which I apologize in advance.

Though I live in Toronto, I am no proper Torontonian; I do not consider it the centre of Canada – let alone, of the universe. Like many urban residents, I frequently yearn for country living but would probably find it irksome if I got there. As a city, Toronto is at least (at present) habitable, but the shades of a megalopolitan wasteland are upon it. Besides, Torontonians bother me. The number of phoneys per acre is growing rapidly. I dislike the weekend men in their slightly jazzed-up business suits, while the parody human beings with buttons on their lapels and slogans on their sweatshirts are acutely depressing. An epiphany (though not, perhaps, in Hood's sense): I am walking close to Casa Loma when a burst of acid rock blares forth behind me; I am passed by a jogger clutching a transistor like a teething-ring. Irving Layton's lines from 'Family Portrait' (about another class altogether) spring to mind:

and I think:
'Thank heaven I'm not
Jesus Christ –
I don't have to love them.' (194)

Hugh Hood *does* love them, and this is a fact of considerable importance. And not with any of the weak, pitying love that disturbs Layton in his brother Jesus. Hood's love takes the form of an open and compassionate interest in ways of life far removed from those of most of his readers. I almost wrote 'of himself' but Hood appears to be interested in *everything*. Perhaps the greatest problem of the arts in an age of fragmented mores, attitudes, and beliefs (or lack of them) is the capacity of artists to comprehend and embody the life of their times. If sensitivity is the hallmark of artists, one wonders how they can be anything but outsiders in a crassly insensitive age.

In this new volume of inter-related short stories, Hood offers a clue in the first narrative, 'God Has Manifested Himself Unto Us as Canadian Tire' (a bold title – what story could live up to it? – but this one does). Here we are confronted by A.O. and Dreamy, who seem at first sight bitterly satiric creations crudely symbolizing a consumer society run riot. Hood saturates his prose with the rhythms and slogans of advertising. The couples are surrounded by the latest buys ('Tonight we've got a Coffee Magic superactivated dripolator' (8)); their culture consists of reading about the next sale ('Canadian Industries 402, the natural shotgun.... Kills at any reasonable distance' (1)); Dreamy is physically enveloped by bargains ('Hairspray, underarmspray, vaginaspray, and ... Desenex Foot Powder. Dreamy is covered, ... triple-armour-proofed from head to toe' (2)). But by the end of the story they are revealed as a pathetically unfulfilled pair, babes in a commercialized artificial-*bonsai* wood, only half convinced that they must be happy since they have everything, aware of a lack but unable to name it. For careful readers, however, the pathos of a self-imposed barrenness is intimated as early as the first paragraph: 'Baby Car Seat by Travl-Gard conforming to all government safety needs. We'll never need one of those' (1). Our ultimate response is complex. Contempt is no longer possible, but we are not allowed to relinquish the responsibility of judgement. An achieved insight beyond the reach of direct statement: such is the capacity of Hood's art.

'Ghosts at Jarry' provides another example. Mario is a baseball fan who dislikes the new Olympic stadium in Montreal. His solution is to go with his radio and portable TV to the old, derelict Jarry stadium and enjoy the games in the old surroundings. There he is joined by a solitary girl and then, gradually, by hundreds – whether real or metaphorical ghosts is left uncertain. For myself (another confession), I have never been to a ball-game and never owned a TV, portable or otherwise; this ought not to be my kind of story, yet I am absorbed and moved.

In prose fiction, perhaps only Margaret Atwood can rival Hood in his presentation of the modern city, though I should make clear that Hood writes in this collection about New York, the West Indies, rural Ontario, and 'Sweet Cream, Manitoba' as well as Toronto and Montreal. Atwood offers the same piercing insight into otherwise unknown lives, but neither the range of character nor the sense of full compassionate understanding. In poetry, Raymond Souster can cajole or bully me into looking at Torontonians in a new way – but the effect is only temporary. In Hood alone I find a palpable extension of my sympathies and awareness. And this is achieved partly through the technical sophistication of his art (but Atwood has that), partly through an assured and tested religious and moral position. Hood begins with a faith that the world – even megalopolis – can be redeemed.

He has recently described himself as 'through and through a Catholic novelist' (Struthers 'Interview' 81). Although fundamentally true, this has the unfortunate effect, for those without a religious commitment, of suggesting pious sentiments, limited subject matter, and sugared pills. On the contrary he offers a joyous acceptance, a healthily positive response to the things of this world, and above all a considered, anything-but-cloistered confidence remarkable in this day and age when believers rather than unchallenged agnostics are under pressure to defend their position. Hood is, I suppose, Canada's most learned, most intellectual novelist. His philosophical *credo,* as offered recently, is as follows: 'I think Truth, Beauty, and Goodness are co-extensive and that they stem from the Divine Being, and I think all created being, insofar as it is a being, is good and beautiful.' This leads in turn to an artistic stance: 'I think of art without Hope as inoperative. It won't work' (Struthers 'Interview' 37, 36). A refreshing change from 'All's shit' – and far more firmly based.

From this religious foundation, it is only a short step to the idea of literature as 'a secular analogy of scripture' – Hood's sole point of agreement, he says, with Northrop Frye (Struthers 'Interview' 32). But once again this sounds too solemn, too pretentious, for Hood's own practice. Comparisons with Dante, which Hood has made himself and which are reiterated here in Keith Garebian's introduction (of which more later), may be intellectually comprehensible but give the wrong impression. Ultimately, Hood is Hood and no one else. His viewpoint allows him to see the sacred in the profane, to turn even casual expletives back to the religious meanings which they originally defied. Set within his achieved context, religious allusions in ordinary speech regain their pristine impact. These stories are littered with instances ('Miracle Mart', 'stigmata', 'the real presence'). Sometimes they do not even need to be included. In 'Ghosts at Jarry', the text 'where two or three are gathered together' (Matt. 18.20) haunts the story without ever being quoted. Hood never insists on his allegorical or emblematic meanings. They are available in his fiction because he recognizes them as available also in the reality out of which his stories emerge.

In Hood's work, then, words can be rescued from banality. Like the world, they too are redeemable. One of the progressions in this book concerns language. In the opening stories it is reduced to the subworld of advertising and, in 'Breaking Off', bureaucracy. Hood can revel in jargon:

> 'Here's the constant-estimate-adjustment sheet for the third week of the current quarter, and the departmental breakdown, oh, and the extrapolation for the remainder of the quarter, and ... the in-field operations costings, and this is the divisional operations summary with three-previous-year comparison parameters.' (18)

But this is more than mere parody ('the departmental *breakdown*' alerts us, once we have learned to read Hood, to the central image presented in the title); it is the first recorded conversation between the main characters, whose affair inevitably breaks off. 'Breaking Off' has both the pathos and the half-absurd comedy of real life.

The stories become increasingly intricate as the book proceeds. Inter-relations are frequent. In the title story (it is typical of Hood that the actual human signature in the narrative should be a fake), an advertising campaign is initiated, and we are – or should be – reminded of the language of the opening tale. Three stories involve song-writers or singers, Hood's artistic equivalent in this collection to the painters in his earlier work. A 'SOCIAL WORKER for God's sake' (7) appears briefly in the first story; in 'Gone Three Days' the phrase takes on a literal meaning. The narrator of the final story, 'Doubles', eschews the solemnity of Mann's *The Magic Mountain* and explores his own 'magic plain' – the terrain we come to recognize as the 'strange geography' (168) of all the stories here – and, indeed, of all Hood's work.

Hood's final distinction, in my view, is one that his critics have often denied him: he has extended the boundaries of fiction. Ironically, because he is seldom conspicuously innovative in technique, his firm artistic control is always in danger of passing unnoticed. One can read a long way in *The Camera Always Lies*, for instance, before the larger meaning beyond the Hollywood routines becomes manifest. Yet so multifarious are his interests that, in his more recent work, the normal limits of narrative form, whether in novel or short story, are inadequate to contain his vision. History, philosophy, politics, sociology, art theory – these and many other subjects are grist to his mill, and he refuses to confine fiction to the traditional elements of plot and characterization. Often (and the numerous allusions to and quotations from Wordsworth are relevant here) he employs an essentially poetic form, as in *A New Athens* – which I believe to be his masterpiece to date – where the incidents are unified by image and emblem rather than by narrative succession. He has described himself as 'probably not a novelist but another kind of fiction writer' (Struthers 'Interview' 27), and he is doubtless referring to an encyclopaedic form that remains as yet unnamed. But if he isn't a novelist, he certainly isn't a short story writer either, since, here as elsewhere, his stories lose much by being extracted and belong not only to the volume as a whole but even to the order within the volume.

No doubt because his verbal, structural, and allusive effects are so delicate and therefore so easily missed, Hood's new publishers, ECW Press, have felt impelled to preface this collection with a scholarly introduction. I can understand the motive, sympathize with it, and admit that my own reading has been stimulated and improved by Keith Garebian's interpretations. But I still think it a mistake. Ultimately, I suppose, Hood is a didactic writer, but he is not a pedagogic one, and this arrangement smacks of the classroom and the schoolteacher. I am reminded of those tiresome academic occasions when a 'difficult' play is framed by a lecture and a panel discussion. Hood can speak for himself and should be left to do so. If the reader needs assistance, there are literary-critical discussions available – notably *Before the Flood: Hugh Hood's Work in Progress,* a re-issue of *Essays on Canadian Writing* No. 13/14. But the first appearance of a fictional work should contain no mediator between author and reader.

This, however, is a minor matter. Much more important is the fact that *None Genuine Without This Signature* offers what we have come to expect from Hood – precision of detail, delicacy of nuance, firmness of (albeit inconspicuous) structure, a smooth felicity of language, and warmly human compassion. It is a worthy successor to the writing that so many of us have come to read in the last few years with ever-increasing admiration. The ramifications of the title are complex but on one level the reference is to the writer and his work. Hood's signature here is undoubtedly genuine.

Two Reviews of Rudy Wiebe

In 1981 I published a critical study entitled *Epic Fiction: The Art of Rudy Wiebe* with the University of Alberta Press. *The Mad Trapper* (1980) had appeared after the manuscript had been completed, and I was able to insert only some very brief references. *My Lovely Enemy* (1983) was, of course, published after my book had appeared. I reviewed both books, one in *Fiddlehead* in 1981, the second in *Canadian Forum* in 1983. These reviews enabled me to relate these later works to the general view of Wiebe's fiction that I had worked out in *Epic Fiction*.

1. THE MAD TRAPPER: On the day that *The Mad Trapper* was published (13 September 1980), the Toronto *Globe and Mail* reported that Frank Hersey, last survivor of the party that hunted down Albert Johnson in 1932, had condemned the book as 'inaccurate and ridiculous'. Hersey, of course, read the novel as a participant, not as a literary critic; he could hardly be expected to accept anything that conflicted with his own memories (one recalls Jessie Chambers, the Miriam of *Sons and Lovers*, rejecting as false all D.H. Lawrence's deviations from the facts of their relationship). The extent to which an artist is obligated to remain faithful to historical events is debatable; oddly enough, however, Hersey's strictures can help us to understand Wiebe's intentions and achievement more clearly.

Hersey maintained that Wiebe 'just didn't do his homework'. That charge can be laid against Hersey himself. Had he followed Wiebe's career as a writer, he would have known that Wiebe wrote his short story 'The Naming of Albert Johnson' as early as 1972-73 and that he has made a long, serious study of the 'mad trapper' story, as his article 'The Death and Life of Albert Johnson: Collected Notes on a Possible Legend' reveals. The most detailed and clear-headed discussion of the mystery may be found in Dick North's *The Mad Trapper of Rat River* (1972);

Wiebe praises the book in his article as 'the most complete study yet written' (226), and it is clear that, while writing his novel, he drew upon North's book for details that could not have been obtained elsewhere. That Wiebe has radically altered many of the historical facts is true; it is also true that he is noticeably less faithful to the historical record here than in *The Temptations of Big Bear* and *The Scorched-Wood People.* But the changes are made not because of ignorance but for reasons that are primarily structural and artistic. Wiebe is creating, not reporting.

The earlier life of 'Albert Johnson' remains a blank. Although North makes a convincing case for identifying him with a trapper named Arthur Nelson, this casts no further light on his motivation and behaviour. Wiebe does not try to construct a motive – indeed, he clearly wishes to maintain a sense of mystery – so he cannot penetrate into the mind of his leading character as he did with Big Bear and Louis Riel. Instead, he concentrates on creating an artistic balance around the central core of mystery. This is a remarkably artful book. If Wiebe were a Henry James (but thank goodness he is not), one could imagine his writing an elaborate 'preface' concentrating on the artistic problems integral to his story.

In *The Mad Trapper* Wiebe is intent upon creating order out of seeming absurdity and meaninglessness. It is therefore a highly patterned work: parts 1 and 2 each have 9 sections while parts 3 and 4 each have 15, and the balancing titles of parts 3 and 4 ['The First Manhunt: Rivers and Wilderness'; 'The Second Manhunt: Mountains and Sky'] show the author consciously moulding his material into a discernible and comprehensible shape. The narrative works on various levels of significance. For example, Wiebe creates a scene in which Johnson watches a grizzly killing a caribou; in terms of plot it is an excrescence, but the 'ultimate meeting between antlers and claws' (46) provides an admirable proleptic image for the final confrontation of Mountie and outlaw. Wiebe is at once recounting a familiar story and in a most literal sense making it his own.

Wiebe's developing of Spike Millen into a central figure in the manhunt as a structural balance to the hunted Albert Johnson represents his most radical departure from the historical record. In actuality, Millen was shot dead by Johnson on 29 January 1932. Wiebe substitutes a fictional Paul Thompson on that occasion and has Millen survive until 17 February when he can come face to face with Johnson at the climax. Here an awareness of the discrepancy between fact and fiction helps us to appreciate the formal structure that Wiebe is creating. Millen and Johnson become focal points. In the opening scenes of the novel a description of Johnson silently floating downriver on his raft is juxtaposed with the noisy celebrations at Fort McPherson in which Millen is prominent. The two who begin as opposites thus draw together, meet for a moment, and then separate until their appointment with destiny at the close of the book. Wiebe builds up an extraordinary sense of converging courses, recalling Hardy's lines about how the iceberg and the *Titanic* 'were bent/By paths coincident/On being anon twin halves of one august event' (289).

But the connection between Millen and Johnson is more than merely structural. Wiebe skilfully develops the Mountie's obsession with the capture of Johnson so that, in a fascinating if rather chilling way, Millen takes on some of Johnson's distinguishing characteristics. Wiebe achieves this effect by subtly repeating a word or a phrase originally used of one man when describing the other. Each tends to 'explode' in 'rage' or 'fury' (all important recurring words in this book). If Johnson is 'the mad trapper', Millen is 'Arctic crazy' (123), 'half mad himself from chasing that devil' (169). The Mountie gains an uncanny insight into the outlaw's mind. There comes a point, indeed, in which it seems as if Millen 'were reading Johnson out of the very air they were breathing' (166).

One reason for Johnson's seeking the Arctic is to get away from men, machinery, and noise. Millen, too, yearns for the old simplicities: 'We don't need radios, planes – all this ... machinery. This is country for men and dogs.' Inspector Eames then asks him: 'You want an old-time shoot-out, eh, man to man?' (110) But this is precisely what Millen cannot have in an age dominated by Hersey with his radio communications and 'Wop' May with his Bellanca. In the later sections May is also presented as a kind of shadow-figure to Johnson. Just as Johnson is seen as a black dot in the Arctic waste, so May's plane is a black dot in the hitherto empty sky. We are told of May that 'the Bellanca was an extension of himself' (153) just as Johnson's rifle was 'part of him like his arm or his eye' (117). May's acrobatic act of flying his plane and shooting with his rifle at the same time may be literally absurd, as Hersey insists, but it is a fitting emblem of the parody-hero of an interfering modernity. Not an authentic historical reconstruction, Wiebe's 'Wop' May is nonetheless an essential part of the creative design.

But Wiebe reserves his greatest criticism – indeed, contempt – for the journalists and news reporters. They, *pace* Hersey, are the betrayers of both story and history because they translate both into cliché. Throughout the book, Wiebe contrasts the serious realities of the situation with the stereotyped, simplistic sensationalism that is spewed out to the world, through radios and newspapers, in the form of 'news'. Their world is that of Hollywood and a cops-and-robbers never-never-land; Wiebe continually distinguishes their preoccupations from the world of art. He may alter the details of history, but he never degrades it. Although Millen at one point rages against 'a stupid Zane Grey movie, all guts and no brain or heart' (132), it is the brain and heart that Wiebe is at pains to provide. His work constantly uses the traditional subject matter of adventure and romance (Indian attacks, trials and executions, police versus outlaw), but he redeems it, wins it back for the world of responsibility and moral choice. So, at the close of *The Mad Trapper*, what looks superficially like 'an old-time shoot-out' is in fact another 'ultimate meeting', the inevitable culmination of an artistic structure that Wiebe has shaped with care and unostentatious skill from the opening pages.

All this helps to explain, perhaps, the two statements that Wiebe makes in his 1978 article that are seemingly contradicted by *The Mad Trapper.* In discussing the backward-spiralling form of his short story on the same subject, he states that 'structurally, the true story of Albert Johnson cannot be approached in chronological fashion' (244). And he also maintains that he 'would find it impossible to write a novel about such a person' as Johnson (246). A novelist is, of course, privileged to change his mind, but I doubt if Wiebe is ultimately inconsistent. He is not attempting in this novel to tell 'the true story of Albert Johnson', and by dividing his interest between Johnson and Millen as well as concentrating, as I have argued, on the complex structuring of his narrative, he avoids the embarrassment (for him) of having a hero who is morally unworthy. The result is a novel that, while fitting readily into the Wiebe canon, extends the novelist's technical range and is in no way a repetition of former successes.

Nonetheless, Hersey's complaint, though in the final analysis it can be dismissed as invalid, suggests that Sir Walter Scott was probably right in choosing 'sixty years since' (to quote the subtitle of *Waverley*) as the lower limit for his historical interpretations. In venturing closer to the present, Wiebe is invading the area not merely of human memory but of active participation. This foray into the twentieth century is, however, an interesting development after his impressive presentation of nineteenth-century Canadian history in his work of the 1970s. Perhaps it heralds a return to the contemporary. At all events, this absorbing novel (at 189 pages it is by Wiebe's standards barely more than a short story) will cause his dedicated readers to look to his future with even greater expectancy.

2. SEX AND THE DEAD: W.B. Yeats once remarked that 'only two topics can be of the least interest to a serious and studious mind – sex and the dead' (730). These are the prime concerns in Rudy Wiebe's extraordinary new book, *My Lovely Enemy,* which forces the novel into imaginative areas that Wiebe himself has never entered before (at least in full-length fiction) and that have seldom been explored even by avant-garde novelists. We are coming to realize that in the house of fiction, as in

the house of God the Father, there are many mansions; here Wiebe inhabits several whose existence is virtually unknown to the literary and religious faithful alike.

This is all strange terrain. If my experience is at all typical, readers will find themselves groping, stumbling – often puzzled, often disoriented; and (if there are any who still recognize the emotion) some will be shocked at the deliberate juxtaposition of what has so often been categorized in the past as the sacred and the profane. Basically, this novel can be seen as the product of Wiebe's earnest (perhaps desperate) attempt to understand and unite two aspects that he recognizes within himself: the religious and the unabashedly sexual man. Robert Kroetsch once described Wiebe as 'in some ways the most profoundly sexual of our novelists' (14), and this book proves how right he was. As might be expected from Wiebe, it is a novel with a theology, but the theology in question is not so much radical as erotic. 'God is love' is extended far beyond *agape* to embrace passion of all kinds.

Wiebe takes enormous risks here, and it will be a long time before the book's implications and significance are fully understood. I suspect that it will be both praised and attacked for the wrong reasons: praised by the pace-setters for a sexually explicit trendiness that Wiebe rightly despises, attacked for a blasphemy which to Wiebe is a profound revelation. *My Lovely Enemy* attempts to combine challenging insight with searing vision. It is not without its snags and problems (what Wiebe novel is completely free of them?), but it is most assuredly a deeply sincere, deeply committed, awesomely courageous book.

When some eighteen months ago I published *Epic Fiction,* a study of Wiebe's writings, I ended by wondering where he would go after *The Scorched-Wood People* (1977) and the novel about Albert Johnson, *The Mad Trapper* (1980). Would he return to modern settings and issues (I noted a recent short story, 'Home for Night') or pursue his fascination with nineteenth-century Indian history (I noted 'In the Beaver Hills', later expanded into

'The Broken Arm' and published in *Canadian Forum* in March 1981)? I should have known that, where Wiebe is concerned, it is wrong to think in terms of either/or. *My Lovely Enemy* is a novel that shifts between present-day Edmonton and the pasts of both the Mennonite settlers and the native peoples. The hero – if hero is the right word – is an ex-Mennonite Professor of History at the University of Alberta researching Indian records of the last century.

At the same time, I was more prophetic than I could reasonably have hoped. Both 'Home for Night' and 'The Broken Arm' are incorporated into the text of this novel, which is a remarkable bringing together of the subjects that have preoccupied Wiebe throughout his artistic career: radical Christianity; intimate human relationships; the impulse towards peace; the impulse towards violence; temptations of all kinds; the tragic conflict between white and Indian in the past of our land; and, of course, voice and where it comes from. James Dyck, the central figure, ran away from an oppressively strict Mennonite father (one remembers the Presbyterian Abe Ross in *First and Vital Candle*) and finds himself tempted into an adultery which in turn leads to some unexpected soul-searching ('Am I being tempted by Christianity?' he asks at one point (169)); Broken Arm, by contrast, is a fierce Indian warrior (he once scalped a wife in a fit of temper) who ultimately becomes a pacifist and a Christian. As so often in this book, one story mirrors and complements another.

I use the word 'mirror' deliberately. The image recurs frequently in *My Lovely Enemy*, beginning with a significant reference to Jorge Luis Borges's short story about the planet Tlön. And as the novel progresses Wiebe probes more and more into 'this mirrored world' (232). He insists that, within the ambience of this particular novel, there can be no boundaries or limits beyond which the questing novelist may not go. Even Jesus himself can appear (in dream? in vision? in the flesh?) to comment startlingly on the problems of our contemporary world. The so-called 'magic realism' of the South American writers blends –

sometimes awkwardly, sometimes supremely – with a modern Christian vision that (shades of Wiebe's first novel) will destroy the peace of many.

Much of the difficulty that confronts the reader of this book arises from the shifts within the narrative. All factors of James Dyck's life – his intellectual interests, his personal past, his sexual drives – are always present and inter-relating. We move not only from present to past as we follow the convolutions of his stream of consciousness, but from a hellish descent to an earthly or at least fleshly paradise (I am being only slightly metaphorical here), from one fictional convention to another, from the bleak mundane world to one of intense imaginative possibility. And these shifts take place not only between sections or paragraphs but even within sentences.

Above all, the book shifts in tone between humour and seriousness. What I have so far written may suggest, despite an extension of range, the rather solemn, angular Wiebe of the first two novels. In fact, however, the opening is richly comic, and there are scenes here that should destroy once and for all the myth that Wiebe lacks a sense of humour. As the book proceeds, however, humour and seriousness become inextricably intermingled. A serious theological discussion takes place while James and his wife are sorting laundry; the presence of Jesus is manifest in a Calgary hotel and the stacks of a university library. Throughout, the sublime and the ridiculous are two sides of the same coin, co-existent within eternity.

My Lovely Enemy demands to be read at least twice. It is a gigantically conceived, often magnificent, sometimes exasperating, always tormented novel that cannot possibly be absorbed and appreciated the first time around. This is especially true of the ending which I defy any reader to anticipate or to come to accept without considerable inner debate. For myself, the first time I encountered the closing pages, I read them with a sense of shock, almost of outrage; the second time, a sadder and wiser man, I read them literally with tears in my eyes. It's that sort of book.

Jack Hodgins and the Sources of Invention

The following article was first published in *Essays on Canadian Writing* in 1987. Though it stands, I think, on its own, it began as an elaboration of another author's research-article in the same journal. Here I try to demonstrate how scholarly historical research needs to be approached imaginatively in order to produce an enhanced reading of a literary text.

IN THE TWENTY-EIGHTH ISSUE of *Essays on Canadian Writing* (Spring 1984), JoAnn McCaig discussed the extent to which Donal Keneally, one of the main characters in Jack Hodgins's *The Invention of the World*, was based on the story of Brother XII, a disreputable religious leader and cult founder who created a bizarre community on Vancouver Island in the late 1920s. This is a useful article in many respects, since it gathers together a good deal of information with which most Hodgins readers had not been familiar, though in my opinion it does not pursue its subject far enough. McCaig confines her investigations to the relation between the historical facts or rumours concerning Brother XII's community and certain narrative events in Hodgins's novel. But the information about Brother XII comes to us in various forms of writing with their own conventions and special qualities. I hope, in the following pages, to develop McCaig's findings by raising a more challenging literary-critical aspect of the subject.

One difficulty with McCaig's article lies in the excessively simple fact/fiction dichotomy upon which it is, for the most part, based. She offers what appear at first sight to be hard facts about Brother XII, but, when we turn to her notes, we discover that they are often drawn from highly untrustworthy sources. Most intriguing is the book-length account by Herbert Emmerson Wilson, who claims to be Brother XII's brother. This is a tricky text, which I shall be considering in some detail later. The rest are pieces of popular journalism with titles like 'The Swindling Swami of British Columbia' or 'Brother XII, Master with a Whip'. The best of these is Pierre Berton's account, 'The Strange Case of The Brother, XII', published in *My Country* (1976). But even this article, which seems to have drawn upon press information sources, provides no documentation, so the authority for individual statements is difficult, if not impossible, to check. In terms of detail, all these accounts differ drastically; as McCaig fairly remarks, 'The story of Brother XII's Aquarian Foundation is a maze of contradictions and mysteries, of unanswered and unanswerable questions' (131). One is reminded, indeed, of Strabo Becker's tale in *The Invention of the World*, which 'exists somewhere ... in the confusion of tales and lies and protests and legends and exaggerations' (xi). A historically trained literary detective might well uncover further evidence after a careful search in contemporary newspaper and legal records, but this (interesting as it might be) would not be likely to cast further light on Hodgins's methods in creating his novel. More can, however, be said about the way Hodgins read and adapted his sources – which would not, incidentally, have included Berton, since *The Invention of the World* was written before *My Country* appeared.[1] My own interest is not so much in the truth or falsehood of the available records as in the stimulus that they gave to Hodgins's creative imagination.

It is worthwhile to begin with a piece of evidence that McCaig did not cite. In an interview dating from 1979, Hodgins made the following statement about *The Invention of the World* and this particular cluster of sources:

1 Hodgins has stated that the first draft of *The Invention of the World* was written 'in the fall and winter of 1974-75' (Hancock 61). In addition, Macmillan held up publication of the completed manuscript so that it did not appear too soon after *Spit Delaney's Island* (1976).

> I toyed with the idea of writing a novel about the infamous Brother Twelve and his colony of religious followers.... I discovered very early in my attempt at research that people didn't want to talk about it. So I couldn't get very far if I wanted to be faithful to fact. And then, while I was making these attempts, some other story began to tell itself in my head, much more interesting to me. I abandoned Brother Twelve very early and got on with the job of the Donal Keneally story. (Hancock 76)

This observation is of considerable interest. It implies that the original conception of the novel was much closer to historical fiction than is *The Invention of the World* as we now have it; it suggests that Hodgins himself began with a project not all that far removed from Becker's in the completed novel; and it is reasonable to assume, because of his original intention 'to be faithful to fact', that he had gathered a good deal of whatever information was available about Brother XII.

The most detailed account in print at that time was *Canada's False Prophet: The Notorious Brother Twelve* (1967), written, as I have already indicated, by the man who claimed to be a brother of his subject. (For convenience, I shall refer throughout this paper to the author of *Canada's False Prophet* as Wilson and to its subject as Brother XII.) McCaig describes Wilson as 'somewhat suspect as a source' (139n3), a remark which can only be classified as sublime understatement. Although it offers itself as 'a true story' (7), his book ought to provoke extreme mistrust even in the most gullible of readers. The trickiness of the book is signposted in the preface where Wilson begins with a text from the New Testament ('*Many false prophets shall arise and deceive many*'), introduces himself as 'Reverend Wilson, ordained minister', and then promises a story of 'degradation' and 'orgies, of weird sexual rites, of cruelty, of greed, of free love, and of black magic'. All this is presented 'out of a sense of atonement' (7). Later, as McCaig notes, he claims to have known the notorious Madame Zee before she became Brother XII's last wife, casually remarking: 'She had been my mistress for several years, and had often preached with me at revival meetings' (118). Wilson possessed considerable comic gifts. It may also be worth noting that he wrote another book, *I Stole $16,000,000,* in collaboration with Thomas P. Kelley, author of *The Black Donnellys*.[2]

Canada's False Prophet is a journalistic narrative that, although purporting to be non-fiction, tells its story in a fictional mode complete with dialogue and suspenseful climaxes. Once again, no documentary evidence is forthcoming, and the writing gets suspiciously vague whenever specific dates and places would seem to be most important. Above all, it shows distinct signs of being written by a ghost-writer; the language, idiom, and slang all seem most unlikely for a man who would be in his eighties at the time of publication. There is also an extraordinary *naïveté* about the attempt to maintain an illusion of non-fiction. Without any conceivable motive, Brother XII is always writing convenient letters to the author to give him information that he could not otherwise obtain. All in all, this book belongs to the kind of popular fake biography that Robertson Davies describes so amusingly in *Fifth Business* – though *Phantasmata,* the 'official' story of Magnus Eisengrim, would have been far more skilfully and elegantly written than Wilson's book!

For the sophisticated reader, the first reaction to Wilson's narrative must surely be that it is an enormous confidence trick. He is continually marvelling at the way in which Brother XII would deceive people – many of them efficient and apparently intelligent people – into accepting his obviously phoney religious vision. Yet, while Wilson is insisting upon this, we get the uneasy sense that he is at the same time revelling in his own power to make his readers believe in an account which, while it clearly contains versions of factual events, entangles them in a web of fairly standard and even tawdry fictional convention. The final

2 It is now known that *Canada's False Prophet: The Notorious Brother Twelve* was ghost-written by Thomas P. Kelley (MacIsaac 78). [1989]

chapter outdoes itself in invented fantasy. While most authorities agree that Brother XII died in Switzerland in 1934, Wilson is not content with so tame an ending. Instead, he claims that in 1943, while he was himself operating a store in Brisbane, Australia, Brother XII appeared on his doorstep, a dying man. He gave Wilson a map showing where his treasure was buried at the Vancouver Island colony, but 'for reasons that I myself have never understood', Wilson remarks drily, '[I] have still to investigate the map's authenticity'. When Brother XII died, Brisbane was in the middle of a gravediggers' strike, so Wilson had to make private arrangements. The book ends: 'Three days after he died, I buried my wonderful and beloved Brother Edward, under the name of Mrs William Knight, in Sydney, Australia' (144). Hodgins's fantasy ending to *The Invention of the World* seems almost staid by comparison.

That Hodgins was familiar with Wilson's book before embarking on *The Invention of the World* seems obvious. It would be a mistake, however, to suppose that he used it straightforwardly as a factual source for his own fiction. He would soon have recognized the fictive elements in this supposedly factual story, and must surely have been fascinated by the blatant literary deceptions ('inventions') that the book practises by its deliberate and, to a novelist like Hodgins, its refreshingly vigorous blurring of the boundary-lines between fact and fiction. As one reads *Canada's False Prophet* with *The Invention of the World* in mind, one continually encounters hints to suggest that Hodgins studied it as a stimulus to his own brand of imaginative creation. Words, attitudes, incidents reappear subtly transformed. At the opening of Wilson's book, for instance, we find this: 'The following story, then, is that of my brother, Edward Arthur Wilson, and of the religion he *invented*' (7; my emphasis). The immediately following insistence that it is 'a true story' recalls a number of places in Hodgins's novel where the outrageous or unlikely is offered jokingly as the truth. Thus the narrator of 'The Eden Swindle', after recounting the myth of Keneally's fight with the bailiff, remarks, 'The truth of it was simpler' – and goes on to maintain that Keneally twisted the bailiff's arm till it came out of its socket and the wounded man left 'a trail of blood behind him that scorched the grass and melted stones' (88). A related effect occurs when Edward Guthrie in the 'Scrapbook' section tells Becker, 'You're a fool and more than a fool if you believe one word anybody tells you about that Keneally,' and almost at once continues: 'So listen to this, I won't bullshit you, it's the truth' (207). The climax to this particular comic *leitmotif* comes at the opening of 'Second Growth', when Becker introduces the fantastic conclusion with the words: '*This is the true story of what happened*' (339). One might even argue that Hodgins reverses Wilson's fictionalized version when he offers an explanatory note in the prefatory material: 'This is a work of fiction; its characters and situations are imaginary.' This usual diplomatic statement of limited liability now serves as one strand in an elaborate joke about the relativity of truth and 'invention'.

Despite Hodgins's denial that any of the Vancouver religious colonies has served as a model, there are undoubted echoes, if not of historical truth, then at least of Wilson's sensationalist version. In the opening chapter, Brother XII is supposed to have made a local girl pregnant while he was still a young man, and Wilson observes: 'she had assumed that he was truly a god' (14). The equivalent girl in Hodgins learns in a dream 'that her child would be fathered by a bull-god from the sky' (69). Wilson goes on to assert that 'on one of his trips to his beloved Vancouver Island, he was struck by a blinding light' (18). Hodgins eschews the cliché, turning the scene into comedy when Keneally discovers a seacoast as rainy as Ireland where his people would feel at home. Later references in Wilson to Brother XII's 'stiff catatonic trance', 'an imitation of an epileptic fit' (23), and the claim that one of his early followers was 'a partial cripple' (30) are taken up and transformed by Hodgins. Even the word 'crazy', which Hodgins employs almost as a verbal trademark, is to be found in Wilson in references to Brother XII's 'crazy notes' (22) and his 'crazy trance acts' (25). Other characteristics that Keneally shares with Brother XII are weaknesses for women and luxurious travel (Wilson *passim*; Hodgins 209, 210). According to Wilson, when Brother XII was in England spreading his message and appealing for funds, he called his redecorated hall his 'Temple of Revelation' (38); the biblical allusion is obvious enough, but this is nonetheless a phrase that Hodgins may well have picked up for the name of Keneally's Revelations Colony of Truth (the main dwelling-house, 'the House of Revelations' in *The Invention of the World* [xi], was 'the House of Mystery' in Wilson (62)).

The list could be continued. In Wilson's version, Brother XII claimed that he would lead his followers to an 'Eden on Earth', a 'paradise' (48, 59-60); in Hodgins, the Eden is a swindle, and the only paradise in the vicinity is the 'Paradise Beer Parlour' (95). As McCaig has noted, the story of Nell Keneally and Christopher Wall that Becker tries to piece together in 'Scrapbook' is based on Wilson's highly unlikely account of the relationship between Alma, Brother XII's first wife, and a young man named Graham (72-85). McCaig also compares Keneally's assertion, 'There is no God' (100), with one of Brother XII's statements – though both read like vulgarized Nietzsche. To this may be added the suggestion that Keneally's trick involving smoke without fire (99-100) seems clearly derived from one of Wilson's anecdotes: 'To further convince [his followers] of his divinity, he took to carrying with him "a flaming stone whose fire did not burn him."... I believe he said that it was done with a piece of naphtha' (46). And at this point it may be worth noting that, although Keneally is an authentic and not uncommon Celtic name, Hodgins may have been encouraged to employ it by the fact that Mary Connally was the name of one of Brother XII's duped followers.[3]

But these resemblances of detail, though often interesting and

3 Wilson altered proper names as a gesture towards members of the colony who were still alive. The woman he calls 'Mrs Boyd' (75 ff.) is given her real name, Mary Connally, in other accounts, including Rasky's and Berton's.

enlightening, are ultimately less important than the stimulus that Wilson's book offered to the tone and general direction of Hodgins's novel. There came a point, as we have seen, when Hodgins decided that he could not write a novel on the Brother XII material. In Hodgins's own terms, the Brother XII story gave way to the Donal Keneally story; what this means, I suggest, is that Hodgins became aware of a rich body of subject matter in the complex inter-relations between such concepts as history, fact, truth on the one hand and myth, fiction, falsehood on the other. Hodgins asserts that the character of Maggie Kyle eventually developed as a 'gradual revelation ... opposed to the character of Donal Keneally', and that he became fascinated 'with a pattern that began to grow involving various types of counterfeits – maps, fake historical sites, alter egos, idols, imitation Edens' (Hancock 76). I would argue that Wilson's book served as a catalyst in bringing this material into creative focus.

Brother XII was a counterfeit, and Wilson's 'true story' of his adventures is also a counterfeit. In commenting on the significance of his title – that it is concerned with the invention rather than the creation of the world – Hodgins has remarked that his novel 'is a story about counterfeits' (Hancock 62). Characteristically, he creates a series of inventions alongside those of Brother XII / Keneally. Thus Wade Powers's phoney fort ('STEP INTO HISTORY' (130)) acts as both a parallel and a counterpart to Keneally's phoney community, providing additional evidence of the ease with which people are deceived – and even desire to be deceived. Indeed, as we read through the novel, we become aware that Wade, though offered as a basically sympathetic figure, shares some surprising and disturbing similarities with Keneally. On his first appearance, Maggie tells the story of his exposing himself to her when she was still a child 'and thought he had some ugly growth between his legs' (23); we are reminded of this later when we encounter the myth of Keneally and his 'sack of turnips' (72, 73, 250). In discussion with Horseman, Wade openly describes his fort as a tourist-trap – 'Like magic, it fools them' (160) – and the simile recalls Keneally once again. Even Wade's protest against the work ethic is not just a matter of laziness, but a counter to the appalling prospect of ceaseless work without adequate reward that is the lot of Keneally's enslaved colonists.

But Wade, unlike Keneally, is redeemable. We first see him at a tree-climbing contest where he is significantly more successful on the ascent that on the descent (30). Although reluctant to accept the idea of his 'buried twin' (315), he at last comes to realize (on another ascent in the 'Pilgrimage' section) that he belongs on the side of the genuine rather than the phoney. *The Invention of the World* may be 'a story about counterfeits', but it is also – unlike Wilson's book – about 'Second Growth'. After Wade has set his affairs in order by tearing down his fort, his marriage to Maggie Kyle (the most obvious contrast to Keneally in the novel, representing a life-celebrating genuineness) becomes a union for good, and at the end of the book the two are magically transplanted back to the colony by the divine Horseman to create the paradise that Keneally has promised but failed to deliver.

At the same time, Hodgins's presentation of Wade's fort serves as a commentary, within the fiction, on Strabo Becker's attempts to penetrate to the truth of history. The validity of Becker's archives, the scrapbooks and newspaper clippings and old photographs and cassette tapes and notebooks described in the prologue (x), is continually undercut in the course of the novel. The recordings and newspaper clippings in 'Scrapbook' contradict each other: 'they'll lie just to please you, they'll pass on what some other stupid bugger told them and call it gospel, and the truth is they don't know *nothing*' (207). Moreover, Lily Hayworth tells Becker: 'I get a kick out of knowing I can tell you any kind of lie and you'd believe it' (261). Ultimately Becker, who begins in the belief that he can 'absorb all this chaos' and 'make it finally his own' (xii), is forced to admit that Keneally's story '*has returned to the air where I found it, it will never belong to me, for all my gathering and hoarding*' (339). The nearest that we can come to the 'truth' of Brother XII/Keneally's story is not in

Wilson's 'invented' counterfeit, nor in Becker's archival gatherings (which turn as we read into the kind of historical fiction that Hodgins abandoned), but in Hodgins's own creative overview that offers a complex but genuine myth.

Asked by an interviewer to define myth, Hodgins replied: 'Lies that tell the truth' (Hancock 76). 'Myth', said Becker on the top of the Irish mountain, 'like all the past, real or imaginary, must be acknowledged.... Even if it's not believed. In fact, especially when it's not believed' (314). Once again, I suspect that Wilson may have obliquely influenced this aspect of *The Invention of the World.* Throughout *Canada's False Prophet* he insists, reasonably enough, that Brother XII's beliefs were no more than a composite of ideas culled from many of the world's existing religions. In *The Invention of the World,* Hodgins adapts this principle to the presentation of myth. We might say that Hodgins creates a myth that is both a celebration and a parody of myth, and he does so by inserting allusions to, and echoes of, a variety of mythic traditions into his basic story. Judaeo-Christian myth is represented not only by the Eden references, but also by the parallel to Moses and his leading of the Israelites towards the Promised Land, by various references to Messiah figures, and by the Yeats-like parody-annunciation that sets the whole book in motion. Classical myth is similarly quarried, as the section entitled 'The Wolves of Lycaon' indicates. Christopher Wall encounters Nell Keneally in circumstances that are doubtless based on Wilson's phoney-historical account, but the scene is also reminiscent of Odysseus's meeting with Nausikaa, just as the demonic annunciation simultaneously recalls the story of Zeus and Europa. Moreover, as Jan Horner has noted, bulls are also prominent in Celtic myth (*The Cattle Raid of Cooley* provides occasional subtextual analogues for the novel), and 'The Eden Swindle' is littered with references to Cuchulain and Brian Boru and Finn MacCool and Cathleen ni Houlihan. This is not just a whimsical exercise in comparing mythologies; in one sense Keneally's story provides Hodgins with a serious illustration of the way 'myth' can shift in meaning from 'sacred story' to 'deceptive fiction'. By the same token, a skilled artist like Hodgins can transform the material of Wilson's deceptive fiction into a story that, if not sacred, is complex and richly satisfying.

Finally, I wish to demonstrate how Wilson may have stimulated the technical high spirits that Hodgins displays to such advantage in this novel. At one point Wilson writes: 'incredible as it may seem, there are records to prove that ...' (90). As we might expect, no records are forthcoming. Hodgins must have delighted in this kind of blatant flaunting of rhetorical gimmicks. He may also have picked up an idea from a curious passage in which Wilson relates a conversation between Alma and Graham, the equivalents to Nell Keneally and Christopher Wall in the novel. Since Alma is murdered and Graham disappears, there is no way in which Wilson could credibly have obtained the details. In Hodgins's version, this is made possible by Christopher's telling the story to his brother, who in turn tells it to Becker. The set-up is intriguingly reminiscent of the whole organization of Wilson's book in which brother confides in brother. Hodgins adds an extra turn of the screw by having Morris Wall comment: 'it sounded too much like one of those book stories to be true' (185).

But Hodgins makes even bolder play with the problem of sources. The whole story is based upon a logical deception: '*Donal Keneally's mother started it all.... When she was told in a dream that her child would be fathered by a black bull from the sky, she fell off the side of her bed in alarm and knocked all memory right out of her skull*' (xii). If the last clause is true, no memory of the dream can possibly exist. Similar jokes are played in 'The Eden Swindle'. Thus the Irish story-teller comments on the scene in which Keneally turns God into a machine: 'The memory of that day was never mentioned by any of them to another and was not even passed on to the following generations, so that when the youngest child there, a Miss Kitty Daly, drowned in the tide at Rossbeigh as a lady of seventy-three in nineteen hundred and sixty-one, the final trace of the day's memory was completely erased' (100). Similarly, the narrator quotes a letter from Daniel

Doherty written the night before he was executed; but we are also told that the jailer tossed it into the fire without opening it (104). These seem to be deliberate reminders of the essential deceptiveness of fiction. That Hodgins openly draws attention to them might be said to rob them of their insidiousness; on the other hand, they may be examples of the way in which we as readers, like Brother XII / Keneally's followers or the tourist-visitors at Wade's fort – or, for that matter, the readers of *Canada's False Prophet* – are eager to be deceived.

The Invention of the World, then, thanks in part to the example of Herbert Emmerson Wilson and other fictional inventors who provoked Hodgins to do likewise but also otherwise, is a novel about the fictive art. It was published at a time when post-modernist attitudes and slogans ('*il n'y a pas de hors-texte*', and all that) were becoming fashionable. Small wonder, then, that the book has attracted a good deal of attention from the newest new criticism. But it would be a mistake to assume that the book is in any way written to a post-modernist formula. On the contrary, *The Invention of the World* is an important novel because Hodgins is insistent that 'the forms of my stories have to grow out of the subject matter'. His earlier unpublished novels failed because, as he notes, 'I was writing the novels I had already read somewhere.' And he is adamant in denying that he is 'in danger of joining those writers who are interested in nothing but playing games with language' (Hancock 63, 61, 57). Hodgins revels in the game, but knows that the end must lie elsewhere. Ironically, *The Invention of the World* is original because it presents the traditional ingredients of fiction – absorbing plot, rich characterization, stylistic energy – in a startlingly new form. Magic realism is a popular, convenient, and initially helpful label, and Hodgins has openly admitted the influence upon him of writers such as Gabriel García Márquez, Jorge Amado, and Mario Vargas Llosa (see Hancock 56, Ohm 4). But, like all labels, it ultimately proves insufficient. Reality, Hodgins reminds us, can be idealistic (Platonic) or down-to-earth (materialistic). His own brand of realism attempts to unite all parts of the spectrum. The vivid immediacy of his presentation of northern Vancouver Island should not prevent us from recognizing his quest for what he has called 'the Reality that exists beyond this imitation reality that we are too often contented with' (Hancock 61). In the last analysis, Hodgins's vision of reality, created rather than invented, is uniquely his own.

Hodgins's 'Pack of Crazies': *The Resurrection of Joseph Bourne*

This review of *The Resurrection of Joseph Bourne*, Jack Hodgins's third book and second novel, was written for *Fiddlehead*, where it appeared in 1980. Despite its winning of the Governor General's award, the novel has not yet received the attention it deserves. I try here to isolate the special qualities of the book while at the same time relating it to the effects achieved in his earlier writings.

'WHAT A PACK OF CRAZIES!'(271) In these words one of Jack Hodgins's characters sums up the rest on the last page of *The Resurrection of Joseph Bourne.* It is a judgement that readers may very well be tempted to take over, and it is one that could also be applied to *Spit Delaney's Island*, Hodgins's collection of short stories (1976) and *The Invention of the World*, his first novel (1977). This latest book can certainly be enjoyed at a simple level of zany make-believe – as one rip-roaring tall tale after another. But is there more to be said about it? Admirers of Hodgins's earlier writings are likely to have approached this one, as I did, with a combination of expectation and foreboding. Surely he would not risk providing the same mixture as before? Yet where could he go after *The Invention of the World*? The answers to these queries, as we might have expected from Hodgins, are predictably unpredictable. We find the same blend of exuberant fantasy and deeply moving pathos (in the words of the novel, 'terribly funny and horribly sad at the same time' (44)), but Hodgins has moved on from Genesis to Revelation. This novel is about the destruction of a world, the apocalypse in question taking place in a northern Vancouver Island logging town, Port Annie, christened (if that's the word) after a grotesque character – the 'God of This World', as Hodgins notes in Blakean mood (145) – with the decidedly Hodginsian name of Fat Annie Fartenburg.

Hodgins has evolved, in fact, a literary medium that can draw upon and successfully combine the magic realism we associate with Gabriel García Márquez and the colloquial blarney of the traditional Irish story-tellers. More to the point, perhaps, he has transformed the myth-and survival-ridden preoccupations of the Canadian literary consciousness into something fresh and compelling, something rich and strange. There is nothing either ponderous or pompous about his mythological adaptations, no sense of a combination of encyclopaedia and midnight oil. On the first page, a woman appears out of the sea like Venus, but she has the contours (and the effect) of Marilyn Monroe; later, a giant wave washes a Peruvian sailor into the bed of a Port Annie virgin, and the situation replays, parodies, and extends the scene of Odysseus's meeting with Nausikaa in Homer. The 'progressive' mayor, continually appearing in different costumes, may be seen as a sort of slapstick Proteus; on the other hand, Jenny Chambers, the ex-stripper Jenny Flambé, is a positive, constructive Salomé. And Joseph Bourne himself – derelict, poet, ideal social worker, and resurrected man – is all things to all men and as the book proceeds manages to suggest (among others) Christ, Joseph, Melchizedek, Prometheus, Ernest Hemingway, and Malcolm Lowry.

If all this sounds strained, I can only insist that, on the contrary, it is both delightful and exhilarating. Wide-ranging in its allusiveness and serious in its overall purpose, the novel is anything but solemn. Although 'the sense of an ending' broods over it in characteristic late twentieth-century fashion, the sense of a beginning is, refreshingly, more conspicuous. Canadian novelists have, after all, combined myth and fantasy before (one thinks immediately of Robert Kroetsch and Roch Carrier). But Hodgins's humour, though occasionally bitter, is never black, cynical, or sick. And the energy that pulsates throughout the book is essentially creative. The resurrection of Joseph Bourne, against all the rules and odds, is offered with remarkable confidence as a defiance of the gloom-and-doom school. He is in hiding at Port Annie, 'on the edge of nothingness', because he has already died to the world: 'the sudden feeling ... had come over him that his life was over, that it added up to nothing at all, that he belonged nowhere in the world, belonged to no one, no place, that he was a homeless friendless purposeless man' (100). It is Venus the goddess of love, in the guise of Raimey the sea-bird ('that cormorant with the cheeky behind' (1)), who makes him snap out of 'the dark despair which was leading him straight to death' (157). As Chaucer knew when he engraved the motto on the Prioress's brooch, *Amor vincit omnia* is a truth that operates on many levels.

The whole novel is based on the conviction that there is 'lots of room for new ways of looking at things' (205). Hodgins's strategy is to undercut the now conventional view of a meaningless world with disturbing intimations of mystery and purpose. Contemporary assumptions are impudently turned on their heads. With the resurrection of Bourne, indeed, 'the marvellous seemed to be perfectly natural, something he couldn't help' (262). In this inverted literature of the absurd, human beings are not diminished but exalted. Even the ridiculous mayor has his moment of dignity when, after the calamitous landslide, he urges the townspeople to 'spring back to life from the ashes of disaster' (265). Their dislocation is even interpreted as 'a chance to find out what they were capable of being' (259), and Jenny the stripper demonstrates the art of 'dancing life back into things' (270).

And all this is offered, not in the spirit of a facile Pollyanna, but as a viable response to the 'miracle' of life. (The words 'miracle' and 'crazy' reverberate through the book.) Hodgins is not just playing with the archetypal symbols of human imagination; he is deliberately rearranging them in fresh yet deeply traditional configurations. Embedded in his text is a series of allusions to modern literary fashion that establish his conscious challenge to the prevailing modes. One of the more 'advanced' members of the Port Annie Creative Writing Club solemnly announces that 'narrative was dead' (63), but her discovery of the principles of the *nouveau roman* prove as outdated as the poetic endeavour of the Canadian Authors Association in F.R. Scott's famous parody. Although Larry Bowman, an avid reader of medieval romance, becomes painfully aware of 'the less romantic minute-by-minute hazards that lay in wait for the heroes of real-life dramas' (120), a case for a modern heroism is ultimately, though playfully and amusingly, made: 'After all, it was only in modern novels that believers were always made to look like fools, with empty hands. In the poems and romances that Bowman read, hoping was not considered to be a crime' (143). When such passages are quoted out of context, they may suggest a tiresomely uplifting didacticism. But in fact, within a novel that encompasses the horrendous and the hilarious, that combines the lusty with the tender, the flamboyantly grotesque with the humanly pathetic, this positive stance contributes to a sense of rich completeness. Hodgins's depiction of life seems not only more attractive but more accurate and more 'real' than that of the post-modern cynicism which has become the convention of the supposed avant-garde.

If *The Resurrection of Joseph Bourne* doesn't quite offer the same sense of delighted surprise that greeted readers of *The Invention of the World*, this is doubtless because we approach the later novel with a more definite awareness of Hodgins's remarkable gifts. The new novel represents the bolstering rather than the establishing of an unusual literary reputation. The advance is, I think, technical. Reading *The Invention of the World*, I was constantly aware, despite my deep admiration, of the precariousness of the achievement. I was never sure whether, on the next page, the whole fictional house of cards might not collapse into a series of accomplished but disunited short stories. *The Resurrection of Joseph Bourne* is more of a controlled whole than its predecessor. The centre of attention is Port Annie, and, although Hodgins moves boldly but dangerously in and out of the consciousness of more than a dozen of its eccentric inhabitants, the centre always holds. We may sometimes, it is true, encounter problems. Initially I found the disappearance of Bourne at the climax of the novel puzzling, and I'm still doubtful if the intellectual justification for this turn of plot – that Bourne can show the way but must not dictate it – excuses what in artistic terms seems a structural wobble. In the main, however, the technical resources here, though less conspicuous than those in *The Invention of the World*, are more stable and ultimately more satisfactory.

It will be a long time, I suspect, before literary criticism develops an adequate approach to novels like *The Resurrection of Joseph Bourne* – or, for that matter, García Márquez's *One Hundred Years of Solitude.* (Attempts are, of course, being made, the most recent – and for Canadian readers one of the most interesting – being Robert Rawdon Wilson's discussion of Robert Kroetsch within the context of magic realism in the Spring 1979 issue of *The Compass.*) The critical tools that suffice for the discussion of traditional realist fiction do not work here. Certainly a brief review cannot even begin to grapple with these complex matters, but I must not end without making reference to Hodgins's stylistic power. Reviewers of *Spit Delaney's Island* and *The Invention of the World* naturally responded to his rhetorical vigour, but I know of no one who commented on the sheer beauty of his prose. This is not something that can be illustrated by brief quotation, nor can it be established by allusion to the standard literary devices. I can only assert that Hodgins writes a flexible, controlled, exquisitely modulated prose. He can move from sensitive description to the colloquial interior monologues of his characters at will, without in any way disturbing the smooth flow of his narrative. His rhythms are clear-cut and finely sculptured, the emphases falling easily and decorously. His prose has an enviably rounded quality; without any sense of self-conscious artifice or the kind of 'fine writing' that is usually so irritating, the sentences shape themselves into a smooth appropriateness that is deeply satisfying. Call it rhetorical eloquence, high style, the gift of the Irish gab, or what you will, it is a faculty that sets Jack Hodgins, with three fine books to his credit, in a class by himself. He is easily the most exciting and original of the younger Canadian fiction writers who have come into prominence in the last few years. And once again we ask with awe and amazement: where will he go from here?

On the Edge of Something Else: Jack Hodgins's Island World

This article began modestly as a review of *The Barclay Family Theatre* for *Canadian Forum* at the time of the book's first publication in 1981. Later, when preparing a collection of Hodgins material, J.R. (Tim) Struthers invited me to extend it to include a review of *The Honorary Patron.* Since *Spit Delaney's Island* is also discussed briefly, the article's appearance here rounds off a discussion of Hodgins that considers all his major books published up to the end of 1989.

THERE CAN BE NO DOUBT that Jack Hodgins has written himself into Canadian literature. *Spit Delaney's Island* (1976), a collection of linked stories, was followed by two novels in quick succession, *The Invention of the World* (1977) and *The Resurrection of Joseph Bourne* (1979), by *The Barclay Family Theatre* (1981), another series of linked stories, and now, after a longer interval than usual, by another novel, *The Honorary Patron* (1987). Here I shall be concentrating on the last two books with glances back, where appropriate, to the earlier work. The qualities – hilarious, haunting, half comic, half disturbing, often touching, always technically masterful – that we have come to expect in Hodgins's writing are again exhibited by *The Barclay Family Theatre.* So they are, in a sense, by *The Honorary Patron,* but this new novel further develops certain Hodginsian preoccupations, and even breaks new ground in exploring, sometimes poignantly and even wistfully, 'the giant comedy of growing old' (293). More important, Hodgins's fictions are beginning to form a varied yet distinct corpus – suggesting that he deserves more detailed and extended attention. Both *The Barclay Family Theatre* and *The Honorary Patron* need to be read not merely for themselves but within the context of all of Hodgins's work to date.

TO BEGIN AT THE BEGINNING, *Spit Delaney's Island* is made

up of a medley of stories connected by a common locale. The protagonists are all Vancouver Islanders, mostly from the logging and pulp-mill communities in the north; more to the point, all of them are vigorous, independent, irrepressible 'characters'. Spit Delaney himself appears in the first and last stories – 'book-ends', Hodgins has called them in an interview by Geoff Hancock (73) – and so provides a loose frame for the whole. But the stories are linked in other ways. Since Spit's marriage is breaking up, the first story is called 'Separating' – and separation becomes an important word, and concept, in the book as a whole. Spit expands the image into something close to a philosophy of life. '*Where is the dividing line?*' he asks – between sea and land, between man and animal, between people and things, '*Between what is and what isn't*' (7-8) – and one can extrapolate that Spit's creator is also exploring the dividing line between what is and what is not possible in fiction. Again, Spit sees himself as 'on the edge' (3) and Vancouver Island, in an image subsequently to be developed, is portrayed as being on the edge of a continent. The second story in *Spit Delaney's Island,* 'Three Women of the Country', takes place in an isolated community called 'Cut Off', and Mr Porter's remark, '"I guess you never really know anybody else"' (41), develops the idea of separation still further. While *Spit Delaney's Island,* as a whole, may be a magnificently vivid evocation of life in the country north of Nanaimo, it has something significant, and universally relevant, to say about what separates man from man.

Hodgins's art is one of subtle interconnections: *The Barclay Family Theatre,* we discover, is also enclosed in a frame. The book begins and ends with first-person reminiscences by Barclay Philip Desmond, who appears in another story, 'The Lepers' Squint', as an author in the process of writing a novel. But *The Barclay Family Theatre* – and here the interconnections become even more complex – takes its germ from a sentence in *The Invention of the World*: 'Mr and Mrs Barclay had raised seven daughters who'd grown up and married loggers and mill workers and truck drivers and moved off in every direction, leaving the two of them alone ...' (140). The centrifugal pattern implied there becomes centripetal here.

By the time we reach the last story, 'Ladies and Gentlemen, the Fabulous Barclay Sisters!', we realize that the individual tales are linked by intricate familial relationships, though these relationships are sometimes fairly remote. 'Mr Pernouski's Dream', for example, is about the second husband of Christina Barclay, who, by her first husband, is the mother of Maggie Kyle, heroine of *The Invention of the World.* Another sister, Mabel (though we – and perhaps Hodgins – were unaware of it at the time that *The Resurrection of Joseph Bourne* was published), is the wife of Jacob Weins, mayor of Port Annie in Hodgins's second novel, who is himself now resurrected in the literary sense to become the main character in 'The Sumo Revisions'.

Tracing these interconnections may seem excessively complicated, like finding one's way through the tangled relationships in William Faulkner's Yoknapatawpha series – and Hodgins admits in the Hancock interview that Faulkner was a major, and initially crippling, influence on his early unpublished work (54). But, as in the case of *Spit Delaney's Island,* the frame for Hodgins's second collection of linked stories is by no means the only unifying device. The provisional title for *The Barclay Family Theatre* was *Invasions,* and Hodgins told Viveca Ohm that the stories are 'about the same family of people, invading other parts of the world, and in return being invaded themselves' (6).[1] As we are reading the book, we may not immediately recognize 'the same family of people'; but we quickly become aware of the preoccupation with invasion, just as we discern the importance of 'separating' in *Spit Delaney's Island,* of 'invention' (and counterfeit) in *The Invention of the World,* of 'resurrection' (and apocalypse) in *The Resurrection of Joseph Bourne.* These invasions can be literal, as in 'Invasions '79', which ends, on an international

---

1 J.R. (Tim) Struthers has informed me that Hodgins also considered the title *Allied Invasions.*

political note rare in Hodgins, with the Russian invasion of Afghanistan, or in 'The Plague Children', the story closest to 'magic realism', in which a section of the island is overrun by hordes of hippies in search of a science-fiction crop of hallucinatory mushrooms. Elsewhere in the collection, the invasions are more personal; in the last paragraph of the last story, one of the sisters emphasizes Hodgins's concern by observing that 'All fiction was an invasion of one kind or another, or it had no point' (299).

But *The Barclay Family Theatre* is also a book about dreams (which rarely come true), about coming to terms with both the possibilities and the limitations of life, and especially (as the title suggests) about acting and role-playing. Moreover, it is a book about art and creativity (there are stories concerned with music, painting, novel-writing, and *kabuki*), though such intimations of high culture make the volume sound pompous, and it is certainly not that. Hodgins's books are rich and packed with implication, but they are compulsively readable and are written to be enjoyed. There is no intellectual barrier between Hodgins's fiction and the general reader (though readers of *The Honorary Patron* will be more comfortable if they have a basic awareness of the history of modern painting). To appreciate his work all that is requisite is an openness to imaginative creation. Yet much more is going on than the surface high jinks and high spirits may suggest.

Take, for example, 'The Sumo Revisions'. Jacob Weins has been dragged to a *kabuki* performance in Tokyo by his wife, and wishes he were at a wrestling tournament instead. His unsympathetic description of the performance is hilarious – more so if one is acquainted with *kabuki*, but highly comic in any case. Eventually he escapes, and his response to the *sumo* bouts is equally funny. But then, gradually, the humour develops into something more serious. An aging wrestler loses an important fight, is demoted, and will have to retire. What will be his future? Weins wonders, and suddenly remembers that he is himself a mayor without a town. The grotesque 'tub of lard' (see 181) suddenly transforms into an alter ego, as Weins wonders: what will be *my* future? The connection is underlined later when he meets another ex-wrestler and finds that they are the same age. A curious sadness takes over the story, and all sorts of subtleties become evident. Weins, who was always dressing up in flamboyant costumes as mayor, is here the only ordinarily clothed figure (from his viewpoint) in a strange world of apparent fancy dress. Presented with a portrait of himself by a native, he is suddenly faced with an image of how he looks to others: '"A Japanese with big ears and a long nose"' (232). What seems to have begun as Hodgins's zestful reaction to an exotic and unfamiliar world develops into a still amusing but ultimately poignant portrait of a man – like Spit Delaney – at a critical juncture in his life. The Barclay family theatre is one in which the dramatic masks can change suddenly from laughter to something close to tears.

This tonal pattern recurs throughout the book. As in Shakespearean comedy, and perhaps in all great comedy, there comes a moment when each story teeters on the edge of something else – sometimes tragedy, sometimes horror, sometimes the sad realization of what is unattainable. Such moments happen, of course, in Hodgins's earlier work, but they are more apparent here. We begin to perceive that 'magic realism' is no longer an adequate description for his fiction. In 'More than Conquerors', the idea that Anna Payne may rise from the dead exists merely as a horrifying illusion in the mind of her unbalanced mother. This story exists in another dimension from *The Resurrection of Joseph Bourne* – closer to 'realism', perhaps, but at this point literary terms bend and break under the burdens we try to put upon them. Ultimately, Hodgins's realism – and his work warrants this term – is neither 'magic realism' nor the official kind that reproduces the diurnal round; and certainly it is nothing like 'photographic realism' or 'socialist realism'. Instead, Hodgins's realism portrays that strange world of wonder, farce, challenge, and terror that impinges upon us at all times and from all sides. Mirrors occur in a number of the stories in *The Barclay Family Theatre,* and it is not too far-fetched to insist that this book holds the mirror up to a nature that is all around us but that too many people fail to recognize.

WHERE *The Barclay Family Theatre* is expansive in the sense that characters move outwards from Vancouver Island to such places as Ottawa, Ireland, and Japan, *The Honorary Patron* presents a contrasting pattern. Here the central figure, Jeffrey Crane, is another aging man at a critical juncture in his life. An islander who has lived in Europe for forty years and become a well-known art teacher, he is suddenly invited back to 'The Pacific Coast Festival of the Arts' (25), an unthinkable venture when he was a young man. This is a book, then, about the return of a native to the scenes of his early years in a town which, though never fully identified, approximates to a no-name Nanaimo. We find here the same 'zany' individuals that have become habitual in Hodgins's fiction, and the setting, though never described in detail, is offered characteristically as 'a backdrop landscape painted by a Hollywood designer with an unlimited budget and a talent for gross exaggeration' (84). At the same time, there is an introspective quality about the book that we haven't encountered before, at least in so sustained a fashion. This is the story of a man who 'had lived for sixty-six years without learning the first thing about how to live what remained' (272), one who had 'to be jarred and shaken and shoved back into what they called life' (55). The vitality and zest of island living is conveyed through an elderly, initially sedate, even chastened protagonist.

But the Island, though clearly recognizable as 'Hodgins Country', is presented with a noticeable change of focus. Whereas in the earlier books the shenanigans of the more obstreperous characters, if violent, were generally innocent and often endearing, here they are threatening, even criminal. The loggers on the wedding rampage at the close of *The Invention of the World* belong to an imaginative never-never-land that doesn't closely impinge upon our own world, and can be enjoyed as absurdly high-spirited rather than dangerous. In *The Honorary*

Patron, however, we are in a world of wanton destruction and terrorism. Crane may imagine himself returning to one of the 'few innocent backwaters in the world' (104), but the inhabitants are soon to realize that 'Evil had been discovered in the town' (220). The area that had been described in *The Resurrection of Joseph Bourne* as 'the ragged green edge of the world' (20) comes to recognize itself as part of Marshall McLuhan's 'global village'. Indeed, in some respects this is a novel about the relation of British Columbia – and Canada – to History. Crane left his up-island backwoods for Europe '"as European history was coming to an end'" (52); he returns to Vancouver Island in the process of realizing 'that being a part of things meant being a part of the horror' (285).

Ultimately, however, many of the elements that we first register as new and different are found to have been anticipated in Hodgins's earlier works. In particular, the struggle between art and philistinism, which has been a minor but continuing preoccupation before (Spit and the poetess Phemie Porter in 'Spit Delaney's Island', the cultural attitudes of Mayor Weins in *The Resurrection of Joseph Bourne,* the responses of his neighbours to Eli Wainamoinen's exhibition of paintings in 'More than Conquerors'), becomes a central concern here. Crane soon discovers that the contemporary islanders are no more ready for The Pacific Coast Festival of the Arts than they were in his day. '"Thought those guys'd never stop talkin' and get on with it"'(65) is a typical reaction after a performance of *Macbeth*; the standard word for cultured people is '"artsy-fartsy"' (68, 215); the town's 'one annual big event', its 'one true enthusiasm' (264), is stock-car racing (= bathtub weekend?). That this problem, too, has a national as well as a regional relevance is underlined in the scene in which, on the plane from Toronto to Calgary, Crane is surrounded by loud-mouthed businessmen and businesswomen wearing cowboy boots, and by an excessively rambunctious baseball team. Hodgins has frequently spoken in interviews about his need as a child to keep his literary interests secret in order to avoid ridicule; that necessity still rankles, and here he presents the anti-intellectualism of his compatriots with his usual zest but also with the trenchancy of a John Metcalf.

Another feature of the novel which helps to highlight effects in previous books is the undisguised allegorical intention that is manifest here. Careful readers of Hodgins have always been alert to larger meanings beneath the beguilingly humorous surface of his fiction. Spit Delaney, drawn down to the seashore in 'Separating' and lured up the mountain in 'Spit Delaney's Island', represents one instance. Hodgins himself in the Hancock interview has acknowledged 'seven different levels' (65) on which the story of *The Invention of the World* could be told, and the (very different) 'supernatural' qualities of Donal Keneally and Horseman can hardly be interpreted except in an allegorical way. Furthermore, the story of Wade Powers and his phoney fort (which he eventually destroys himself) clearly implies deeper meanings. In *The Resurrection of Joseph Bourne* most of the scenes seem to cry out for allegorical interpretation. For David L. Jeffrey, in 'A Crust for the Critics', the novel 'portrays a contest between charity and cupidity' (74) while J.R. (Tim) Struthers, in 'Thinking about Eternity', has pointed out that it is structured 'between a Flood and an Apocalypse' (129). In *The Barclay Family Theatre,* to confine myself to a single example, Mr Pernouski doesn't represent 'Eden Realty' (72) by accident.

Such readings have always been available. In *The Honorary Patron,* however, an allegorical meaning is explicit, insisted upon within the text. When Crane is about to return to Canada, one of his European cronies exclaims: '"A mythic journey! An old man in search of his dream children, deep into the caverns beneath the unfabled city at the edge of the western world!"' (55). True, we have just been told that 'Literary Karl could find an allegory even in the way you tied your shoelaces or failed to tie them' (55), but this only drives home the point. And in a climactic scene, where Crane, Elizabeth Argent, and Blackie Blackstone look down into a seemingly bottomless pit that has opened up beneath his childhood home, and where they are in the company of a young parachutist referred to as '*Der Engel vom Himmel*' (313), we are close to the medieval three-tiered universe and the obsessively allegorical cast of the medieval mind.

So much for the ways in which *The Honorary Patron* fits into the established characteristics of Hodgins's earlier work. But there are significant developments that I have not yet considered. We find here a more demanding fictional structure than before, but less sustained vigour of style. Technically, the book operates through an authorially-imposed limited perspective: Crane is 'on stage' from start to finish, like Strether in Henry James's *The Ambassadors*. This is a new challenge for Hodgins – the mirror image, we might say, of the situation in *The Resurrection of Joseph Bourne*, where the town is the centre and attention is split among a large and rich cast of characters. Perhaps it is this concentration on an intellectual and (albeit against his will) essentially passive protagonist that contributes to the comparatively sober quality of the prose. While there are many vintage Hodgins eccentrics here, all with their appropriate speech rhythms – I particularly enjoyed Marisa Boreski and her passion for playing Chopin amid the beauties of nature – I must confess to a slight disappointment in the narrative style, which seems to lack the rhythmic variety and verbal dexterity that have been, for discriminating readers, a prominent feature of Hodgins's writing. Individual sentences still sparkle (I have given in to the temptation to quote several), but they do not accumulate to form a rich prose-texture.

Still conspicuous, however, is Hodgins's fundamentally positive attitude to life, which has always been so refreshing. Though Crane takes his destined part in an absurd plot, he rejects an absurdist philosophy. Even if he had 'made himself enough of a clown and a sad, sad fool to be taken at last for a genuine specimen of twentieth-century man' (263), he refuses to accept as inevitable what one of Hodgins's British Columbian artistic forebears, Ethel Wilson, in *The Innocent Traveller*, characterized as 'the appalling wreckage of our time' (9). Earlier on, Crane had protested against a world of relativity: 'What else was the twentieth century about, if not an attempt to recover from Einstein's blow?' (24). By the end of the novel, a promising young local artist (whom Crane has, to his chagrin, neglected) displays a series of canvases in which '"the tunnel walls"' of subterranean Nanaimo (which are also the abysses beneath all our crumbling houses) are portrayed with '"the old guy's face just sort of peeking out"', as if in search of '"something that would sort of balance out what he scared everybody with before"' (317). The hesitant phrasing is that of the angel parachutist, but it embodies a youthful confidence from which Crane takes hope. Much earlier – in equally hesitant phraseology – Crane had offered his own decidedly traditionalist aesthetic: '"the fashion has been to acknowledge little more than excellence of form. Yet beauty, dignity, that sort of old-fashioned thing is what I've gone on looking for – amongst other things, of course'" (47). So, one might add, has Hodgins. *The Honorary Patron* works throughout in this extraordinarily intricate way. Passage echoes passage across the expanse of what, at 333 pages in the first edition, is by modern standards a more than usually substantial novel. It certainly displays 'excellence of form' but also embodies a quest for beauty and dignity. As a result, it is a book of disorienting shifts of tone, some daring effects, and even (I think) some occasional longueurs, but it is a novel that demands to be read deliberately and imaginatively. If approached in this spirit, it will ultimately yield up some valuable secrets.

I HAVE SUBTITLED THIS ESSAY 'Jack Hodgins's Island World' because, for me, his fiction exists in the fabulous realm he has created between island and world. Like most writers, Hodgins is uneasy about being labelled a regionalist; but he is a regional writer in the most profound sense of that term. He transforms his local backyard into an image of the whole creative universe. He creates (not invents) a world which is (like Thomas Hardy's Wessex and William Faulkner's Yoknapatawpha and Margaret Laurence's Manawaka) both a mirror image of a particular part of the earth's surface and a looking-glass land (there is at least a hint, surely, of Lewis Carroll in his work) – an imaginative space, a world with its own laws and logic. Above all (and this feature is what makes him so inimitable a writer), Hodgins's world is an organic one. The stories grow out of each other. A character from an earlier work suddenly pops up again in a new environment so that we see new aspects of that individual's personality; a minor theme in one story becomes a major preoccupation in another. Who knows what image or phrase in *The Honorary Patron* may not germinate and become the starting-point for a subsequent fiction? There is a remarkable richness, energy, even genius here; long may it continue.

Interpreting and Misinterpreting 'Bluebeard's Egg': A Cautionary Tale

The writing of this article, which has not yet been published elsewhere, coincided with the planning of this book. The subject provides a suitable conclusion for two reasons: first, I have earlier had some hard things to say about Atwood as critic, and it is a pleasure to discuss a piece of fiction that reveals her greatest creative strengths; second, this is an article about both criticism and fiction, and therefore serves as a reminder that the two sections into which *An Independent Stance* has been divided are ultimately inseparable.

THIS ARTICLE HAS ITS ORIGIN in a specific incident. Some months ago I was asked in the course of my academic duties to read an unpublished essay that offered a strictly feminist reading of four short stories by Margaret Atwood. I was especially interested in the treatment of 'Bluebeard's Egg' because the interpretation turned out to be radically different from what I had remembered of the story; on checking the text I discovered that the reading was based on highly selective evidence and could not be reconciled with a careful response to the subtleties of the narrative. Such an experience is not, in itself, uncommon, but the particular example seems to me important as a peculiarly contemporary phenomenon. This circumstance provides an unusually clear instance of what can happen if one begins from a theoretical position and imposes it upon a work of art to which it is not suited. The example therefore deserves more detailed attention. I shall begin with a brief summary of the essay's argument and an explanation of why it seemed to me inadequate. I shall then go on to offer what I hope to be a more satisfactory response to the challenge of the text.

THE PAPER BEGAN BY ASSERTING that Atwood's was a subversive art concerned with the overturning of the accepted myths of a 'patriarchal' society. In such a society, the writer continued, women are inevitably alienated. The purpose of the essay was to show how Atwood documented this alienation in the female protagonists of 'Bluebeard's Egg' and three other stories. The argument is, of course, to all intents and purposes circular: the result is implicit in (even guaranteed by) the terms of the original – I believe, questionable – assertion. In introductory remarks, much was made of the psychological patterns said to distinguish female from male. The underworld, I read, was an emotional world associated with the feminine but feared and misunderstood by men, and so for the most part a feminine domain. Fair enough. I would not pick any quarrel with that formulation. A difficulty came, however, a few pages later when details of the opening of the story were being examined.

'Bluebeard's Egg' begins with Sally, the protagonist, looking out of her kitchen window at the garden lot that 'sweeps downwards, into the ravine; it's a wilderness there ...' (*Bluebeard's Egg* 133). She wanted 'to have a kind of terrace ..., but Edward [her husband] says he likes it the way it is' (133). Sally, however, is disturbed by drunks who, she claims, live in the ravine and occasionally wander over the broken-down fence 'to emerge squinting like moles into the light of Sally's well-kept back lawn' (133). The critic referred to this passage, but drew attention only to the suggestion of male dominance ('Edward says he likes it the way it is'). No mention was made of the surely significant fact that, in this case, it is the woman who fears the ravine and that the supposedly feminine domain is specifically described as inhabited by men. (Ravines, it should be noted, are used in this virtually archetypal sense throughout Atwood's fictional writing, from *The Edible Woman* through *Lady Oracle* to *Cat's Eye,* and this symbolism is clearly insisted upon here as the drunks 'emerge ... into the light'.) Oddly enough, two pages later, the critic went on to quote Frank Davey (from *Margaret Atwood: A Feminist Poetics*) on the language of the male formal garden without apparently noticing that in 'Bluebeard's Egg' we are concerned with a *female* formal garden (Sally's 'terrace', 'well-kept back lawn'). What we must surely deduce from all this is that Atwood does *not* work in terms of these simple dichotomies. 'Bluebeard's Egg' would seem to challenge rather than to uphold the kind of interpretation that the commentator tried to force upon it. One might even go so far as to suggest that, major writer as she is, Atwood uses her subversive art to deconstruct the inadequate clichés of certain kinds of feminist theory.

A similar instance occurred a few pages further on. Here the critic made the acceptable, indeed perceptive observation that in this story Atwood often encloses her characters' true feelings in parentheses. Several instances of such parentheses were quoted, all designed to back up the paper's feminist thesis. Again, fair enough. But here is an example that wasn't quoted:

> Why did she choose [Ed] (or, to be precise, as she tries to be with herself and sometimes is even out loud, *hunt him down*), when it's clear to everyone she had other options? (135; Atwood's emphasis)

The implications of this passage are interesting. The title (and, so far, only the title) has alerted us to read Sally's situation in terms of the original Bluebeard story, which is, of course, a 'patriarchal' fairy tale with a vengeance. Yet there is surely something odd about a potential Bluebeard story in which the woman hunts down the wizard instead of vice versa! The critic presumably ignored this example of parenthetical usage because it didn't fit the essay's thesis; I would argue, however, that it is important for the very reason that it undercuts the thesis. Atwood is indeed being 'subversive', but not in the way the critic thought; on the contrary, Atwood is careful to *balance* the insights derived from these parenthetical passages, to *complicate* the meaning of her story so that it cannot be read as a simple tract, feminist or otherwise.

I have written enough, I think, to cast doubt on the adequacy of the interpretation of 'Bluebeard's Egg' that was proposed. Let me now offer an alternative reading, which will concentrate on the actual use of the traditional fairy tale within Atwood's story (a central topic about which the critic had virtually nothing to say). As I have already indicated, the title provides an initial clue, though Bluebeard is not otherwise mentioned until two-thirds of the way through the narrative. Careful readers, however, will be put on their guard by the title, and will begin to draw certain conclusions. Within a few paragraphs a very different 'fairy tale' reference occurs. Ed, we are told, is 'a child of luck, a third son who ... manages to make it through the forest with all its witches and traps and pitfalls and end up with the princess, who is Sally, of course' (134-35). On the other hand, a reference soon follows to 'Ed's two previous wives' (136) that neatly fits the Bluebeard story. Ed, however, seems an unlikely candidate for a modern Bluebeard. He is presented as stupid, easy-going, apparently considerate, a bit pompous, and (when his profession as 'heart man' (139) is concerned) earnestly serious. At the opening of the story, there is no evidence that he is a woman-chaser; on the contrary, women chase him – they 'corner him on sofas, trap him in bay-windows at cocktail parties' (139). If he has a secret room, it is not in their house but in the hospital, the room where a new X-ray facility is located; moreover, Sally persuades him with little difficulty to take her into it – there is nothing forbidden about it.

It is possible, nonetheless, to entertain some doubts about Ed. Can he really be as stupid as Sally paints him? Indeed, Sally herself sometimes 'sees his stupidity as wilfulness, a stubborn determination to shut things out. His obtuseness is a wall, within which he can go about his business ...' (135). He professes not to know 'what happened with [his earlier] marriages, what went wrong' (136), which causes Sally to consider – in a reference which again recalls fairy tale, that 'she isn't the true bride after all, but the false one' (136). And the X-ray room, however different from the traditional forbidden chamber in the 'house in the forest' (157), still conceals a hint of Bluebeard: '"it was clearly a dangerous place. It was like a massage parlour, only for women. Put a batch of women in there with Ed and they would never want to come out' (147).

Apart from the title, as I have said, any specific reference to Bluebeard is delayed until comparatively late. Eventually we learn that Sally has been taking a night-course entitled 'Forms of Narrative Fiction' (154). After exploring 'The Epic' by reading '*The Odyssey* (selected passages, in translation, with a plot summary of the rest)' (154) – Atwood's subversive art, again – and poking around in Joyce's *Ulysses* in order to suggest Toronto equivalents for the Dublin locales, they go on to discuss 'The Ballad' and are now studying 'Folk Tales and the Oral Tradition' (155). The instructor introduces them to orally transmitted stories and sets them an exercise in which, after listening to a story, they must 'write a five-page transposition, set in the present and cast in the realistic mode' (156). The tale chosen (Atwood reproduces the Grimm version in her text) is the story of Bluebeard. Above all, they are not allowed to use the Universal Narrator, which they have already exploited: 'This time they had to choose a point of view' (156).

That last sentence is, I would submit, the crucial statement in Atwood's story, one that causes us to reconsider all that we have been told in the story so far. If point of view is central to Sally's assignment, it is also central to 'Bluebeard's Egg'. We now realize, if we haven't noticed before, that Atwood is employing limited third-person narration. An authorial voice is invoked, but everything is seen from Sally's viewpoint and consciousness. Moreover, it is now clear that everything we have so far been told has come from the perspective of a Sally who has, throughout the action of the story, had this point-of-view assignment on her mind. (We learn a little later that she first received the assignment 'a full two weeks ago' (158).) If we have speculated about the application of the Bluebeard story to Ed, it may be only because Sally is herself superimposing the story upon the pattern of Ed's life. This is a variant of the characteristic satiric trap that Atwood introduces into so many of her fictions. The whole story, we now see, is about 'point of view'. Once we have assimilated the full implications of this insight, we have to reconsider and reassess all that we have been told.

If we return to the opening of the story with Sally's possible bias in mind, the identification of Ed as Bluebeard begins to look decidedly doubtful. This is our first sight of him: 'He's puttering around the rock garden now; some of the rocks stick out too far and are in danger of grazing the side of Sally's Peugeot, on its way to the garage, and he's moving them around' (134). In other words, he is considerately making things easier for his wife. (The description of the car 'on its way to the garage', as if self-propelled, is a brilliant stroke. It can be interpreted either as Ed's polite refusal to acknowledge Sally's poor driving or Sally's own reluctance to admit this fact.) A few lines earlier, when she has been trying to imagine Ed at high school, she observed: 'Girls would have had crushes on him, he would have been unconscious of it; things like that don't change' (133-34). Hardly a Bluebeard characteristic! The implication, surely, is that Sally's attempt to interpret him as Bluebeard conflicts hopelessly with the evidence.

A little later in our rereading, we shall be struck by the extent to which Sally sees Ed and her relationship with him in specifically literary terms. In the third paragraph, she associates him with A.A. Milne's Winnie the Pooh: '*My darling Edward,* she thinks. *Edward Bear, of little brain. How I love you*' (134). Soon afterwards, she switches to detective fiction:

> ... she was spoiled when young by reading too many Agatha Christie murder mysteries, of the kind in which the clever and witty heroine passes over the equally clever and witty first-lead male, who's helped solve the crime, in order to marry the second-lead male, the stupid one, the one who would have been arrested and condemned and executed if it hadn't been for her cleverness. Maybe this is how she sees Ed.... (135)

Maybe. But if so, this is once again a very different Ed from the one who is offered as a stand-in for Bluebeard – not to mention the interesting association of Ed with a character who is wrongly suspected of a crime. It may also be significant that the first reference to 'Ed's two previous wives' (136) with its Bluebeard implications, occurs within a few lines of the passage just quoted, as if to point up an incongruity.

A children's book, a murder mystery, and now a fairy tale. Sally responds more fully to these than to the abridged and translated *Odyssey* or the brief dip into *Ulysses*. However, these two classic texts may now set up some interesting though complicating reverberations. Homer's hero is a womanizer who eventually returns to an archetypally faithful wife; in Joyce, however, positions are reversed – not only is Molly Bloom unfaithful to Leopold, but Leopold knows it. 'Bluebeard's Egg' is clearly a complex, post-modernist narrative that both flaunts its artifice and depends upon an elaborate intertextuality.

It is evident that 'Bluebeard's Egg' has to be read very warily indeed, and at this point it may be worthwhile considering the section about Sally's job – a section that doesn't immediately further the basic plot. Of her current job we read: 'Luckily Ed has no objection; he doesn't have much of an objection to anything she does' (140). In other words, he is *not* a male chauvinist who interferes with his wife's freedom of action. We are presumably intended to regard this as the opposite of Bluebeard's giving his wives orders as to what they must and must not do. The job in question, second-in-command to the incompetent male editor of a business magazine who does none of the work but receives all the official credit, enables Atwood to make fun of various business attitudes. But even these details are double-edged. Sally's boss was a failure in management but 'couldn't be fired because his wife was related to the chairman of the board' (141). This is (one must assume, deliberately) ambiguous: perhaps the chairman is protecting one of his own sex; but it is equally possible that the editor's wife is exerting indirect but effective female pressure on her male relative. Two paragraphs later, Atwood makes reference to a perennial 'sexist' controversy: do a female employee's duties include making coffee for her male boss? Atwood's detail is incisive: 'she stops short of behaving like a secretary: she doesn't bring him coffee. They both have a secretary who does that anyway' (142). The undermining force of that last sentence contains an almost Swiftian intensity. Clearly, Atwood cannot be easily pigeon-holed in any clear-cut feminist category.

We need to be fully aware of all these complexities of interpretation before we approach the tricky final pages of the story. The immediate emphasis, once the Bluebeard story has been told, is upon Sally's efforts to produce 'her present-day realistic version' (158). And her first response is to reject precisely those versions which, as careful readers, we have been testing: 'The great temptation is to cast herself in the role of the cunning heroine, but again it's too predictable. And Ed certainly isn't the wizard; he's nowhere near sinister enough' (158). But then she decides that 'the intriguing thing about the story, the thing she should fasten on, is the egg', and from there it's a short step first to 'the brilliant idea of writing the story from the point of view of the egg' and then to the parenthetical realization: '(Ed isn't the Bluebeard: Ed is the egg ...)' (159). Clever; perhaps too clever – on Sally's part, not Atwood's. In the fairy tale 'the wizard met his come-uppance' (158); in 'Bluebeard's Egg' it appears to be Sally herself. At her party, imaginative as ever, she decides that one of the guests, Walter Morly, is paying far too much attention to her friend Marylynn for Sally's comfort. She therefore directs her to show Ed the antique she has just bought. Marylynn is quick to read her motive: '"Don't worry," she says, "I won't rape Dr Morly"' (162). But soon afterwards Sally sees Marylynn and Ed together and convinces herself that Ed had his hand on Marylynn's thigh.

Is Ed a candidate for the role of Bluebeard after all? The feminist critic assumed this, but Atwood is not so clear-cut. A few minutes later, Sally begins to doubt the evidence of her own senses: 'Now she isn't sure whether she really saw what she thought she saw' (164). As in *Lady Oracle,* the world of creative fantasy and that of real life have become thoroughly snagged. Ed may be guilty, but if we think back we shall remember how, in the past, Sally has continually fantasized about Ed and other women. I have already shown how she imagines girls having crushes on him when he was a schoolboy, and have commented on her readiness to notice women cornering him on sofas. Earlier in the day she has teased him about women '"hiding in the forsythia"' (148), though she is aware that 'she's made them up' (149). The possibilities of interpretation are now manifold. Perhaps he has been having an affair with Marylynn all along; perhaps Sally is imagining it all; perhaps, with her perpetual teasing, she has actually put the idea into his head; perhaps she is projecting the Bluebeard story on to a very different reality without being aware of it. Later, in the kitchen, Ed makes a general reference to the cleaning-woman as if he doesn't remember her name. Sally, now suspicious, is bothered by this in a way she had never been before, yet it could well be a sign that he doesn't notice – is not interested in – other women. Yet as soon as she begins to interpret, to imagine other versions and other points of view, all seems ambiguous.

And inevitably the story itself ends on a note of ambiguity. After the party, Ed goes to bed while Sally roams the house like a ghostly visitant. When she eventually goes upstairs, we are told that Ed 'is breathing deeply as if asleep. *As if*' (165; Atwood's emphasis). The critic took this at face value, assuming that Ed, having transferred his attention to Marylynn, is feigning sleep in order to avoid his marital obligations, but the italicized phrase draws attention to the ambiguity of the point of view. Once Sally doubts, anything can become 'as if'. We are trapped with her in her limited perspective. The story ends with Sally in a state between sleep and waking, imagining first her own heart in black and white, as on Ed's X-ray screen, and then the egg, pulsing, alive, and in colour. The two images are either opposite or complementary. Her heart is 'cold and white and inert' – as hearts should not be; the egg, previously associated with Ed, is 'glowing softly as though there's something red and hot inside it. It's almost pulsing ...' (166). Each manifests the basic qualities of the other.

The story ends enigmatically on a question – 'what will come out of it?' (166) – but we have already been informed that an egg is a symbol with numerous possible meanings. It can be 'a fertility symbol, or a necessary object in African spells, or something the world hatched out of' (159). Or, in this story, it may be 'a symbol of virginity' (159). And if 'Ed is the egg', what then? If the story closes on a puzzling vision of the egg, this is because Sally has chosen to interpret the story from the egg's point of view and finds that the possibilities are endless. Atwood's story is called 'Bluebeard's Egg' and *is* Bluebeard's egg – an object with a multiplicity of possible interpretations.

THE ABOVE READING lays no claim to comprehensiveness. I have inevitably stressed some aspects of the story and passed over others. But I would submit that it is reasonably faithful to the tone that Atwood establishes and the general narrative movement of the story. In emphasizing the centrality of interpretation rather than advocating *one* interpretation, it at least avoids a blinkered narrowness. Others may well draw attention to further subtleties and refinements, but I see no reason why my reading should not be regarded as an acceptable foundation for further literary-critical discussion.

I must return now, however, to the writer of the unpublished essay. The difference between my reading and hers is that mine arises out of what the story actually says while hers forced the story into a preconceived and distorting pattern. What happened, I suspect, is that, having accepted the ideological attitudes of feminist criticism, the critic jumped to the unjustified conclusion that, because Atwood is a writer interested in feminist issues, she *must* accept this viewpoint and that, as a result, her stories *must* be compatible with the theory. The critic therefore searched 'Bluebeard's Egg' for any evidence that seemed to fit the theoretical imperative and failed to notice the numerous details that conflicted with it.

I write all this not just to cast doubt on one extreme application of feminist theory but to register a warning against excessive reliance on *any* theory. Art, to put the matter bluntly, is larger than theory. If the two conflict, then it is the theory that must be adapted or discarded. The critic came to grief because she had become bemused by theory and assigned to it an authority that it could not sustain. There is, when we come to think of it, something absurd in supposing that a work of art of any complexity can be adequately discussed by attempting to demonstrate that it conforms to some general and independent principle. Unfortunately, of course, it is much more difficult to formulate the unique qualities of an individual work than to force it into a pre-existent mould. A full reading requires response to tone, nuance, and the numerous stylistic effects that, however neglected in some quarters, remain the stuff of literature.

This, then, is a cautionary tale. I have written it, not to show up the errors of an inexperienced commentator, but rather to take a convenient opportunity to draw attention to the dangers that beset all literary critics. We need to approach literature not with made-to-measure theory but with a flexible, verbally sensitive critical practice that attempts, tentatively, humbly, sometimes painfully, to develop a tradition of close and accurate reading. Such a reading should highlight literary complexities instead of obscuring them. Above all, we must encourage our students – and ourselves – to recognize what is there on the page rather than to read simpler and perhaps inappropriate notions into works that have so much more to offer. I must end, however, with a sincere acknowledgement. The writer of the unpublished essay persuaded me that 'Bluebeard's Egg' is a supremely effective work of art by goading me into challenging her own reading. This is an important way in which the discipline of criticism proceeds. Her essay provoked me into a deeper realization of the complexity and artistry of Atwood's story – and for that I am grateful.

Works Cited

Abrams, M.H. *A Glossary of Literary Terms.* New York: Holt, Rinehart and Winston, 1957.

Arnason, David, ed. *Nineteenth Century Canadian Stories.* Toronto: Macmillan, 1976.

Arnold, Matthew. *Poetry and Criticism of Matthew Arnold.* Ed. A. Dwight Culler. Boston: Houghton Mifflin, 1961.

Atwood, Margaret. *Bluebeard's Egg.* Toronto: McClelland and Stewart, 1983.

———. 'Face to Face'. *A Place To Stand On: Essays by and about Margaret Laurence.* Ed. George Woodcock. Western Canadian Literary Documents 4. Edmonton: NeWest, 1983. 20-27.

———. *Second Words: Selected Critical Prose.* Toronto: Anansi, 1982.

———. *Survival: A Thematic Guide to Canadian Literature.* Toronto: Anansi, 1972.

Auden, W.H. *The Dyer's Hand and Other Essays.* New York: Random House, 1962.

Berton, Pierre. 'The Strange Case of The Brother, XII'. *My Country: The Remarkable Past.* Toronto: McClelland and Stewart, 1976. 100-21.

Borges, Jorge Luis. *Labyrinths: Selected Stories & Other Writings.* Ed. Donald A. Yates and James E. Irby. New York: New Directions, 1964.

Bowering, George. 'That Fool of a Fear: Notes on *A Jest of God*'. *Canadian Literature* 50 (1971): 41-56.

Brown, Russell M. 'Critic, Culture, Text: Beyond Thematics'. *Essays on Canadian Writing* 11 (1978): 151-83.

Callaghan, Morley. *Such Is My Beloved.* 1934. New Canadian Library 2. Toronto: McClelland and Stewart, 1957.

Cameron, Barry. *John Metcalf.* Twayne's World Authors Ser. 771. Boston: Twayne, 1986.

———. 'The Practice of the Craft: A Conversation with John Metcalf'. *Queen's Quarterly* 82 (1975): 402-24.

Cameron, Barry, and Michael Dixon. 'Mandatory Subversive Manifesto: Canadian Criticism vs. Literary Criticism'. *Minus Canadian: Penultimate Essays on Literature.* Ed. Barry Cameron and Michael Dixon. *Studies in Canadian Literature* 2 (1977): 137-45.

Cameron, Donald. *Conversations with Canadian Novelists: Part One.* Toronto: Macmillan, 1973.

Cameron, Elspeth. *Hugh MacLennan: A Writer's Life.* Toronto: U of Toronto P, 1981.

Connolly, Kevin, Douglas Freake, and Jason Sherman. 'Interview: Alice Munro'. *What* [Toronto] Sept.-Oct. 1986. n. pag.

Davey, Frank. 'Surviving the Paraphrase'. *Canadian Literature* 70 (1976): 5-13.

Davies, Robertson. *The Enthusiasms of Robertson Davies.* Ed. Judith Skelton Grant. Toronto: McClelland and Stewart, 1979.

———. *Fifth Business.* Toronto: Macmillan, 1970.

———. *High Spirits.* Harmondsworth, Eng.: Penguin, 1982.

———. *Leaven of Malice.* 1954. Toronto: Clarke, Irwin, 1964.

———. *The Manticore.* Toronto: Macmillan, 1972.

———. *A Mixture of Frailties.* Toronto: Macmillan, 1958.

———. *The Rebel Angels.* Toronto: Macmillan, 1981.

———. *Tempest-Tost.* Toronto: Clarke, Irwin, 1951.

———. *The Well-Tempered Critic: One Man's View of Theatre and Letters in Canada.* Ed. Judith Skelton Grant. Toronto: McClelland and Stewart, 1981.

———. *World of Wonders.* Toronto: Macmillan, 1975.

Dooley, D.J. *Moral Vision in the Canadian Novel.* Toronto: Clarke, Irwin, 1979.

Dudek, Louis. 'Can Lit Notes 1'. *The Bumper Book.* Ed. John Metcalf. Toronto: ECW, 1986. 40-41.

———. *En México.* Toronto: Contact, 1958.

———. *Europe.* Toronto: Laocoön (Contact), 1954.

———. *In Defence of Art: Critical Essays & Reviews.* Ed. Aileen Collins. Kingston, ON: Quarry, 1988.

———. 'Interface: Reality and Literature'. *Louis Dudek: Texts & Essays. Open Letter,* Fourth Series 8-9 (1981): 237-44.

———. *Selected Essays and Criticism.* Ottawa: Tecumseh, 1978.

———. *Technology & Culture: Six Lectures.* Ottawa: Golden Dog, 1979.

Duffy, Dennis. 'Space/Time and the Matter of Form'. *Essays on Canadian Writing* 13/14 (1978-79): 131-44.

Engel, Marian. 'Steps to the Mythic:*The Diviners* and *A Bird in the House*'. *Journal of Canadian Studies* 13.3 (1978): 72-74.

Fabre, Michael. 'From *The Stone Angel* to *The Diviners*: An Interview with Margaret Laurence'. *A Place To Stand On: Essays by and about Margaret Laurence.* Ed. George Woodcock. Western Canadian Literary Documents 4. Edmonton: NeWest, 1983. 139-209.

Fogel, Stan. 'Lost in the Canadian Funhouse'. *Queen's Quarterly* 88 (1981): 690-707.

———. *A Tale of Two Countries: Contemporary Fiction in English Canada and the United States.* Toronto: ECW, 1984.

Frye, Northrop. *The Bush Garden: Essays on the Canadian Imagination.* Toronto: Anansi, 1971.

Frye, Northrop, Sheridan Baker, and George Perkins. *The Harper Handbook to Literature.* New York: Harper & Row, 1985.

Gibson, Graeme. *Eleven Canadian Novelists: Interviewed by Graeme Gibson.* Toronto: Anansi, 1973.

Graff, Gerald. *Literature Against Itself: Literary Ideas in Society.* Chicago: U of Chicago P, 1979.

Graves, Robert. *Goodbye to All That.* 1929. Rev. ed. London: Cassell, 1957.

Grove, Frederick Philip. *Fruits of the Earth.* 1933. New Canadian Library 49. Toronto: McClelland and Stewart, 1965.

———. *In Search of Myself.* Toronto: Macmillan, 1946.

———. *It Needs To Be Said....* Toronto: Macmillan, 1929.

———. *The Letters of Frederick Philip Grove.* Ed. Desmond Pacey. Toronto: U of Toronto P, 1976.

———. *Our Daily Bread.* 1928. New Canadian Library 114. Toronto: McClelland and Stewart, 1975.

———. *Settlers of the Marsh.* 1925. Introduction by Thomas Saunders. New Canadian Library 50. Toronto: McClelland and Stewart, 1965. [N.B.: In recent reprints, this introduction has been replaced.]

———. *Tales from the Margin: The Selected Short Stories of Frederick Philip Grove.* Ed. Desmond Pacey. Toronto: Ryerson/McGraw-Hill, 1971.

———. *The Yoke of Life.* Toronto: Macmillan, 1930.

Hancock, Geoff. *Canadian Writers at Work: Interviews with Geoff Hancock.* Toronto: Oxford UP, 1987.

Harding, Anthony John. 'Field of Vision: Hugh Hood and the Tradition of Wordsworth'. *Canadian Literature* 94 (1982): 85-94.

Hardy, Thomas. *The Collected Poems of Thomas Hardy.* 4th ed. London: Macmillan, 1930.

Hoar, Victor. *Morley Callaghan.* Studies in Canadian Literature 4. Toronto: Copp Clark, 1969.

Hodgins, Jack. *The Barclay Family Theatre.* Toronto: Macmillan, 1981.

———. *The Honorary Patron.* Toronto: McClelland and Stewart, 1987.

———. *The Invention of the World.* Toronto: Macmillan, 1977.

———. *The Resurrection of Joseph Bourne.* Toronto: Macmillan, 1979.

———. *Spit Delaney's Island: Selected Stories.* Toronto: Macmillan, 1976.

Hood, Hugh. 'The End of Emma'. *Canadian Literature* 100 (1984): 148-56.

———. *The Governor's Bridge is Closed.* Ottawa: Oberon, 1973.

———. *A New Athens.* Ottawa: Oberon, 1977.

———. *None Genuine Without This Signature.* Downsview, ON: ECW, 1980. [Some copies contain an introduction by Keith Garebian.]

———. *A Short Walk in the Rain.* The Collected Stories II. Erin, ON: Porcupine's Quill, 1989.

———. *The Swing in the Garden.* Ottawa: Oberon, 1975.

Hopkins, Gerard Manley. *The Poems of Gerard Manley Hopkins.* Ed. W.H. Gardner and N.H. MacKenzie. 4th ed. London: Oxford UP, 1967.

Horner, Jan C. 'Irish & Biblical Myth in Jack Hodgins' *The Invention of the World*'. *Canadian Literature* 99 (1983): 6-18.

Jeffrey, David L. 'A Crust for the Critics'. Rev. of *The Resurrection of Joseph Bourne,* by Jack Hodgins. *Canadian Literature* 84 (1980): 74-78.

Johnston, George. 'Yet Another Slim Vol.'. *The Bumper Book.* Ed. John Metcalf. Toronto: ECW, 1986. 106-07.

Jones, D.G. *Butterfly on Rock: A Study of Themes and Images in Canadian Literature.* Toronto: U of Toronto P, 1970.

Keith, W.J. *Canadian Literature in English.* Longman Literature in English Ser. London: Longman, 1985.

———. *Charles G.D. Roberts.* Studies in Canadian Literature 1. Toronto: Copp Clark, 1969.

———. 'Editors and Texts: Reflections on Some Recent Anthologies of Canadian Poetry'. *Canadian Poetry: Studies, Documents, Reviews* 12 (1983): 77-86.

———. 'Text and Subtext: Davies's *World of Wonders* and Robert-Houdin's Memoirs'. *Canadian Literature* 104 (1985): 176-78.

Klinck, Carl F., gen. ed. *Literary History of Canada: Canadian Literature in English.* 1965. 2nd ed. 3 vols. Toronto: U of Toronto P, 1976.

Kroetsch, Robert. 'Mirror, Mirror Show Us All'. Rev. of *The Scorched-Wood People,* by Rudy Wiebe. *Books in Canada* Jan. 1978, 14.

Laurence, Margaret. *A Bird in the House.* Toronto: McClelland and Stewart, 1970.

———. *The Diviners.* Toronto: McClelland and Stewart, 1974.

———. *Heart of a Stranger.* Toronto: McClelland and Stewart, 1976.

———. Introduction to *The Lamp at Noon and Other Stories.* By Sinclair Ross. New Canadian Library 62. Toronto: McClelland and Stewart, 1968. 7-12.

Lawrence, D.H. *The Collected Letters of D.H. Lawrence.* Ed. Harry T. Moore. 2 vols. New York: Viking, 1962.

Lawrence, Robert G. and Samuel L. Macey, eds. *Studies in Robertson Davies' Deptford Trilogy.* ELS Monograph Ser. 20. Victoria: English Literary Studies, Department of English, U of Victoria, 1980.

Layton, Irving. *A Red Carpet for the Sun.* Toronto: McClelland and Stewart, 1959.

Leavis, F.R. *The Common Pursuit.* London: Chatto & Windus, 1952.

———. *The Great Tradition: George Eliot Henry James Joseph Conrad.* London: Chatto & Windus, 1948.

———. *The Living Principle: 'English' as a Discipline of Thought.* London: Chatto & Windus, 1975.

Lecker, Robert. *On the Line: Readings in the Short Fiction of Clark Blaise John Metcalf and Hugh Hood.* Downsview, ON: ECW, 1982.

———. 'A Spirit of Communion: *The Swing in the Garden*'. *Essays on Canadian Writing* 13/14 (1978-79): 187-210.

Lewis, Gertrud Jaron. 'Vitzliputzli Revisited'. *Canadian Literature* 76 (1978): 132-34.

Lucas, Alec. *Hugh MacLennan.* Canadian Writers 8. Toronto: McClelland and Stewart, 1970.

MacDonald, R.D. 'Serious Whimsy'. *Canadian Literature* 63 (1975): 40-51.

MacIsaac, Ron, Don Clark, and Charles Lillard. *The Devil of De Courcy Island: The Brother XII.* Victoria: Porcépic, 1989.

MacLennan, Hugh. *Cross-Country.* Toronto: Collins, 1949.

———. *Thirty & Three.* Ed. Dorothy Duncan. Toronto: Macmillan, 1954.

———. 'Victory'. *The Other Side of Hugh MacLennan: Selected Essays Old and New.* Ed. Elspeth Cameron. Toronto: Macmillan, 1978. 177-83.

———. *The Watch That Ends the Night.* New York: Charles Scribner's Sons, 1959.

Mathews, Lawrence. 'The Secular and the Sacral: Notes on *A New Athens* and Three Stories by Hugh Hood'. *Essays on Canadian Writing* 13/14 (1978-79): 211-29.

McCaig, JoAnn. 'Brother XII and *The Invention of the World*'. *Essays on Canadian Writing* 28 (1984): 128-40.

Metcalf, John. *Girl in Gingham* [includes 'Private Parts' and 'Girl in Gingham']. Ottawa: Oberon, 1978.

———. *Kicking Against the Pricks.* 1982. Guelph, ON: Red Kite, 1986.

———. *The Teeth of My Father.* Ottawa: Oberon, 1975.

———. *What Is A Canadian Literature?* Guelph, ON: Red Kite, 1988.

Mills, John. 'Hugh Hood and the Anagogical Method'. *Essays on Canadian Writing* 13/14 (1978-79): 94-112.

Morley, Patricia. *Margaret Laurence.* Twayne's World Authors Ser. 591. Boston: Twayne, 1981.

Moss, John. 'Bushed in the Sacred Wood'. *The Human Elements: Second Series.* Ed. David Helwig. Ottawa: Oberon, 1981. 161-78.

———. *Patterns of Isolation in English Canadian Fiction.* Toronto: McClelland and Stewart, 1974.

———. *Sex and Violence in the Canadian Novel: The Ancestral Present.* Toronto: McClelland and Stewart, 1977.

Munro, Alice. 'On John Metcalf: Taking Writing Seriously'. *The Malahat Review* 70 (1985): 6-7.

Neuman, Shirley, and Robert Wilson. *Labyrinths of Voice: Conversations with Robert Kroetsch.* Western Canadian Literary Documents 3. Edmonton: NeWest, 1982.

New, W.H. 'Every Now and Then: Voice and Language in Laurence's *The Stone Angel*'. *A Place To Stand On: Essays by and about Margaret Laurence.* Ed. George Woodcock. Western Canadian Literary Documents 4. Edmonton: NeWest, 1983. 171-92.

———. 'The "Genius" of Place and Time: The Fiction of Ethel Wilson'. *Journal of Canadian Studies* 3.4 (1968): 39-48.

Ohm, Viveca. 'Jack Hodgins: Story-Teller'. *UBC Alumni Chronicle* 34.4 (1980): 4-6.

Ondaatje, Michael. 'O'Hagan's Rough-Edged Chronicle'. *Canadian Literature* 61 (1974): 24-31.

Pacey, Desmond. *Ethel Wilson.* Twayne's World Authors Ser. 33. New York: Twayne, 1967.

———. *Frederick Philip Grove.* Toronto: Ryerson, 1945.

———. 'The Innocent Eye: The Art of Ethel Wilson'. *Queen's Quarterly* 61 (1954): 42-52.

———. Introduction to *Swamp Angel.* By Ethel Wilson. Toronto: McClelland and Stewart, 1962. 5-10. [N.B.: In recent reprints, this introduction has been replaced.]

Peterman, Michael. 'Margaret Laurence'. *Journal of Canadian Studies* 13.3 (1978): 1-2, 100-04.

Piercy, Marge. 'Gritty Places and Strong Women'. Rev. of *The Diviners,* by Margaret Laurence. *Margaret Laurence.* Ed. W.H. New. Critical Views on Canadian Writers. Toronto: McGraw-Hill Ryerson, 1977. 212-13.

Powe, B.W. *A Climate Charged.* Oakville, ON: Mosaic, 1984.

Radford, F.L. 'Heinrich Heine, the Virgin, and the Hummingbird: *Fifth Business* – a Novel and Its Subconscious'. *English Studies in Canada* 4 (1978): 95-110.

Rasky, Frank. 'The Swindling Swami of British Columbia'. *Gay Canadian Rogues: Swindlers, Gold-diggers and Spies.* Toronto: Thomas Nelson and Sons, 1958. 72-86.

Rehak, Peter, and Beverley Slopen. 'The Myth and the Master'. *Time* (Canada), 3 Nov. 1975: 8-12.

Rhodenizer, V.B. Rev. of *Settlers of the Marsh,* by Frederick Philip Grove. *Frederick Philip Grove.* Critical Views on

Canadian Writers 5. Ed. Desmond Pacey. Toronto: Ryerson, 1970. 116-17.

Richardson, John. *Wacousta; or, The Prophecy: A Tale of the Canadas.* 1832. Ed. Douglas Cronk. Centre for Editing Early Canadian Texts. Ottawa: Carleton UP, 1987.

Richler, Mordecai. *The Apprenticeship of Duddy Kravitz.* London: André Deutsch, 1959.

Roberts, Charles G.D. 'A Note on Modernism'. *Selected Poetry and Critical Prose.* By Charles G.D. Roberts. Ed. W.J. Keith. Literature of Canada: Poetry and Prose in Reprint. Toronto: U of Toronto P, 1974. 296-301.

Ross, Sinclair. *As For Me and My House.* 1941. Introduction by Roy Daniells. New Canadian Library 4. Toronto: McClelland and Stewart, 1957. [N.B.: In recent reprints, this introduction has been replaced.]

Skelton, Isabel. 'One Speaking into a Void'. *Frederick Philip Grove.* Ed. Desmond Pacey. Critical Views on Canadian Writers 5. Toronto: Ryerson, 1970. 24-44.

Smith, A.J.M. 'A Survey of English-Canadian Letters'. Rev. of *Literary History of Canada: Canadian Literature in English,* gen. ed. Carl F. Klinck. *University of Toronto Quarterly* 35 (1965-66): 107-16.

Spettigue, Douglas O. *FPG: The European Years.* Ottawa: Oberon, 1973.

———. *Frederick Philip Grove.* Studies in Canadian Literature 3. Toronto: Copp Clark, 1969.

Steele, Charles R., ed. *Taking Stock: The Calgary Conference on the Canadian Novel.* Downsview, ON: ECW, 1982.

Stegner, Wallace. 'The Provincial Consciousness'. *University of Toronto Quarterly* 43 (1974): 299-310.

Struthers, J.R. (Tim). 'An Interview with Hugh Hood'. *Essays on Canadian Writing* 13/14 (1978-79): 21-93.

———. 'Thinking about Eternity'. Rev. of *The Resurrection of Joseph Bourne,* by Jack Hodgins. *Essays on Canadian Writing* 20 (1980-81): 126-33.

Tallman, Warren. 'An After-Glance at MacLennan'. Rev. of

The Watch That Ends the Night, by Hugh MacLennan. *Canadian Literature* 1 (1959): 80-81.

———. 'Wolf in the Snow'. *Canadian Literature* 5 (1960): 7-20 and 6 (1960): 41-48.

Thomas, Clara. 'The Chariot of Ossian: Myth and Manitoba in *The Diviners*'. *Journal of Canadian Studies* 13.3 (1978): 55-63.

———. *The Manawaka World of Margaret Laurence.* Toronto: McClelland and Stewart, 1975.

Thrall, William Flint, Addison Hibbard, and C. Hugh Holman. *A Handbook to Literature.* Rev. and enlarged ed. New York: Odyssey, 1960.

Tierney, Frank M., ed. *The Crawford Symposium.* Reappraisals: Canadian Writers. Ottawa: U of Ottawa P, 1979.

Traill, Catharine Parr. *The Backwoods of Canada.* 1836. Introduction by Clara Thomas. New Canadian Library 51. Toronto: McClelland and Stewart, 1966.

Twigg, Alan. *For Openers: Conversations with 24 Canadian Writers.* Madeira Park, BC: Harbour, 1981.

Watters, R.E. 'Ethel Wilson, the Experienced Traveller'. *British Columbia Library Quarterly* 21.4 (1958): 21-37.

Wiebe, Rudy. 'The Death and Life of Albert Johnson: Collected Notes on a Possible Legend'. *Figures in a Ground: Canadian Essays on Modern Literature Collected in Honor of Sheila Watson.* Ed. Diane Bessai and David Jackel. Saskatoon, SK: Western Producer Prairie Books, 1978. 219-46.

———. *The Mad Trapper.* Toronto: McClelland and Stewart, 1980.

———. *My Lovely Enemy.* Toronto: McClelland and Stewart, 1983.

Wilson, Ethel. 'The Bridge or the Stokehold?: Views of the Novelist's Art'. *Canadian Literature* 5 (1960): 43-47.

———. 'A Cat among the Falcons: Reflections on the Writer's Craft'. *Canadian Literature* 2 (1959): 10-19.

———. *The Equations of Love: Tuesday and Wednesday – Lilly's Story.* 1952. Laurentian Library 19. Toronto: Macmillan, 1974.

———. *Hetty Dorval.* 1947. Laurentian Library 6. Toronto: Macmillan, 1967.

———. *The Innocent Traveller.* 1949. Toronto: Macmillan, 1960.

———. *Love and Salt Water.* Toronto: Macmillan, 1956.

———. *Mrs Golightly and Other Stories.* Toronto: Macmillan, 1961.

———. 'Reflections in a Pool'. *Canadian Literature* 22 (1964): 29-33.

———. 'Series of Combination of Events & Where Is John Goodwin?' *The Tamarack Review* 33 (1964): 3-9.

———. *Swamp Angel.* 1954. New Canadian Library 29. Toronto: McClelland and Stewart, 1962.

Wilson, Herbert Emmerson. *Canada's False Prophet: The Notorious Brother Twelve.* Richmond Hill, ON: Simon & Schuster, 1967.

Woodcock, George. *Hugh MacLennan.* Studies in Canadian Literature 5. Toronto: Copp Clark, 1969.

———. 'When the Past Becomes History: The Half-Century in Non-Fiction Prose'. *University of Toronto Quarterly* 50 (1980): 90-101.

———. *The World of Canadian Writing: Critiques & Recollections.* Vancouver: Douglas & McIntyre, 1980.

Yeats, W.B. *The Letters of W.B. Yeats.* Ed. Allan Wade. London: Rupert Hart-Davis, 1954.

Index

Biographical Note

W.J. KEITH is a member of the Department of English at University College, University of Toronto. A former editor, for many years, of the *University of Toronto Quarterly*, he has written extensively on both British and Canadian literature. His books on British literature include the study *Richard Jefferies* and three acclaimed volumes on rural British non-fiction, poetry, and novels: *The Rural Tradition*, *The Poetry of Nature*, and *Regions of the Imagination*. His numerous discussions of Canadian literature include the single-author studies *Charles G.D. Roberts* and *Epic Fiction: The Art of Rudy Wiebe*, the critical survey *Canadian Literature in English*, *A Sense of Style: Studies in the Art of Fiction in English-Speaking Canada*, and the present volume, *An Independent Stance: Essays on English-Canadian Criticism and Fiction*. W.J. Keith is a Fellow of the Royal Society of Canada.